WHAT PEOPLE ARE SAYING ABOUT
THE BOOK ON . . . BUSINESS FROM A TO Z

"Business is demanding. This book sits on my desk within arms-reach so that I can refer back to it as new challenges arise. In fact, it is required reading for my entire management team because it really does contain the answers from A – Z."

David Fisher, Founder & President of the Southern California Manufacturing Group

"This book is a great resource and is recommended reading for all entrepreneurs. It provides excellent information and advice for the entrepreneur covering a broad breadth of topics including capital markets."

John K. Paglia, Ph.D., CFA, CPA; Denney Academic Chair; Associate Professor of Finance; Senior Researcher, Pepperdine Private Capital Markets Project; Graziadio School of Business and Management; Pepperdine University

I must confess that I am generally not a big fan of compilations when it comes to business literature. However, "THE Book of Business...From A to Z" might change that preconceived opinion.

The authors have compiled series of interesting material related to various issues and situations that business owners and managers experience in their "corporate life". The contributing authors have achieved the successful marriage of practical relevance and theoretical accuracy in the book, allowing the reader to leave with substantial take-away rooted in 26 business topics.

The book goes beyond classic, oft-vague principles and "recipes" to offer real substance in managerial disciplines and topics as varied as: Accounting, finance, risk-management, innovation, networking, quality, business turnaround, business valuation, and "Z score".

The reader can use the book as a first-diagnosis and orientation tool, but also as a source for more specialized knowledge. It answers classic questions and helps to frame more complex issues.

For business owners, managers, and everyone interested in management and business, this book is definitively an excellent resource."

Daniel Degravel, PhD.; Association of Strategic Planning, Los Angeles Chapter Board Member, Assistant Professor at California State University, Northridge, College of Business & Economics, Department of Management; Consultant in Management, strategic management

THE Book on...

Business from A to Z:
The 260 Most Important Answers You Need to Know

Compiled and Edited by Daniel Feiman, MBA, CMC©

Published by Build It Backwards Publishing

200 South Juanita Avenue

Suite 312

Redondo Beach, CA, 90277-3438

310-540-6717

Want more? Look for these other titles in our *Build It Backwards* series:

- THE Book on…Improving Productivity by Fair Means or Foul

- THE Book on…Business From A to Z

- THE Book on…Continuous Process Improvement

- THE Book on…Business From A to Z II

- THE Book on…Leadership

- THE Book on…Strategy: From Planning through Implementation

- THE Book on…Where to Go When the Bank Says No

- THE Book on…Financial Modeling

- THE Book on…Budgeting and Forecasting

- THE Book on…Accounting: Making Sense of the Numbers

TABLE OF CONTENTS

DEDICATION

*THIS LABOR OF LOVE IS DEDICATED TO MY THREE WONDERFUL
SONS; CLIFFORD, MARCUS
AND BENJAMIN. THEY MAKE ME WANT TO CONSTANTLY DO BETTER
AND CONTRIBUTE SOMETHING GOOD TO THE WORLD.*

FOREWORD

The business of doing business is the backbone of every profession. An effective, efficient and financially sound business is borne out of solid decisions and practices, and solid decisions and practices come from a deep understanding of relationships between and among business disciplines and professional areas of practice.

This book's unique format delivers a practical approach to answering the 10 most important questions in each of the subjects. This provides an expansive ready-made guide to be turned inward for thought, discussion and action. Roll up your sleeves to tackle *THE Book on… Business A to Z: The 260 Most Important Answers You Need to Know.*

What is cash flow? Do you have the right people? Should you care about innovation? Can you build boundaries around the concept of knowledge and how to harness it to your advantage? In the book's Chapters A to Z -- from Accounting to Z-Score – you will find dialogue and guidance over a wide range of topics.

If you want to brush up on a business subject or learn something new, you'll find a friend in this book. The easy-read design and breadth of subject matter will give you what you need to be a business professional first.

You will come away satisfied you now have a grasp on, and solutions for, some of the most perplexing business concepts.

Paul Novak, CPSM, C.P.M., A.P.P., MCIPS

Chief Executive Officer

Institute for Supply Management™

PREFACE

Someone had to write it... and that's why we did. ***THE Book on ... Business from A to Z; The 260 Most Important Answers You Need to Know*** is the result of trying to constantly answer clients' questions across a vast range of business topics. After frequent discussions about some of our most challenging engagements, we (the co-authors) realized that we had one thing in common: Clients who were regularly asking questions about many areas beyond our individual areas of expertise. We did our individual best to answer them and/or put the clients in touch with other experts who could.

However, we wanted to be able to go beyond this and to provide an ongoing resource for those questions that arise when we are *not* in front of our clients. We wanted to make a lasting resource for our past, present and future clients. The result is ***THE Book on ... Business from A to Z; The 260 Most Important Answers You Need to Know.*** This book covers 26 of the most important business topics in the world today. Although each chapter is worthy of a complete book of its own, we have condensed each down to the 10 most frequently asked questions and their answers.

We hope you find the information in this book as useful as many of our clients have. Please let us know your thoughts and opinions by dropping us an email at info@BuildItBackwards.com.

This book is available at Amazon.com, at bookstores everywhere, and on our website: www.BuildItBackwards.com.

CHAPTER A – ACCOUNTING

By Rick Norris

1. **What is accounting?**

According to Merriam Webster, "Accounting" is *the system of recording and summarizing business and financial transactions and analyzing, verifying, and reporting the results.* This generic definition does not do justice to the nature of accounting in the real world. Accounting processes are used in almost every level of business, but the basic function is to track all financial transactions, which in turn measure a company's financial position at any point in time.

To illustrate this point, let's use a fictitious towel manufacturing company, *Sloppy Towels*. Sloppy's sales manager computes sales commissions, mark-ups and markdowns in a normal course of business. Though the department is sales, the manager is using accounting information and processes to determine whether or not a salesperson is above or below a sales quota. Moreover, the sales manager will need accounting information to measure the gross profit margin when determining whether mark-ups or mark-downs make sense, as well as other calculations related to the accounting information.

In effect, the *Sloppy Towels* sales manager uses accounting, but is not an accountant; he is not part of the accounting department and probably doesn't have an accounting degree. But this does not preclude him from practicing some form of *accounting* in his sales department as he uses the information provided to make decisions.

What the Sloppy's sales manager may not see is that the information he uses is created in a system called *double-entry* accounting. Double-entry accounting is a standard accounting method that involves each transaction being recorded in at least two accounts, resulting in a debit to one or more accounts and a credit to one or more accounts. Double-entry accounting provides a method for quickly checking accuracy, because the sum of all accounts with debit balances should equal the sum of all credit balance accounts.

Almost every accounting software program for business uses double entry accounting; without this feature an accountant would have difficulty preparing year-end reports and tax records. Below is an example of the double-entry approach for the balance sheet:

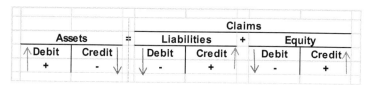

Assets		=	Claims					
			Liabilities		+	Equity		
Debit	Credit		Debit	Credit		Debit	Credit	
+	-		-	+		-	+	

2. What is the difference between financial and managerial accounting?

Financial accounting processes gather information for producing standard financial statements. These accounting processes usually follow U.S. accounting standards, rules and procedures known as the Generally Accepted Accounting Principles. These standards are enacted and enforced by the American Institute of Certified Public Accountants (AICPA) and the Financial Accounting Standards Board (FASB). The most basic financial statements are the balance sheet, statement of income and retained earnings, and the statement of cash flow. These financial accounting statements analyze a company from a broad perspective and are used to provide information to persons both inside and outside of the organization. Outside individuals and organizations, like banks and shareholders, may use the financial statements for different purposes than those inside the company.

Managerial accounting (also referred to as financial analysis), however, considers a business's accounting practices from a more "micro" point of view. This form of accounting uses the same information, but in light of an organization's managerial goals. As indicated above with our sales department example, a managerial accountant may give the Sloppy Towel's sales manager specific information. This information may be used to determine the price of a product or service. The information may consist of the business's cost of goods or the services sold. This type of managerial accounting is called *cost accounting*, because the accountant is determining the *cost* of the company's product. Larger companies usually have accountants that specialize in this type of accounting.

Additionally, there are a few differences in the names used to identify line items to make this *costing* approach easier. In financial accounting, you call the costs incurred to create the product or service you sell the *cost of goods sold*. This is made up of labor, material and overhead costs. When you deduct costs of goods sold from your revenues, the result is *gross profit*; subtract *operating expenses* from gross profit and the result is *operating profit*.

Financial accounting			Managerial accounting	
Revenue		$100,000	Revenue	$100,000
Cost of Goods Sold				
	Labor	$14,300		
	Material	$16,500	Variable Costs	$32,450
	Overhead	$12,750		
Gross Profit		**$56,450**	**Contribution Margin**	**$67,550**
Operating expenses		$43,500	Fixed Costs	$54,600
Operating profit		**$12,950**	**Operating profit**	**$12,950**

While in managerial accounting, you call the direct costs to create what you sell *variable costs (VC)*, as they vary with the sales volume, and these are labor and material costs *only*. Revenue minus variable costs equals *contribution margin (CM)*. CM less *fixed costs (FC)* (those that do not vary with sales volume) leaves you with your operating profit.

Fixed costs are those that are:

- Not related to volume

- Indirect, as they do not go directly into creating the product/service

- Period costs, as they are fixed for a period of time rather than product cost that go into the product

- Frequently unchanged for a period of time, like a year, based on a contract – rent, salaries or insurance

Financial accounting is how a company presents its financial statements to the world so it is externally focused. *Managerial (Management) accounting* is internally focused, and uses different terms to focus on what it cost to produce something rather than if the firm is profitable or not.

3.   **What is the difference between accounting and financing?**
Financing, like most other company functions, depends on accounting input. Financing, not to be confused with financial analysis, is usually defined as the resources needed by a business to operate. Business financing can take two forms: a) Investment by the owners, known as equity or stock, and b)

5

Debt, usually loans and notes. Debts usually have interest attributed to them, and the company is legally required to pay the money back. Accounting is the process of recording and verifying these financial resources.

Corporate finance is primarily comprised of three elements:

- Working capital

- Capital budgeting

- Capital structure

Working capital is the difference between the current assets and current liabilities on the balance sheet, and is a measure of the relative liquidity of your company at a point in time.

Capital budgeting includes the major long-term investments you make to maintain and expand your business. You analyze your options here using the projected financial statements and apply tools like *Net Present Value (NPV) or Internal Rate of Return (IRR)* in order to make the best decision for your organization.

Capital structure refers to the absolute and relative amount of debt and equity capital, on the balance sheet, financing your company over the long-term. (See Chapter D – Debt and Chapter E - Equity for more information).

4.   **What do you need to know about financial statements?**
There are three basic financial statements:

- Balance Sheet

- Statement of Income and Retained Earnings

- Statement of Cash Flow

Each statement has a different function. The Balance Sheet is a snapshot of the business's health. A user must understand what each line and section means in gauging this health. More specifically, the Balance Sheet shows things such as how much money is in the bank, furniture and equipment purchased, how much money is owed to the company, how much money the company owes other companies, and the amount of money invested in the enterprise. In other words, the Balance Sheet summarizes what assets a company owns/controls and juxtaposes these to the liabilities owed to others. The *equity* is the net of those two sections. Equity is also known as Net Book Value. What many people call a "statement" is actually a Balance Sheet, because all assets must *balance* to the total of the company's liabilities and equity.

Sloppy Towels, Inc.		
BALANCE SHEET		
As of December 31 2009		
ASSETS		
Cash		$ 193
Accounts receivable		
Inventory (cost)		
Total current assets		193
Plant, Property & Equipment (net)		500
		$ 693
LIABILITIES & STOCKHOLDER'S EQUITY		
Current Liabilities		
Accounts payable		
Bank notes payable		133
Total current assets		133
Long-term debt (net of current portion)		200
Stockholder's Equity		
Capital Stock		100
Retained Earnings		260
		360
		$ 693

The Statement of Income and Retained Earnings shows operating performance for a specific period of time. For example, a third quarter statement of income and retained earnings will not show any activity from the first two quarters. This differs from the Balance Sheet, which is cumulative. The retained earnings portion illustrates the cumulative profit, losses and other changes to the company's equity, such as dividends, distributions, prior period adjustments, reorganizations, and some treasury stock transactions.

Sloppy Towels, Inc. STATEMENT OF INCOME AND RETAINED EARNINGS For the Year Ended December 31, 2010	
Sales (net)	$ 400
Cost of Goods Sold	200
Gross Profit	200
Expenses	
Selling, general and administrative expenses	135
Depreciation	100
	235
Income from operations	(35)
Interest expense	(23)
Net income before taxes	(58)
Provision for income taxes	-
Net income (Loss)	(58)
BEGINNING RETAINED EARNINGS--January 1 , 20XX	260
Dividends	(2)
ENDING RETAINED EARNINGS--December 31, 20XX	$ 200

The third financial statement, Statement of Cash Flow, looks at the company in a different light. It is divided into the sources and uses of cash. This information is not explicitly found on the other two types of financial statements, but is indirectly related to some items on both of them. In other words, the Statement of Cash Flow explains the changes in the Balance Sheet from period to period, and their effects on cash flow. For example, the section *Net cash flows provided (used) by investment activities* may contain proceeds from the sale of land, cash disbursed for the purchase of machinery, and investments in other companies' stocks.

Sloppy Towels, Inc. STATEMENT OF CASH FLOWS From January 1, 2010 to December 31, 2010	
CASH FLOWS FROM OPERATING ACTIVITIES	
Net income (loss)	$ (58)
Adjustments to reconcile net income to net cash used by operating activities	
Depreciation expense	100
Decrease in accounts receivable	-
Decrease in inventory	(10)
Increase in accounts payable	8
NET CASH USED BY OPERATING ACTIVITII	40
CASH FLOWS FROM INVESTING ACTIVITIES	
Acquisition of property and equipment	-
NET CASH USED BY INVESTING ACTIVITIE	-
CASH FLOWS FROM FINANCING ACTIVITIES	
Plus net new equity capital raised	
Less decrease in short-term notes	(133)
Less dividends paid	(2)
Net new long-term debt	0
NET CASH PROVIDED BY FINANCING ACT	(135)
CASH AT 12/31/2009	193
CASH AT DECEMBER 31, 2010	$ 98

Comparing these financial statements, the Statement of Income and Retained Earnings and Statement of Cash Flow explain how a company has changed between one period and another. In other words, if you have two *Sloppy Towel's* balance sheets, December 31, 2010 and December 31, 2011, the Statement of Income and Retained Earnings and Statement of Cash Flow will display the change between these periods.

5. What else can a Balance Sheet tell you about your company?

Once you understand what each line of the Balance Sheet means, you can do your managerial analysis. There are many ratios (or metrics) that you can compute using the Balance Sheet as your source of information. For example, Sloppy Towels may be making money, but when you look closer, the company may not be as healthy as you might have thought.

One measure is *current ratio*. A current ratio is current assets over current liabilities. A current asset is an asset that is cash or could be converted to cash within 12 months. Examples of these would be a company's bank account and accounts receivables. Current liabilities, conversely, are money that is due to others within 12 months. Examples of current liabilities are accounts payable and short-term loans. If your current ratio is 1 over 2, then you owe more money to your vendors than you have, or will have within 12 months. It's not looking good for the paper towel company, because according to its *current ratio*, it is unable to pay its short–term obligations.

How about Sloppy's leverage? Look at the Balance Sheet under long-term liabilities. This number represents debt owed to others. Is the money owed to others greater than the money invested and earned in the company? If so, that means Sloppy could have a real *leverage* problem where they are using too much debt as compared to funds invested by the stockholders. If the company has too much debt, they may not be able to make timely payments.

6. Why is the Statement of Cash Flow so important?

Business owners probably misunderstand the Statement of Cash Flow more than any other business statement. This financial tool takes a different approach than the Balance Sheet and Statement of Income and Retained Earnings. The Statement of Cash Flow examines your net cash activity, and whether you increased it or decreased it. This financial statement illustrates cash receipts and cash payments in categories of investing, financing, and operating activities. A sale of computers would be an example of a cash receipt investing activity.

The Statement of Cash Flow allows outside viewers to get information about what the company is doing with their cash, and whether they are making good decisions. For example, if Sloppy Towels has large cash balances on their balance sheet, the Statement of Cash Flow tells a viewer where the cash originated; for example, it may come from the sale of Sloppy's manufacturing plant. That may not be a good thing, and may warrant more due diligence on the part of the viewer.

7.   **What else can financial statements tell you about your business?**

Let's say Sloppy's makes $1 million in sales, and the cost of these goods sold amounts to $800,000. The net profit would be $200,000. This information is obvious on the Statement of Income and Retained Earnings financial statement. But, when Sloppy's CEO looks at her bank statement, she only sees $100,000 in the bank. Where did the other $100,000 go? Did someone steal it? She then turns to her balance sheet and sees that the accounts receivable is $100,000. In other words, Sloppy's may have profited $200,000, but the customers have not paid all that is due. This would is obvious from the Statement of Cash Flow, because the net increase in cash is only $100,000.

Below is a generic example. The opening balance shows the financial status of the company at the beginning of the period. The income statement for the year and the resulting cash flow statement follow. The final model is the ending balance sheet, which reflects the results of the activity of the other two. This demonstrates how the three financial statements are linked together. See if you can follow the flow.

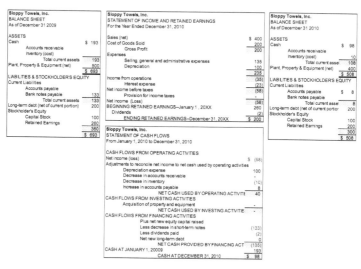

8. Which is more important, profits or cash flow, and why?

What is more important, cash flow or profits? That is a loaded question, because they are both important. As seen in the previous example, you may have a good profit and a bad cash flow. What is also important from the above example is that you may have a long-term profit with a dismal short-term cash flow. As a business owner, or executive, you would not stay in business very long under this scenario. The term *"cash is king"* has much validity. Without the cash, you can't pay your employees. However, the opposite is also true. Let's say that you have $1 million in revenue and $1.2 million in expenses. But you have $400,000 in cash. Where did it come from? There are only two other possible sources: debt and equity. This may be an unprofitable company with large debt or stock, much like some of the technology *dot-com* companies of the 1990s.

9. What is the difference between the Cash Flow Statement and a Cash Budget?

As stated above, cash is important. A cash flow statement can tell you where your cash has gone. But what about looking to the future? Are you planning your company's cash with a budget? A cash budget lays out the cash receipts and disbursements by month. A typical budget forecast will try to predict cash activity in a future period. For example, if you're a seasonal company, you will need to know if you will run out of cash in June, even though you make a large profit in September. If your company has a revolving line of credit, you will have to know the amount of debt you will need, and what your interest payments will be. A company that has a large debt will have interest payments eating into its profits. All of this will become clear when examining the budget from a cash standpoint.

Going back to Sloppy's, its budget can take two basic forms. Does it start with a bottom-up budget process where the managers submit their cash requirements to upper management? Or, does it start with a top-down budget where top management dictates the budget to the lower department levels? Either way can work (see Chapter F – Forecasting and Budgeting for more information).

10. What are financial ratios and why are they important?

I've mentioned financial ratios throughout this chapter. Such things as liquidity, turnover, leverage, and profit percentage, are all helpful…but only if you know what they mean.

Many small and medium-sized business owners have shrugged their shoulders when looking at financial ratios. Why? The reason is because these owners may be excellent at their trade, but they never learned the significance of the ratios that communicate the vital signs of their businesses. What good is a liquidity ratio of 2:1 if you don't know what it means?

Financial ratios are as not useful when displayed alone. They should be compared to *benchmarks*. Benchmarks might be industry or internal company ratios to which you want to compare your financial ratios. For example, if Sloppy's reports that its net profit percentage is 15%, but the industry norm is 25%, investors may leave Sloppy's for more profitable companies. They can seek better returns from one of Sloppy's competitors.

There are a number of metrics and tools that can help improve a business. Financial scorecards are computer-generated reports that show owners and managers a combined view of their business's vital signs on a single screen. Many accounting programs have some sort of scorecard included in their packages.

Scorecards could contain a variety of measurements (or metrics) that can be important in running a business. Common tools that metrics measure in determining whether a company is reaching its financial goals are *Key Performance Indicators* (KPI) and *Critical Success Factors* (CSF). KPI's help management determine the progress an organization has made in reaching its financial goals. Such examples of KPI's are *sales per day* and *customer satisfaction*. CSF's, however, are more refined, looking at no more than six factors that may help an organization reach success.

CHAPTER B – BRANDING

By Christie Harper

The answers to 10 basic questions about branding can help you make sure your organization's branding is on track – regardless of the size of your company.

1. **What is a brand, and what is branding?**
    Although many marketing experts differ on their precise definition of what a "brand" is, there is increasing agreement around the following definition: *A brand is a promise a company makes to its customers, which must be delivered consistently with every interaction.*

    So, if a brand is a promise, branding is the art of developing the right promise to create your desired business results, communicating that promise to stakeholders, and then aligning the organization to keep the promise at every touch point. The branding practice essentially breaks down into three disciplines:

    - Brand strategy – determining the right promise to make to drive business results.
    - Brand marketing – putting the promise out in the market to stakeholders.
    - Brand management – ensuring that the promise is kept at each touch point.

2. **How does a company develop a branding process?**
    The branding process begins with brand strategy, which defines the promise. A brand strategy exercise should examine the *Three C's* of an organization:

    - The Competition
    - The Customer
    - The Company

    You should know who your important competitors are and what they are promising, so that your promise can be differentiated in the marketplace. You should know who your ideal customers are and what they care about, so that your promise can be relevant and deliver compelling functional and emotional benefits. You should also know what your organization is known for now, and what it aspires to be in the future. At the intersection of these three areas of insight is where the brand promise can be found. In marketing-driven organizations, the brand promise can often be developed or refined using internal resources. However, organizations with small or less-developed marketing resources may find benefit in working with a consultant to help them develop the brand promise.

Once the brand strategy is complete, marketing can begin. This is where the promise is made, and it involves aligning all of your communications to clearly convey the brand promise. Everything from your brand identity (name, logo, tagline and visual system) to your collateral, advertising, and even your in-store or office experience, should reflect the brand promise. You can, of course, emphasize other key selling points in your materials, but your primary messaging should always ladder back to the brand promise.

Simultaneous with developing your brand marketing, you should focus on brand management – ensuring that the organization is delivering on the promise at every interaction or touch point. Often the best way to accomplish this is to perform an inventory of all your customer touch points – look at the customer's experience through *their* eyes. How does the *customer* interact with *you*, not how do *you* interact with the customer. List each touch point, and then perform a gap analysis, assessing the gap between the ideal brand experience based on the promise, versus the experience you are currently delivering. Then brainstorm and implement ways that you can close the gap between the current and ideal experience.

3. **Why is a strong effective tagline needed?**

A tagline is a great way to create a concise encapsulation of your brand promise. It helps customers understand the promise you are trying to make, and it helps employees remember the promise they are trying to keep. In a situation where an organization is trying to shift in a new direction, a fresh tagline can also help signal to customers that there's something new going on that's worth paying attention to.

That said, not all great brands use taglines. Apple doesn't use a tagline. Neither does Starbucks or Disney. These brands simply know what their brand promises are and clearly communicate and deliver on them at every interaction. No tagline necessary.

Here's an important point: a bad tagline is worse than no tagline at all. *TaglineGuru.com* has a tagline Hall of Shame that provides excellent examples of poor taglines. Among them: AIG's *The Strength to Be There*, Ames Rubber's *Excellence Through Total Quality*, and Lehman Brothers' *Where Vision Gets Built*. A bad tagline can make you seem unclear, undifferentiated and irrelevant to your customers - even if your brand promise has the potential to be really resonant.

So use a tagline with caution. It can be a great way to signal your brand promise, but if it's not compelling, it can, at best, make you seem like *just another [cleaning/shipping/retail/fast food, etc.] company*. And at worst, can make you seem behind the times. Regardless of whether you find the perfect tagline, what is critical is that you and everyone in your organization understands the brand promise, and can deliver on it in everything they do.

4. **Is a logo critical to creating a brand?**

Let's be clear about one big misconception: Your brand is *not* your logo. Originally, it was. When a cattle rancher put his *brand* (aka *logo*) on a cow, he was signaling, *this is my cow, and this is how my cow is differentiated from all the other cows in the pasture.* But as branding has evolved as a discipline, the logo has become just one component of the overall brand. As with taglines, a logo can be a great way to communicate the brand promise, but it is not the *only* way.

The logo is part of what is commonly referred to as the brand identity. The brand identity includes the organization's name, logo and tagline, as well as what we call *visual vocabulary* – the combined use of color palette, imagery and typography that communicates the brand promise, and, when used well, makes each brand's communication unique and distinctive. It is important that you consider the entire brand identity when evaluating whether or not you need a newer, fancier logo. Sometimes what is needed is not a logo at all, but rather a refreshed visual vocabulary.

One of the best examples of visual vocabulary is Coca-Cola. With the use of Coke signifiers such as the bold, bright red, the script writing, the bubble pattern, and the shape of the bottle, you could see a Coca-Cola ad with no name or logo on it and know that it's Coke. You could probably see a Nike ad with no *Swoosh* or *Just do it* and know that it's a Nike ad. In fact, Nike paid something like $500 to an intern to develop its famous Swoosh, which is one of the most iconic logos in the world. Its power lies not in the fact that it's a brilliantly designed logo, but in the fact that Nike has spent decades and billions of dollars having it stand for the promise of *activating athletic excellence.*

5. **Should you brand your company or your product?**

Within any company, there are actually multiple layers of brands. This is often referred to as *brand architecture*. At the top of the architecture is the Masterbrand. This is generally the company brand that produces products or

15

delivers a service. Then, for a company that offers multiple products or services, those products can be organized into Family Brands. Then, within each family, there are individual Product or Service Brands.

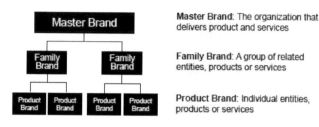

Master Brand: The organization that delivers product and services

Family Brand: A group of related entities, products or services

Product Brand: Individual entities, products or services

A great example of brand architecture at work is at Microsoft. Microsoft is the Masterbrand. Then it has Family Brands targeted to various customer segments – Office for knowledge workers, Visual for software developers, Dynamics for small and large enterprises, X-Box® for gamers, and so on. Then within each family – let's use Office™ as an example – there are products like Word®, Excel®, PowerPoint®, etc.

The question about branding the company or the product comes down to which of three types of brand architecture models you want to pursue.

• Branded House – Here, the Masterbrand is dominant. The Masterbrand endorses all products, as is the case with Microsoft and FedEx. This is the default model, because it is the most cost-effective and provides the most market leverage for a company. You should start with this model and determine whether there's a compelling reason NOT to be a Branded House.

• House of Brands – In this model, the Masterbrand is less prominent, and the emphasis is given to the Product Brands. Proctor & Gamble is the best example of a House of Brands. When you're buying Tide, you aren't thinking that you're buying a P&G product. This model is normally used by consumer packaged goods companies, which may offer multiple products that compete with one another at various price points. The model should be pursued with caution, because it can be very resource-intensive to develop and maintain multiple brands.

• Hybrid – This model generally incorporates a strong master brand with one or more *flanker* brands that target different audiences with differently configured and priced products. Consider Toyota: a strong master brand, with Lexus to address the higher end of the market and Scion to address the lower, younger end of the market. The Lexus brand has complete independence from the Toyota brand, where Scion is more closely linked.

6. **Can you brand your service the same way you brand a product?**

Yes, but generally a service company would follow a Branded House model, so you would be branding your company along with the service. IBM is a good example. Its brand promise is about being *Smart*, its services are always IBM-branded and are aligned to deliver on the *Smart* promise. Interestingly, IBM is one of the only companies that successfully evolved from delivering mostly products to delivering mostly services, and this is because its brand promise was as relevant to services as it was to products.

When companies consider branding a service, the question is generally not about developing a brand promise for the service that is distinct from the Masterbrand's promise. It is generally a question of brand identity – specifically name and logo. In a Branded House model, because the emphasis is on building equity in the Masterbrand, it is best to use descriptive naming for services. Descriptive doesn't necessarily mean *boring*, but it does mean *clear*. You should also avoid developing a new logo for each service – in almost every case the Masterbrand logo should be able to carry the weight of the service offering.

7. **How does branding increase your company's sales?**

Branding works in three direct ways to increase sales: attracting new customers, retaining existing customers, and enabling you to command a price premium. By making a compelling and relevant promise you:

- Attract new customers with that promise.
- Retain customers by providing the experience you have led them to expect.
- Can command a price premium over others who are not making or keeping relevant promises.

This dynamic is easiest to spot in B2C (business-to-consumer) branding, when you consider a pair of brands in the same category. Let's talk about Target and K-mart. Both are discount retailers, providing clothing and household goods at low prices; both have high levels of awareness; both have partnerships with celebrity brands. However, K-mart's brand promise really stops at the commodity *low prices* promise, while Target's promise encourages consumers to aspire to something more: not just low prices, but *great design* at low prices. Target's promise is: *Great design doesn't have to be expensive.* Target's revenue in 2010 was $66 Billion. The entire Sears entity, which owns K-mart, among other retailers, was $44 Billion. Target was also significantly more profitable than Sears.

You can see the same dynamic in B2B (business-to-business) marketing. IBM was ranked #2 on Interbrand's 2010 List of Best Global Brands – ranking right behind Coke. This is astonishing for a "boring" B2B brand. IBM's promise is about smart people doing smart and complex things. Compare this to its closest competitor, Hewlett Packard (HP). While it is still a very powerful brand (#10 on Interbrand's list), it is struggling to rationalize its broad portfolio of products and services. Its new brand promise is *Let's do amazing*, which is emotional, but not particularly differentiating or relevant.

IBM reported a profit margin of 15 percent in 2010, while HP's was less than half of that. On every financial level, IBM is besting HP by more than 50 percent.

8. **How does branding improve your company's bottom line?**
   In one word: *Focus*.

- *Focus* on the customer:

   In developing a brand promise, you'll need to determine which customers are right for your brand, and which are not. This simple ability to determine which customers your organization is *not* right for saves you valuable time and money. And once you've determined who the right customers are, you can focus more clearly on their needs, delivering products and services that are relevant, and eliminating products and services that don't matter to your core customers.

- *Focus* in marketing:

   Your marketing efforts will provide more "bang for the buck" because you are always driving them back to the same core idea, the brand promise. And through the use of a strategic visual vocabulary (see question 4), your designers will be working from a pre-approved template and not reinventing the wheel with each communication. The same marketing dollar provides a lot more impact under a brand-focused program than with a more scattershot approach.

- *Focus* on products and services:

   Many companies find that a clear brand promise allows them to eliminate products and services that aren't relevant to the customer (and don't deliver on the brand promise), while developing new products and services that yield better top-line results. For example, a home building company used to have construction staff spend hours going through each completed home, vertically aligning the screws in the electrical plates, which this company thought was a signal of product quality. The problem was that the customer didn't notice. And if the extra effort was pointed out, the customer didn't care. What they *did* care about was seeing trash on the construction site because they feared that the used hamburger wrapper would end up inside the walls of their new home. A brand promise that focused the company on making the customer confident in their purchase caused the company to apply the same staff to trash collection rather than screw alignment, which significantly increased customer confidence.

9. **How does your company evaluate the effectiveness of its branding?**

Begin with evaluating your brand promise. A good brand promise should be emotional, differentiating, and relevant to customers. Often, companies make the mistake of talking about themselves – when they were founded, their values, what they offer – and don't translate those attributes into customer benefits. These promises lack emotion and relevance. If your promise doesn't mention the customer at all, and is scarce in using words like "you" or "our customers", you need to re-assess your promise.

Once you've determined that you have a brand promise that is emotional, differentiating, and relevant, you then need to assess your brand identity. Is your name, logo, tagline and visual vocabulary doing all they can to clearly communicate the brand promise? Then assess your marketing and communications. Can you clearly see the brand promise communicated directly or indirectly in every single piece? Finally, conduct a gap analysis between brand promise and brand delivery at every touch point. (See question 2.)

Here are some clues that your brand program may not be working for you and needs a revamp:

- Your sales people have a hard time explaining the company and its offerings.
- You can't command a price premium relative to your competition.
- Your marketing spending is not yielding qualified leads.
- Your sales program is struggling to convert good leads to sales.
- Customer retention is low – you get them, but you can't keep them.
- Your employees can't explain what the company does or why it's important, or they are generally disengaged.
- You are expanding your product or service offering into new areas and you're not sure how to explain the change to current or new customers.

10. **Why is Apple considered the most valuable brand?**

Apple is often cited as *the* most successful contemporary brand, simply because it does branding right. At every level, Apple's branding is incredibly clear and compelling. Indeed, no other company does it quite as well. Look at these Apple examples:

- Brand promise: It started around *ease of use*, offering an easy-to-manage alternative to the PC. This functional promise became more emotional over time as Apple started to emphasize what ease of use unleashed – namely, creativity.

- Brand identity: Whether you think its product names are great or not, you must admit that when you see a *Mac, iPad, or iPod, etc.*, you know it comes from Apple. Its logos are simple, imaginative and consistent with one another. The company does not currently use a tagline, but perhaps it is still remembered for an older tagline, *Think Different.* And its visual system – using pops of color against white, or white against fields of color – is so distinctive that you wouldn't need to see a logo on the ad to recognize it.

- Brand communications: Its dramatic, bold visuals of the product experience on billboards or TV ads do not overwhelm viewers with functional details. Rather, they create desire by causing the viewers to imagine what *they* could do with that product. You don't need to know everything an Apple product does, or its functional specs, to know that you want one.

- Brand experience: From product design to packaging to the immersive experience of the Apple Store, the company delivers on its promise of Unleashing Creativity. In every single thing it does, the company pays tremendous attention to detail and inspiration.

Through careful and consistent attention to creating and delivering a meaningful brand promise, Apple has come to dominate its markets. Customers are very forgiving when Apple occasionally stumbles, because they know that over the long term, Apple keeps its promises and values its relationships with customers.

CHAPTER C – CASH FLOW

By Gene Siciliano

1. What does the term *cash flow* mean?

Cash flow is the term used to encompass everything an organization does that changes the balance in its bank account. Cash in, cash out – for whatever reason – is what makes up cash flow. If that were all we needed to know, we could use our bank statement to track it. But just like a budget or a P&L statement, it's the details that matter.

Cash coming *in* from sales or collection of accounts receivable are typically the largest and most important elements of incoming cash. However, cash coming in from a new bank loan, from the sale of stock in the company, from the sale of unneeded company assets, or payments received on money previously loaned out are also all part of cash flow on the incoming side.

Similarly, cash goes *out* for purchases of goods and services, but it also goes out for repayment of loans, cash dividends to stockholders, money loaned to employees or owners, the purchase of new assets for the business, and a host of other typically smaller, but still relevant reasons.

So cash flow is one of the most critical measures of business health and yet, like most metrics, it's a meaningless number if not analyzed and thoroughly understood. The remaining questions in this chapter will help you to understand some of the questions you must ask in order to understand and manage the cash flow of your business.

2. How much cash do you need to run your business successfully?

To answer this question, you will need to have an understanding of the cash flow cycle of your business. If you don't know it, you'll need to guess (and that is not a good option).

The cash flow cycle is most easily understood by imagining a timeline showing the amount of time it takes from the point at which your business lays out cash – for inventory, raw materials, labor, etc. – until the cash is returned to the company from the customers who purchased the company's goods or services. It is usually limited to the company's variable and product-related costs, without considering the cash that gets paid out for fixed costs, such as rent, in order to focus on what is typically the largest demand for cash.

As you can imagine, a company that manufactures a product from raw materials it buys and then processes will have a much longer turnaround of its cash than will a retail store that purchases goods ready for sale and sells them to customers on a cash-only basis. Whichever kind of business you have, you will need enough cash to pay the company's fixed costs during the time you are waiting to get your cash back. So, if you pay cash for inventory, and for processing, and for shipping and handling, etc., you will need enough cash to keep the business running until the customer pays.

Simple enough. Except for one thing. In a typical business, especially a manufacturing business, you will have to order, manufacture, ship and invoice every month if you want to stay in business. If your basic cash flow cycle is 90 days, for example, you will have to order, purchase, process and sell several months' worth of goods before the money from your first month's sales comes in. That significantly increases the amount of working capital you'll need, and if you aim too low, a cash shortage could suddenly force your company to have to slow down production to save money, just when it's beginning to take some market share. And one more thing, *growth* typically means you will need *still more* working capital cash than if sales were flat, because your new purchases will have to be larger than your previous purchases to satisfy that growth.

3. Why do you need a Statement of Cash Flow when you get a reliable Income Statement every month?

The income statement, or P&L statement, shows you how much you earned in a given period, and how much you spent to earn it and to operate the business during that period – usually a month, quarter, or year. It contains important, in fact *critical*, information for the success of your business.

There is one piece of critical information that it doesn't contain, however, and that is how much cash you added to your bank account and where it came from. So unless you run a corner store that buys its merchandise at the beginning of the month and sells it all by the end of the month – for cash – your P&L statement tells you very little about how the cash flow is actually flowing.

As you can see from the answer to question 2 above, this information is rather critical for keeping the doors open. Lots of businesses have been known to generate healthy accounting profits month after month, only to find themselves insolvent because they didn't have enough cash/working capital to continue to operate while they were waiting for the cash to come back in.

Now, add to that the cash items that will never show up on your P&L statement – equipment purchases, loans and loan repayments, etc., and you can see that the change in cash will virtually always be different from the net income, often by material amounts.

In somewhat technical terms, then, the income statement shows your operating results by the *accrual* method, meaning transactions are recorded when they are committed and final in the legal sense, not when they are settled in cash. The statement of cash flow shows all the reasons that net profit (or loss) on the income statement didn't result in an equal increase (or decrease) in cash, and that's a key piece of information that you must have to avoid unpleasant surprises down the road.

4. Why is it so important to have a current cash flow forecast?

Following on the heels of the last two questions, you can see why having a handle on your cash flow is important. When you have a P&L statement and a statement of cash flow in front of you, you can see what happened in the past to cause the business to have a profit and what caused changes in the cash balance.

Now let's look beyond the past into the future, because you will want to know those same things about your business going forward, if possible. And since you can't know the future until it happens, you need to make estimates and assumptions to help you anticipate what will happen. A budgeted P&L is usually the tool used to anticipate the income and expense results you hope to achieve in the future (see Chapter F – Forecasting and Budgeting for more information). You need to manage "to" that budget to get what it says you could get, if everything goes according to plan. Since you've already seen that profit and cash flow are always different, you will need one budget for the profit and a somewhat different one for the cash flow.

The budget for cash flow is most often called a cash flow forecast. It can be a relatively long-term forecast (a year or more) or a shorter term forecast (perhaps only a few weeks or months). The point is that anticipating your cash needs into the future is critical if you want to be ahead of the game. A projection of extra cash in the future – a nice thing to have – will enable you to plan for new asset purchases or short term investments that can enhance the efficiency or profitability of your company. A projection of a cash shortfall will enable you to move proactively to arrange a credit line or defer some discretionary purchases and avoid that awful feeling that comes when you're not sure you can make next week's payroll or next month's mortgage payment.

5. Why should your annual budget include more than just a P&L projection?

The short answer to this question is: because your business is more than just a P&L statement, and you must manage more than just profit in order for the business to succeed. In fact, you must manage cash flow (refer to question 4) and you must manage your balance sheet, especially if you have, or ever plan to have, a bank loan. Every transaction that your company completes will appear on one or the other of those three primary financial statements. So let's look at each of these in relation to the P&L statement, which is the core of most annual budgets, and see why you should plan for all three to properly project your company's future.

Your P&L budget projects sales, expenses, and profits of the business. As you learned in the answer to question 3, it shows transactions when they are firmly committed and binding. Sales are recorded and appear in your budget in the month the product will get shipped to the customer. Expenses are recorded and budgeted in the month in which you incur the expense – inventory arrives on your doorstep, employees put in their time, you use the rented building that houses the business, etc. There is no mention of cash here, as you now know, so you have to go further into your budget.

You will need to budget cash flow changes during the period of the P&L budget. When will those budgeted sales be collected from the customer? When will you have to pay your suppliers? This is the cash forecast addressed in question 4, integrated with the P&L budget so that it shows the anticipated collection of the sales, and the anticipated payment for the expenses. Then it goes further, to include those items mentioned in question 3 that don't appear on your P&L statement: capital expenditures, loans made or repaid, dividends paid out to stockholders, new shares sold to new stockholders, and so on. Since each of these is a producer or consumer of cash, they must be projected to get a complete picture of the company's operations for the year.

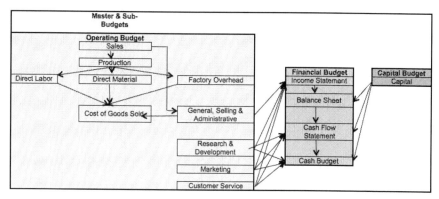

So, do you have the complete picture yet? Not quite. The value of your company is an important element of financial health, and neither the P&L statement nor the statement of cash flow reflects that. They only reflect the changes that will occur over the period of the budget. So you need to include a budgeted balance sheet as well, because it will show the other side of those cash transactions that don't appear in the P&L statement, such as the increase in assets due to new purchases, the reduction or increase in money borrowed, and so on. You can read more about the importance of a balance sheet projection in Chapter F – Forecasting and Budgeting.

6. What should you expect to experience in collecting cash from a mix of credit customers that includes both large and small businesses?

Any business manager who has experienced the collection of accounts receivable knows that patterns are hard to predict, and it's easy to see that the general state of the economy is only one of many factors that affect when a customer will pay the amounts they owe. But since this is usually the largest element of cash flow it bears some analysis and consideration in your credit granting practices. Here are some factors that impact prompt receivables collection:

a) *Size of the customer in relation to the company* – A large customer will typically either pay strictly on time or very late. They will pay strictly on time if they are highly automated and have adopted the policy that it's more efficient to pay on a machine-defined schedule.

b) *Financial health of the customer* – Obviously a customer in financial difficulty, especially cash flow difficulties, will try to pay late whenever possible, and often without advance warning. In a recession this is an important consideration in credit granting.

c) *Cash management policies of the customer* – Some customers may, as a matter of policy, delay payment in order to enhance their own cash flow. Credit granting practices with good research will discover this before goods are shipped.

d) *Billing practices of the company* – It's an easy decision to delay payment when there is a discrepancy in your invoice, regardless of how minor. Ensuring your invoices are always accurate is the best way to remove this factor from the list.

e) *Collection practices of the company* – If your company assigns collection as a collateral duty to someone in the accounting department *when they have time*, this will typically hurt collection activity. See question 9 below for clarification on this.

f) *Role of the company's salesperson in collection* – If your company policy requires the assigned sales person to be involved in the collection process, that often speeds things up, because they know the company and can often get the buyer to intercede to avoid shipment interruptions.

g) *Alternative sources of the product available to the customer* – If your customer can get it somewhere else, they may run up your account balance and then jump to another supplier. This is even more likely if they are having cash flow problems.

7. **What are the principal cash flow considerations in inventory management?**

A large, robust inventory means cash has been invested to build that inventory. So as a general rule: inventory up, cash down; inventory down, cash up. However, as a practical matter it isn't quite that simple. A higher inventory means greater ability to ship on time, lower back orders, quicker response to rush orders, and less time spent by order takers and sales people finding out if you have it in stock. However the flip side of that is greater chance of individual items becoming damaged, soiled, lost or broken. Add obsolescence for technical products, spoilage for perishable products, and theft for anything of value to employees, and it's easy to see that a big inventory is not usually a good idea.

The best balance, then, depends on your customers' needs, the stability of your product, and the quality of your inventory control system. These issues all sound like inventory management issues, and they are. But they're *also* cash management issues, because inventory on your warehouse floor means cash that isn't in your bank account. You can see why it might be a good idea to periodically reduce the margins you hoped to earn on individual items in stock to free up cash for alternative uses. Some of the most common methods that should be periodically used for freeing up cash from a bloated inventory could include: Inventory clearance sales, culling SKUs for slow moving or low margin items, implementing an item-by-item reorder point system so that your inventory never gets below the level needed to satisfy incoming sales, or just-in-time (JIT) arrangements with your suppliers.

If your inventory carrying value is the largest item on your balance sheet, or if your inventory turnover ratio is lower than those of other companies in your industry, you may be investing too much cash in inventory in the hopes of capturing every sale or always getting the best volume purchase price, both good policies if not carried too far.

8. How can you improve your collection of customer receivables?

Collection practices vary widely, especially among middle market and small businesses, as the pressure of stretching staff and strengthening margins can cause collection efforts to be less than ideal. I once had clients who were selling their company at a price based on profit margins, so they froze hiring to save money on salaries. Since their collection department was already understaffed in this marketing-focused company, it made the collection effort nearly unworkable. I revamped the collection department and reduced bad debt losses so significantly it added $5 million to their ultimate selling price…without adding another dollar of sales.

So how can you improve your collection results? Here are some proven ideas from some of my client histories:

- *Improved credit granting practices*
  On the front end, screen new customers more closely before granting a credit line. Get a credit report, and call a couple of their credit references to get a sense of the relationship they have with your potential customer.
- *Committed collection effort, all the time*
  Make collection follow up a key duty of at least one person in your company. Don't make the mistake of giving the job to your controller to handle in her spare time, just because "accounting handles the money." Most importantly, do what you say: If you say you must deny future shipments until an account is brought current, stick to it – every time.
- *Call ahead of time to make sure they're ready to pay*
  Have your collection person call the customer's Accounts Payable department a few days before the due date for payment, *as a courtesy* to your customer, just to make sure there were no problems with the paperwork and the check will be going out on time.
- *Discounts for prompt payment*
  This is an old technique that worked well years ago, but has fallen into neglect in recent years as business practices evolved. The old "2/10 net 30" was, and still is, a fantastic deal if explained to customers clearly. Consider this: A two percent discount for paying 20 days earlier than scheduled amounts to an annual return of 37.24 percent!

THE BOOK ON...BUSINESS FROM A TO Z

9. What's the best way to manage accounts payable to maximize your cash flow?

If you are like most business owners, you extend credit to your customers in order to get them to buy from you, and you hope they will pay you promptly so you can lend the same money to other customers. Well, your suppliers are in that same position with you. They want you to buy from them, they will lend you interest-free money to induce you to do that, and they hope you pay it back promptly.

But what does "promptly" mean? In reality, it means different things to different people. For some, it means payment in accordance with the terms printed on the invoice – the standard trade terms, typically 30 days. Realistically, however, even in good economic times, the average time period for trade payables to be repaid in this country is in the range of 45 days; and it's closer to 60 days in today's challenging economy. If you pay your suppliers in something over 30 days, despite the terms on their invoice, have they threatened to cancel your account for unsatisfactory payment?

So what's the real answer? It depends on what your suppliers think is unsatisfactory payment. Virtually none of them thinks 31 days is unsatisfactory. So how about 35 days? 40 days? 47 days? Well, maybe. The truth is, individual suppliers will probably have a different answer, but if you ask them, they'll all likely refer to the terms printed on their invoices because that's official policy. If they don't follow their own official policies, what policies are they following, and how can you find out what those are?

We call the real answer *Natural Payment Terms*. Each supplier who has customers on credit has an idea in their minds of what constitutes acceptable payment. You know when you've surpassed their acceptable payment terms because they will call you to ask for payment. When that happens, you know you have exceeded their natural payment terms and you should have paid sooner – perhaps a week sooner. But now you know. And if you pay that supplier before they decide to call you, send you a letter or generally agitate for payment, you have paid them in an acceptable timeframe, as defined by their own operating practices. They'll be content – they got paid without having to exert any collection effort – and you'll be happy because you may have extended your trade payables *credit line* by as much as 30 or 45 days or more, just by being aware of your suppliers' real expectations.

10. What are the best tactics to use when you experience a temporary cash shortage?

First, let's define a "temporary cash shortage": You can't quite make payroll next week, but you'll be fine in a month. This can arise because a large customer payment didn't come in when it should have, or you need to snap up a bargain purchase of inventory or a fire sale price on a new machine for the plant, or the bank is taking longer than they said they would to approve your loan renewal after you've paid it off as required.

First, you should ask yourself why you are in this position. Is the cash shortage really temporary or does this happen with regularity? What could you have done to avoid this? Do you really need to spend cash for non-essential items today? Are you clear about the difference between what you *need* and what you *want?*

Now you need to consider a few ideas: You can call that customer and offer a one-time discount if you can pick up the check today; call your largest customer(s) for a particular product and offer a significant discount off the usual agreed-upon price to move inventory now; sell off some inventory at a super bargain price, for cash up front, by calling your largest customer(s) for that product; delay paying a large bill (but call the supplier first so they're not surprised); or you can call your bank and explain to them the problem caused by their processing delay, then ask for an advance against that renewal.

CHAPTER D - DEBT

By Kim D. Defenderfer

1. What is debt?

If you are a business owner, debt is a beautiful thing: You can grow your companies and increase your returns without having to invest more of your own money; and no matter how well your company performs, the lender does not share in the profits[1].

Companies use debt instead of equity because it:

- *Lowers Cost* - Debt is less expensive than equity because it carries less risk. In the event of liquidation, debt holders are repaid before the equity holders. Debt differs from equity because the lender's *return* is limited to the interest it collects.
- *Increases Returns* - Debt will increase a company's Return-on-Equity (ROE) if the assets financed create more income than the cost of the debt.
- *Allows More Control* - Debt holders have no voting power and therefore have no control over the direction, ownership or management of the company.
- *Reduces Required Equity Investment* – By using debt, shareholders may not have to invest more (or as much) capital.
- *Increases Ownership Retention* – Debt financing allows owners to avoid bringing in other investors who would dilute their ownership.
- *It is Easier to Obtain* – Because it is less risky, debt is easier to find than equity. Lending money to companies is the principal purpose of commercial banks, and even as we still feel the effects of the Great Recession, there are still over 8,000 commercial banks in the United States.

---

1   * There are types of *loans* that combine features of debt and equity, such as mezzanine debt, which is debt with warrants and preferred stock. For the purposes of this chapter we will limit our discussion to debt that does *not* include any equity components.

2. What are the principal sources of debt?

The most common sources of debt for middle market companies (from lowest to highest cost) are commercial banks, cash flow lenders, asset based lenders, factors and hard moneylenders.

Banks are the least expensive source, because they have the lowest cost of funds due to their ability to gather FDIC insured core deposits.

When a company has had recurring operating losses, is highly leveraged (see question 3) or has too brief a track record, it may not qualify for a bank loan. However, if it has adequate collateral, it may qualify for financing from an asset based lender, factor or hard moneylender. These alternative lenders all put more emphasis on collateral than profitability.

If a company lacks collateral but has a proven cash flow, even if it is highly leveraged it may qualify for a *cash flow* loan from specialized nonbank lenders or departments within banks. The interest rates paid to these alternative lenders are a reflection of the increased risk and cost of monitoring the debt.

Other options include government guaranteed loan programs. The most popular are the SBA 7A and 504 programs. Detailed information on these programs is available at *SBA.gov* and from banks with SBA departments.

Choosing the Right Lender

Borrowers should obtain bids from at least two worthy competitors and select based on overall long-term value, including:

The quality of the lending team (their experience and understanding of your goals and your business):

a) Price, terms, and conditions
b) Access to decision makers
c) The fit for the institution (is the loan size and type typical for the lender?)
d) The financial strength of the lender
   (see *Bankrate.com or Bauer.com*)

Borrower – Lender Relationship

Borrowers and lenders should build a long-term relationship based on mutual benefit, trust, and open communication. These foundations become especially important in times of opportunity or challenge.

3. **How will lenders underwrite your request?**

Lenders typically use the *Five C's* – Character, Capacity, Capital, Collateral, and Conditions – to underwrite loans.

Character of Management (Owner's and Top Manager's)

There is a saying among lenders: "Numbers don't repay loans – people do." Character (integrity) is an essential building block of trust - the foundation of all lending relationships. Lenders have to trust that when there are challenges the owners and managers will do everything possible to repay the loan. Nothing can overcome a lack of integrity or trust.

Management's reputation and track record are measures of its character. Questions lenders will ask include: What is the company's reputation with employees, suppliers, customers and former bankers? Has management brought the company through challenging times?

Capacity (Cash Flow) – Lending 101

This "C" dictates commercial lenders have at least two independent sources of repayment (cash flow and collateral).

There are a number of definitions of cash flow, but the principle is always the same: whether or not the borrower generates enough cash to repay principal plus interest over the stated term. Lenders will consider future events (projections), but due to the uncertainty of the future, the past is the primary foundation for evaluation. (See Chapter C – Cash Flow for more information.)

A Debt Service Coverage Ratio (DSCR) is commonly used to measure capacity to service debt. As with cash flow, there are numerous definitions. Following is a common definition: (Net Income + Depreciation + Interest)/ (Current Portion of Long Term Debt + Interest). Lenders (and Borrowers) should set a DSCR covenant high enough to assure the Borrower has some *cushion* for a potential downturn.

Capital

Here the question is: Does the company have adequate capital to fund operations and provide cushion for a potential downturn? Capital needs variation by industry depending on the amount of assets required as well as their sales and collection cycles. For example, service businesses generally demand less capital than manufacturers, as they have fewer fixed assets (plant and equipment) to support. Lenders look at the ratio of Effective Debt/Effective Tangible Net Worth to measure leverage. A ratio of 4:1 is considered high by commercial banks. Generally, the higher the leverage ratio the tighter the loan structure, for example more highly levered borrowers may be put on a formal borrowing base, where loan outstandings (the total amount of the loan(s) a customer has with a lender) are limited to an advance rate on eligible assets (see question 8).

Collateral

Lenders look to assets as a secondary source of repayment, and will normally file UCC liens to assure they are in a priority position in front of other creditors (such as trade creditors). These can either be *broad form filings* on all tangible and intangible assets, or *specific filings* on individual assets (such as a single piece of machinery).

Not all collateral is created equally. Lenders assess its quality (value) based on their judgment of the net proceeds they would collect, should they be forced to step into the shoes of the Borrower. The most common types of collateral include:

- *Accounts Receivable (AR)* – The quality (value) of AR's vary widely:
  - *Higher Quality* - Receivables from a diverse client base, where it is clear the product was received (there are no returns or warranties); for example, the sale of a commodity raw material such as raw steel.
  - *Lower Quality* – Receivables from less concentrated or financially viable group of clients, or where it is not clear the service was fully or satisfactorily delivered, such as progress billings for legal fees or contractor services. Other challenging categories are receivables from government entities or from the sale of software licenses, because there are extra steps to legally perfect these liens.
- *Inventory* – As with AR's, the value of inventory to a lender varies widely:
  - The most valuable commodity is raw material inventory, such as steel, lumber and petroleum, where there is a ready market. The least valuable are unique goods or items whose value can be diminished by changing technology or tastes. If a loan has a significant dependence on inventory, lenders may want a professional appraisal so they can establish an *advance rate* based on the appraisal's *orderly* or *forced liquidation* value. Lenders, even Asset Based Lenders, will rarely allow more than 50 percent of the loan outstandings to be based on inventory.
- *Collateral Advance Rates* - The chart below provides a common range of *advance rates,* which vary depending on the lenders outlook of marketability and collection costs.

Collateral	Range of Advance Rates
Cash (pledged CD in lender's bank)	100%
US Treasury Bonds	70% to 90% depending on duration
US Stocks	40% to 60%
Eligible Receivables (excludes concentrations over 20%, foreign and past due receivables)	60% to 85% - depending on nature of product, client diversity and history of dilution.
Commodity Inventory – (raw materials such as steel, lumber, petroleum)	25% to 60% depending on predictability of ready market, format, location, cost of sale.
Finished Goods Inventory	0% to 50% depending on stability of market, format, location, cost of sale.
Equipment	50% to 80% of Forced Liquidation Value

Conditions

This includes both the conditions of the borrower and the overall economy.

- *The Borrower* – In addition to the five *C's,* other conditions include the depth of management, location, access to raw materials, and labor and production capacity.
- *Industry and the Overall Economy* – These conditions relate to all borrowers and include the competitive landscape, availability of raw materials, potential product obsolescence, and need for investment in research and development, as well as overall economic conditions effecting supply, demand and the availability and cost of credit.

4. What is the *right* level of debt?

As mentioned in the beginning of this chapter, debt can increase the returns to owners on a given amount of equity. The other side of the coin is debt increases risk, because it provides lenders with certain contractual rights. If things do not go as planned, lenders may have the right to increase interest rates, charge penalties and ultimately seize their collateral.

The right level of debt, sometimes referred to as leverage, is dependent on the borrower's willingness to increase risk relative to its potential to reap higher returns. The amount of debt should be weighed against the predictability that future cash flows would materialize to repay the loan according to terms.

Let's compare two companies (Company A and Company B). Each company has the same profile, except Company A is borrowing to add a new location, while Company B is borrowing to replace an existing machine. It is obvious Company A is taking on more risk because of the unknowns of opening in a new location (demand, staffing, suppliers, regulations, and competition).

This does not mean they should not proceed; it just means Company A may want to have a lower level of leverage.

5. **How much should debt cost?**

Loan pricing is often quoted as a *spread* over an established index, such as Prime or LIBOR for variable rate loans, or the equivalent term U.S. Treasury for term loans. Common pricing for bank loans can range anywhere from Prime less 1.00% to Prime + 3.00%, or LIBOR + 1.50% to LIBOR + 3.50%. The amount of this *spread* is dependent on a combination of the following:

- *The economy and market conditions* – Market rates vary widely depending on the general interest rate environment. For example, Prime Rate has varied from a high of 21.50% in December 1980 to a low of 3.25% for all of 2009 and 2010.
- *Risk* – Pricing reflects risks associated with the borrowing, economy, and industry. Risk is based on a combination of factors, including potential for changes in supply or demand, the stability of cash flow, leverage, the amount and quality of collateral, debt service coverage, the presence and financial strength of a guarantor, the diversity of customers, geography or products, management's experience, etc.
- *Duration* – Rates are driven by the lender's alternative investment opportunities and ultimately by the wider economy. Rates for longer-term loans are normally higher than for shorter-term loans. The US Treasury yield curve, driven by the global economy, is a good indicator of the cost of money over various time periods.
- *Loan structure/Collateral* – The tighter the structure, the less the risk of uncertainty and therefore the lower the price. A one year line of credit to a distributor, secured by a diverse base of accounts receivables and commodity inventory guaranteed by an owner with ample liquid assets with quarterly reporting and covenant monitoring, would be priced lower than line of credit to a service company with progress billings accounts receivables, semi-annual reporting and a weak guarantor.
- *The competitive environment* – Two or three offers from reputable lenders should be enough to assure a competitive market rate.
- *The lender's cost of funds* - Not all banks have the same cost of funds. A bank's cost of funds is dependent on its mix of deposits (non-interest bearing vs. interest bearing), its ratio of loans to deposits, its level of equity and the quality of its loan portfolio.

- *Associated business with lender* – Lenders use relationship pricing taking into account returns from deposits, loans and fees from the entire relationship.
- *The particular lender's appetite* – Lenders need a diversified portfolio to reduce risk. Lenders may either shy away from, or increase pricing to, industries they are overexposed to, or in which they have had credit problems.

6. **What information should you provide lenders?**

Open book is the best definition of a relationship with a lender. The better a lender understands a borrower's industry, operations, financial condition and goals; the better the lender can meet the borrower's immediate and future needs. More information sooner is almost always better. Suppressing bad news is not only ethically wrong, it will cause the lender to lose faith in the borrower, and could be a violation of federal law.

New borrowers often believe information requests by lenders are invasive. However, adequate information is needed by the lender to properly assess the risks, structure the credit and be supportive of the borrower's needs. This assessment must be included in a *write-up* with all source documents maintained in a *credit file* available to credit administrators and regulators.

Following is a list of the information commonly requested for a commercial loan (often call a *Financial Package*):

Borrower

- Three years of CPA-reviewed financial statements or federal tax returns.
- The most recent internally prepared quarterly financial statement and prior year comparable interim statement.
     Note: If there is seasonality, or if there have been material interim changes, such as losses or rapid growth, the borrower should provide statements showing the last 24 months or 8 quarters.
- Company prepared projections for the period of any term loan.
- Accounts receivable and accounts payables summary agings.
- Inventory summary by location.
- Equipment listing.
- A list of the top five clients by dollar revenue for the each of the past three years.
- Three months of bank account analysis statements.
- Organizational chart showing key management positions and entity chart if there is more than one legal entity.

Guarantors

- Personal Financial Statement.
- Two years tax returns with all K-1's.
- Bank or brokerage statements showing liquidity.

Standard ongoing reporting includes quarterly internally prepared financial statements, accounts receivable and payables agings, annual CPA reviewed financial statements, an updated personal financial statement, tax returns and brokerage statements.

7. **How does purpose dictate structure?**
Purpose (the assets being financed and why) drives the structure (the duration and repayment schedule) and the source of repayment (how the assets financed will generate cash to repay the loan). Below are two common loan structures:

- *Revolving Line of Credit (RLOC)* - A one-year RLOC is used to finance temporary increases in current assets (accounts receivables or inventory). The loan is drawn down to finance the purchase and production of assets (or the cost of providing services) and repaid when the resulting receivables are collected.
    - o The RLOC can be either *an open line* or a *formula or asset based line*. An open line means the company can borrow up to the limit of the line, assuming it is not in violation of its loan terms. If Borrowers are more leveraged, rapidly growing or lack a consistent track record, they may be put on a formal monitoring program where loan outstandings are restricted to a *Borrowing Base* equal to the specified eligible assets multiplied by an appropriate *advance rate*. This monitoring can take place daily, monthly or quarterly, depending on the lender's assessment of the risk. Regardless if a formal Borrowing Base is utilized or not, lenders will estimate the value of the collateral using the advance rate ranges outlined in question 3.
- *Term loan* - A loan to support a piece of equipment lasting five years may be structured as a five-year, fully amortizing loan with the source of repayment being the cash flow generated by the equipment financed. This structure matches the accounting norms of equipment being initially capitalized and then expensed (via depreciation) over its useful life.

8. **What are common loan terms and conditions?**

The terms and conditions of a loan are driven by the structure, source of repayment, purpose and perceived risk. A typical term sheet should provide the following categories:

- Borrower
- Loan amount
- Availability if subject to a borrowing base
- Purpose
- Rate
  - o Fixed
  - o Floating
    - ▪ Margin above/over
    - ▪ What index
- Maturity date
- Repayment schedule
  - o Monthly
  - o Quarterly
  - o Interest only
  - o Fully amortized
- Collateral
- Guarantors
- Reporting requirements
- Financial covenants
  - o Positive covenants
  - o Negative covenants
- Preconditions to funding

9. **What documents will you be signing?**

Many banks utilize standard documents tailored to their state. Complex loans (multiple borrowers, unusual conditions) may require outside counsel. The most common documents include:

- *Loan Agreement* – includes terms, conditions, covenants of all loans (one Loan Agreement may cover multiple notes)
- *Promissory Note* – one for each loan, states amount, maturity, rate, default rate, and repayment schedule
- *Security Agreement* – allows lender to take a security interest in collateral
- *UCC Filing* – document filed (electronically) with each state where collateral is held; identifies the collateral and perfects lenders interest in collateral via a public record

- *Borrower Resolution* – grants authority from management to borrower
- *Disbursement Agreement* – states conditions of loan disbursement
- *Agreement to Provide Insurance* – provides insurance agent borrower's authority to name lender as loss payee
- *Guarantee/s* – those who promise to repay the loan if the borrower(s) do not

10. What are the biggest mistakes you should avoid?

- *Choosing the wrong lender*

   The wrong lender is one who is either not interested in, or capable of, meeting the borrower's needs now and in the future. Please see the section entitled *Choosing the Right Lender* in question 2 of this chapter.

- *Failing to communicate*

   Consistent open communication is always important, but is crucial to laying a solid foundation for unforeseen but eventual opportunities or challenges. Experienced lenders, like other professionals, can be good sounding boards for ideas. Also, knowing at least one senior person in addition to the loan officer is a good idea, in case the officer leaves the institution or is not responsive.

- *Agreeing to terms the borrower cannot meet*

   Borrowers should read and understand all agreements before they sign. If they have questions, they should ask for clarification. Financial covenants should be understood and tested to ensure enough cushion exists for normal swings in operations, while simultaneously being meaningful triggers to allow the lender to assert its rights early enough to protect its position, should things not go as projected.

- *Violating the terms of the agreement and not proactively communicating with the lender*

   It is important borrowers establish a track record of performance with lenders. This means reporting information in a timely manner, not running overdrafts, making payments on time, tracking their own covenants, and proactively informing the lender of problems and future needs. Trust is the foundation of the lender-borrower relationship: It will either be strengthened by consistent open communication, or weakened by a lack thereof.

CHAPTER E – EQUITY

By David Cohn

1. What is equity financing?

Equity is share capital invested in a business for the medium to long-term in return for a *share of the ownership* and a negotiated element of control of the business. Because equity investors are co-owners of the business, they may be exposed to personal liability for all business debts unless the business is a corporation, limited partnership, or limited liability company. If you recruit equity investors for what has been your sole proprietorship, your business will now be treated as a general partnership. This means your equity investors will be considered to be general partners, whether or not they take part in running the business.

There are three common ways to organize your company so that you can offer shares of ownership with limits of liability to the investors:

- Form a corporation and issue stock.
- Form a limited partnership and make the investor(s) a limited partner.
- Form a Limited Liability Corporation (LLC) in which the investors become members.

Unlike lenders, equity investors don't normally charge interest or expect to be repaid by a particular date. Instead, their return is usually paid in the form of dividend payments, and those payments depend on the growth and profitability of the business. Because the investors share the risks your business faces, this form of funding is often referred to as *risk capital.*

Many times there will be an element of control of the business that must be negotiated, and that usually depends on the circumstances in which the money is invested. Money invested in a healthy business with growth prospects is unlikely to have any provisions for operating control, unless there is a dramatic deterioration of the firm's performance. And then those provisions would be in the form of pre-negotiated triggers that would change control of the board. Money coming in to fix a company's balance sheet, or shore up operating cash flow is a different story. It is likely that the *new* money will have some element of control, or least some influence in key operating decisions made by management.

In the United States, equity investing in the form of *seed capital* has been the most robust form of capital formation for the last 20 years. The following examples illustrate the fact that the U.S. remains number one in the environment for new business formations, especially taking ideas and turning them into reality[2]:

- *Starbucks* was started by an English teacher with venture capital.
- The first computer was sold in 1976 by *Apple*, which was started with seed capital.
- The *Intel Venture Fund* was responsible for the first microprocessor.
- *Amazon* was started with venture capital money in 1996.
- *Google* was started with $100,000 of venture capital money.
- *Fed Ex* was started with seed money in 1973.
- Venture capital money was used to start *Home Depot* by two fired and unemployed managers from an established hardware chain store operation.

2. What are the basic differences between debt and equity?

Debt is borrowed money that you must pay back regardless of the success of the firm, as discussed in Chapter D. Securing debt financing does not entail *selling* or diluting your ownership interest, but is *borrowing* against assets. Your ability to repay the loan's principle and interest are what is important.

Equity is selling partial ownership in your firm. The owners share proportionally in the risk and only receive cash dividends if your firm is successful. As there are many forms of debt financing, there are also many forms of equity structures.

Beware of prospective equity investors who want to "have their cake and eat it too", in the form of guarantees on the return of their money, regardless of the performance of the company. In addition, they will expect their money to be repaid before your money comes out. This is something you should be aware of. If someone invests equity, they normally wait until the company is profitable enough to pay dividends. It is very unusual that an equity investor "double dips" by receiving investment repayment AND dividends.

Many early stage companies turn to private commercial financing, factoring (selling accounts receivable), or equipment leasing until they are strong enough to secure traditional bank debt.

---

2 *National Venture Capital Association (www.nvca.org)_*

3. What are the advantages and disadvantages of raising equity?

The 2008 recession tested millions of borrowers whose loan *covenants* (restrictions) caused many businesses to make tactical decisions they had never contemplated. The main advantage of using equity to finance your business is flexibility within the covenants of the investment agreement with investors. Since equity funding does not require repayment, it allows your business to evolve with economic factors.

Equity investors only realize a gain on their investment if the business is doing well and there is a liquidity event down the road, such as a public offering or a sale. Another alternative is to bring in business angels and/or venture capitalists, which are discussed further on in this chapter. They bring valuable skills, contacts, and experience to your business. They may also assist in strategic and key decisions during the relationship. Investors have a vested interest in the business' success, its growth, profitability and increase in value. If there is a good experience with these types of investors, often they will provide follow up funding as the business grows.

Keep in mind that raising capital is demanding, costly and time consuming. Your business may suffer, as you need to devote large spans of time to the deal with prospective investors. These potential investors will be seeking a multitude of data, including background information on you and your business, that you may not have readily available. They will closely scrutinize the past results and forecasts. They will probe into management competency throughout the company as well.

However, in the end you might find this process to be very useful, regardless of whether or not you actually receive any funding. This is because of what you learn during the process - Your business strategy and objective folks will have put your model under the microscope, so you must prove to them and yourself that they are viable. The aftermath usually involves some warranted yet constructive changes to the business. You learn and grow.

Depending on the investor, when you secure equity financing, you may lose a certain amount of your ability to make management unilateral decisions. You now have a team to consult. You will have to put in place reporting systems, if not already there, and invest management time to provide regular information for the investor(s) to monitor. In the end, you probably need these disciplines regardless of the path you take.

As a result of the sale of some ownership, you will have a smaller share in the business. However, your reduced share may become worth a lot more in absolute monetary terms if the investment leads to your business becoming more successful. You have provided a platform to share risk.

At various times in the life of most companies, there are going to be requirements for outside capital in order to grow the business. Choosing which type of financing vehicle is best for your company is very important. Deciding whether to seek equity capital or debt financing may be the first step. At this stage, bringing in professionals to assist in this process is highly encouraged. These professionals can wear different hats, but still help you get to the right conclusion.

4. **Is equity financing right for your business?**

Consider the following challenges and questions that need to be answered:
- What exactly is the funding for?
- How much control are you hoping to retain?
- What skills does the business need that the investor could bring?
- How long do you need the funds for?
- What are the core issues in your business plan?
- Are your plans for the business realistic?
- Are your plans the result of a collaborative effort or just you?

Your business plan should address these issues in detail. The plan should include a series of detailed financial forecasts and how you'll repay the investor. Your management's level of participation is key. The effort must be collaborative, and the investors need to sense that.

5. **When should you consider equity financing?**

Your business may not be attractive to lenders because of lack of cash flow to service interest costs, or lack of assets to borrow against, and therefore you have only the equity route to follow. Making the effort to raise equity is most likely to make sense when:

- Your company does not have a balance sheet capable of attracting debt financing, and if so it would be at very high cost.
- Your business does not have enough cash flow to pay interest on a loan after funding operating expenses.
- Your business requires capital expenditures in order to get to the next plateau.

After you have reached the conclusion that raising equity is the route you would like to take, other questions arise, which can include:

- Are you prepared to give up a share in your business and some control?
- Are you prepared to have outside parties monitor progress and possibly have them involved in significant decisions regarding operating the business?
- What industry experience and knowledge does your management team have?
- Could you use additional skills?
- Are you prepared to deal with the investor(s) having expectations of a higher return than maybe you do?

After reviewing the above, ask yourself again, "Do I need outside professional help?" You will find the more the investors can understand your business and what makes it tick, the less the aforementioned topics become problems.

6. **Who provides equity?**
   There are various sources of equity as we move away from sources of debt.

   Friends and Family
   This is probably still the most popular source for seed money. In many cases, it could be family with prior exposure to the project, and quite possibly involved in the startup activities of a new business. However, just because you are close with this funding source, you still cannot take relaxed approach to seeking the funds. Proceed as if these folks were strangers and professional. Friends and family members may not be that objective, and won't always ask all the right questions. Therefore surprises surface during the investment relationship. Understanding the salient issues in the business and why the money is needed is still quite important.

   Angel Investors
   Angel investors are often retired entrepreneurs or executives who may be interested in investing for reasons that go beyond pure monetary return. These can include: wanting to keep abreast of current developments in a particular business arena, mentoring another generation of entrepreneurs, or making use of their experience and networks on a less-than-full-time basis. These investors can often provide valuable management advice and important marketing strategies. They get their deal flow from their trusted sources and other business contacts, investor conferences, symposiums, and at meetings organized by groups of angels.

Companies seeking this type of funding will be expected to pitch directly to investors in face-to-face meetings on a regular basis. Many of these groups have full time screeners, who can assist you in organizing your pitch, if they think your offering merits a presentation. This group of investors can offer capital, particularly in the early or growth stages of project, in return for generous amounts of equity.

The average angel investment for any one deal can be from $500,000 to $1million, with individual contributions between $50,000 and $75,000. The past few years, particularly in North America, we have seen the emergence of networks of angel groups. If go to the website for the *Angel Capital Association* (www.angelcapitalassociation.org), you will find the angel groups in your area.

Venture capital

Is most often used for high-growth businesses destined for sale or to be taken public. Venture capital (VC) money is generally sourced from pension funds and university endowments. Also, there is an abundance of money coming in from larger corporations to serve their own specific interest in corporate development. Most VC funds are operated to find and invest in specific industry sectors; in fact, it is rare to find a VC that will jump their self-imposed boundaries or be a generalist. You will discover that they have the same appetite for a percentage of ownership as the *Angel Investors,* plus a sizable amount of control on the exit strategy of the company. You will be expected to operate the business, with a formal reporting structure, and a formal approval process on capital expenditures beyond a certain amount. One of the common websites that you can use as a resource for finding funds of this type is *National Venture Capital Association* (www.nvca.org).

Private Equity

Private Equity (PE) groups operate very similarly to VC, except that their appetite for investments is much broader, and they generally look at later stage companies. Their style of managing their portfolio of invested-in companies varies from weekly reporting to passive reporting. These folks have an affinity for attracting skilled managers, because of their passive investment nature to begin with. Their portfolios consist of either platform companies, which are used to purchase similar companies in what is called a *consolidating environment*, or portfolio companies, which depend on internal or "organic" growth. There is one caveat that you need to be aware of with PE: These groups making non-controlling investments in companies are still in the minority. It is estimated that only about 12% of the PE groups currently in existence will entertain a minority investment. Most the PE groups are financially oriented in their investments, and they generally buy controlling interest in the company. A good website for this information, along with a robust search platform, is *Private Equity Info* (www. privateequityinfo.com). The website is relatively inexpensive to use; the data is very current and is widely accessed by M&A (mergers and acquisitions) professionals.

Government Grants

In today's world, you almost have to be Sherlock Holmes to find government sources of money, but they do exist. Many of these grants have such *liberal* return of funds clauses that the so-called debt looks more like equity. The government also provides resources and funding for minorities. If you are a minority founder and/or owner of a startup or existing business, the *Minority Business Development Association*, a part of the U.S. Chamber of Commerce, is an excellent resource for this purpose. Their website is www.mbda.gov. This organization is not your direct source of financing, but they know where to send you and can give you the right tools to work with.

7. **Where do you find equity investors?**

Finding parties to fund your idea or growing company is not a mystery today, especially with so much online data available. Having said that, you need to consider how much time you personally can devote to *the hunt*. Remember, simply identifying a source of capital can be an exhausting search and a tiny fraction of the total time required to negotiate and complete a deal. Engaging outside professionals to manage the entire process and to do the legwork might be a good idea, depending on how you manage your time. Your personal banker, attorney, accountant, or other professional advisors can possibly be your starting point. They will know investment bankers and similar advisors that can manage this process to a successful conclusion.

Professional organizations, such as the *Association for Corporate Growth*, (www.acg.org), have chapters organized in most large metropolitan areas. They will have monthly events, to which nonmembers are welcomed. By joining organizations like *Association of Merger & Acquisition Advisors*, (www.amaaonline. org), you will have access to middle market investment bankers, valuation professionals, attorneys, and accountants. This organization thrives on the exchange of information related to capital formation, structuring, and sourcing of debt and equity.

8. **When securing equity financing, what are the important steps?**

The ultimate goal is to eventually get to a short list of potential investors, whether you are doing it on your own or through professionals. Remember that many private investors are interested in specific industry sectors or geographical regions, so that by itself may shorten your list.

Pitching your plan or proposal to potential investors is important. Try to anticipate the concerns the investors may have and show the benefits of their involvement, placing emphasis on the:

- Investment required
- Terms you're proposing - such as share of control, bringing in new skills and exit plan
- Ability of the management team to proceed with the plan
- Likely return on any investment

Make sure your presentation is informative, relevant and engaging. Include other members of your team in the presentation whenever possible. Potential investors are more likely to invest in someone they feel they can trust and has a clear business strategy. Specify how the investment relationship will be managed, and what involvement they'll have in the company. Discuss how your corporate governance can accommodate their wishes.

After an arduous round of negotiating the deal, the validation and verification process will begin. Most investors, from part time semi-professionals to full-time professionals, want outside advisors running the due diligence process. The main reason for this is *objectivity*. The savvy investors will check everything that relates to the business and its history. They may want to do a *quality of earnings study* to determine how valid your profit margins are. They may want to talk to your key customers, and other personnel in the field. All this effort is called due diligence. The prospective investor also may suggest changes in your corporate governance.

9. What else should you know about equity?

As the owner of a business idea, plan, or company, understand that the value of your ownership is subjective. There will always be a constant movement of *perceived value* between the buyer and seller until there is a transaction, and that is the ultimate test of any valuation. When a company does not use a professional to market itself (meaning the company tries to sell itself without the benefit or the experience or advice of a professional broker), there are other paths to narrow down the range of value. You may need to engage an independent professional valuation firm to establish the value (see Chapter V – Valuation for more information). I also recommend that you browse www.asabv.org, the *American Society of Appraisers* website.

The individual investor is interested not only in the total changes to equity, but also in the increase/decrease in the value of his own personal share of the equity. This reconciliation of equity should be done both in total and on a per-share basis. Accountants use a standard method of accounting for your economic value as a shareholder, adjusting for net income or loss, minus dividends paid if any, along with any changes in shares outstanding.

One form of debt, called *Convertible Debentures,* sometimes ends up as equity. These debenture (unsecured bond) holders do not have rights to vote in the company's general meetings of shareholders, but may have separate meetings or votes; e.g., they may weigh in on changes to the rights attached to the debentures. The interest paid to them is a charge against profit in the company. These instruments can be converted into *equity shares* of the issuing company after a predetermined period of time.

10. What are the key ingredients to successful negotiations with equity investors?

It is most important to carefully examine any business's cultural issues and the investors' tolerance for risk. The key question: What are the investors' tolerances for negative events, and will they be patient if reversals or slowdowns occur? Another important checkpoint is to agree on the growth metrics for the company, and on whether or not the goals are reasonable. Regardless of the structure of the investment, the level of knowledge your investor has about your business will dictate the collaborative effects in running the business, and how effective fresh ideas from outsiders can become a part of improving the business model.

There needs to be an alignment in timetables for exiting the business. For example: "*We will sell in x years…*" Or: "*We will sell when we get to a certain plateau in growth…*" Quite often there will be provisions in the contract for "buy backs", or "puts", to address disagreement in exit timing if that should occur.

A "buy back" is the scenario where the business will pay the investor back at $X amount. The number is predetermined and set at the beginning of the investment. A "put" is a contractual right of the investor to sell (to the original shareholders) his share of ownership at a predetermined price or formula. A "buy back" gives a little more control to the buyer, where a "put" reverses this and gives slightly more control to the seller.

In the absence of 20/20 vision in forecasting the environment, you should be careful in allowing such provisions without a well-thought-out financial plan. In all cases of capital injection, you must be prepared for uncertainty, and that all expectations may not be met.

When seeking outside capital, many sources of funds have particular industry niches they are more comfortable working in. Take the time to look around and be sure that the source you are considering is well acquainted with your type of business.

In closing, there are three salient points that bear no compromise in the capital raising process:

1. Find investors familiar with your industry.
2. Make sure their risk tolerance matches yours.
3. There is total agreement on the strategic plan and estimated of time of exit for both the investor and the company receiving capital.

CHAPTER F – FORECASTING AND BUDGETING

By Daniel Feiman

1. What is forecasting?

"Everything that can be invented has been invented." – Commissioner, U.S. Office of Patents, 1899.

The quote above was a forecast. It was completely wrong; but it was a forecast. So what *is* a forecast? According to Merriam-Webster, a forecast is:

a: to calculate or predict (some future event or condition) usually as a result of study and analysis of available pertinent data; *especially* to predict (weather conditions) on the basis of correlated meteorological observations

b: to indicate as likely to occur

In business forecasting, it is vital that you make the forecasts for your company as accurate as possible, because you will base many of your decisions and the related actions on your forecast.

Most of the synonyms for a forecast relate to some version of a calculation. But how do you calculate a forecast? You gather assumptions, apply some reliable formulas to the assumptions, and calculate results.

The standard approach to calculating business forecasts is by using a *model*. A mathematical model is nothing more than a spreadsheet that has built-in formulas. You build them in yourself (if you have the time and experience to do so), you have someone else build it for you, or you buy it. Simply put, a model is nothing more than a spreadsheet with areas for inputs (assumptions), the formulas, and areas for outputs (results).

The example below is a model to forecast what the current market price of a corporate bond should be based on assuming a *rate, number of periods until maturity, coupon (interest) payment and percentage of original value returned at maturity*. With these inputs, you apply the *formula, -PV(B3,B4,B5,B6)* and calculate the *Price*. This is not a guarantee of anything it is merely a forecast of what the market price would be *if* all of the assumptions are correct.

You are looking at a bond that has 25 years to maturity. The coupon rate is 9% and coupons are paid semiannually. The yield-to-maturity is 8%. What is the current price?		
RATE	4.00%	(8%/2)
NPER	50	(25*2)
PMT	4.5	(9%*100/2)
FV	100	(%)
Price	$110.74	Formula: -PV(B3,B4,B5,B6)

Forecasts can be for very short duration, such as how long it will take to read this chapter, or much longer term, such as how many years it will take to cure cancer.

2. **How do you know when you have a good forecast, and what is the benefit of having one?**

A *good* forecast is one that leads to an accurate, achievable budget. The best way to consistently have this result is to research and validate your assumptions. These assumptions should include at a minimum:

- Product lifecycle
- Customer base
- Competition
- Technology
- Risk
- Availability and cost of materials
- Availability and cost of personnel
- Market share
- Pricing
- Obsolescence
- Financing
- Seasonality
- Cycles over multiple years
- Economic conditions
- Industry trends
- Market conditions
- Production requirements

When you take all of these variables (and any others you deem critical to your success) into account in building your forecasts and the resulting budgets consistently are within the company's variance tolerances, you have a good forecast. In other words, it takes time to know *if* you have the forecasting process and that the results are reliable.

Now, the benefit of a *good* forecast is that you have more confidence when relying on it to make decisions or create budgets. With a higher level of confidence in the results, you can move more aggressively into actions based on this forecast.

3. What are the steps to developing a good forecast?

There is a *best practice* for developing forecasts that yield consistently reliable results. This practice includes:

a) Determining the use of the forecast

b) Selecting the items to be forecast

c) Determining the time horizon of the forecast – short-, medium- or long-term

d) Selecting the forecasting model(s) (see below)

e) Gathering the data you need – internal, external, first vs. second-generation

f) Creating the forecast

g) Validating the forecast

h) Implementing the results

4. What are the most common types of forecasting used in businesses today?

Qualitative Forecasts

These are used when situations are vague; little data exists (e.g., new products and technologies) and no model is necessary. It involves intuition and experience. Some techniques in producing a qualitative forecast include:

a) *Expert opinion*

A small group of highly respected experts in a given area are polled on a critical subject or topic. Over some period of discussion, they eventually arrive at a consensus.

b) *Sales force polling*

Each salesperson is asked to project his or her sales. Since salespeople are the ones closest to the marketplace, they should have the capacity to know what the customer wants.

c) *Delphi method*

Set up exactly like expert opinion above, with one significant difference: Instead of having the experts discuss their opinions in a group trying to come to a consensus, each is interviewed individually. Their views are tabulated to see *if* there is consensus. If not, and this is usually the case, the outliers are interviewed again to determine their reasons for the positions they took. The interviewers make the forecast based on all of the data.

d) *Consumer market survey*

The customers (commercial or individual) are asked about their purchasing plans and their projected buying behavior. A large number of respondents are needed here to be able to generalize certain results.

Quantitative Forecasts

These forecasts are those you use when the situation is stable and historical data exists. There are several commonly used mathematical techniques including:

a) *Time series models*

These models look at a series of data points over time, including:

1. *Naïve Approach* – This assumes that demand in the next period is the same as demand in most recent period. Unfortunately, demand patterns may not always be that stable. An example would be if July sales were 50, then August sales will also be 50.

2. *Moving Average* – This is a series of arithmetic means and is used if little or no trend is present in the data. A moving average provides an overall impression of data over time. A simple moving average uses average demand for a fixed sequence of periods and is good for stable demand with no pronounced behavioral patterns. For example, if you want to forecast a value in period four you might use this equation: $F4 = [R1 + R2 + R3] / 3$. Which means you take the result (R) for periods one, two and three, then divide the total by three (as the number of periods of data you have) and use the result to forecast what will happen in period four.

3. *Weighted Moving Average (WMA)* - A weighted moving average adjusts the moving average method to reflect the most recent data by giving it more weight. This assumes the older data is less important. The weights are based on intuition and lie between 0 and 1 for a total of 1.0. An example might be - Equation: WMA for period 4 = (W)(R3) + (W)(R2) + (W)(R1). W=Weight; R=Result.

4. *Exponential Smoothing* - The exponential smoothing is an averaging method that relies more on recent changes in demand by assigning a smoothing constant to the most recent data so it has a greater impact on your forecast than older data. This is more useful if recent changes in data are the results of actual changes (e.g., seasonal patterns) instead of just random fluctuations. The formula is Ft + 1 = a R t + (1 - a) Ft. Where Ft + 1 is the forecast for the next period; Rt is the actual result in the present period, Ft is the previously determined forecast for the present period; a = a weighting factor referred to as the smoothing constant. The smoothing constant is derived through trial and error.

b) *Causal models*

1. These models attempt to show the "cause and effect" relationship between one or more independent variables on a single dependent variable to predict the results. An independent variable is one you research and/or control. This is also called an assumption. The dependent variable's value is the result of the impact of the independent variable(s).

2. Regression

   i. Simple (Linear) regression is a form of forecasting that calculates the relative relationship between a single dependent variable and single independent variable. You take a set of historical actual data and attempt to determine if a change in the independent variable causes a predictable result (effect) on the dependent variable. For example, will an increase in your advertising investment of $100,000 actual cause sales to increase $250,000?

   ii. Multiple regression is how you test the relationship between several independent variables and a dependent variable. For example, as a real estate agent you might record the size of homes, the number of bedrooms, the average income in the respective neighborhood and the curb appeal. From this you might be able to determine that the number of bedrooms is a better predictor of the price for which a house sells in a particular neighborhood than the curb appeal.

5. How do you make your forecast more reliable/useful?

The first thing you need to do is test it. Start with some actual data from several previous periods; apply it to your forecasting model(s) then see how reliable the results are compared to what actually happened. If they are consistent, you have a reliable forecast. If not, there probably one of two reasons: 1) the current condition is not consistent with previous ones, or 2) the model is the not the right one for your situation. If that's the case, try alternative models.

6. What is the difference between forecasting and budgeting?

Since we have established that forecasting is applying one or more formulas to one or more assumptions to calculate one or more potential results, how is that different from budgeting? A budget is a *result* of a forecast. Once your forecast results in what you can commit to achieving during your operating period you convert it into a budget (see the example below). The goal of the budget is to give you a roadmap to achieving your strategic and tactical goals.

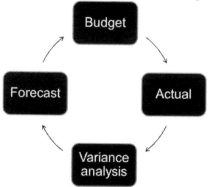

7. What are the three kinds of budgets your company may want to create?

There are two types of budgets every company must develop every year as parts of the *Master budget*: the *operating budget* and the *financial budget*. The operating budget is what you use to manage the business. It is comprised of a series of linked sub-budgets that represent *sales, production, labor, material, overhead, cost of goods sold, headcount, general and administrative areas,* and the *income statement*.

The income statement is calculated as a result of the other sub-budgets and is the "bridge" between the operating and the financial budgets.

The financial budget starts with the income statement and then adds the budgeted *statement of cash flow* and *balance sheet* before getting down to the detail of the *cash budget.*

If a company wants to invest in major projects (buildings, equipment, facilities, etc.) to grow, it will develop a *capital budget* for this purpose, which would be the third kind of budget. The capital budget shows the revenues (if any) generated by the investment, the related variable and fixed costs, the net profit or loss and the net cash flow per period. From this you determine *if* the project increases or decreases the value of the firm by using one or more of the standard analysis tools such as *Net Present Value (NPV), Internal Rate of Return (IRR) or Profitability Index (PI).* Or the capital budget might simply show the timing of purchases and the amount of cash/borrowing committed to the purchase.

8. **What are the most common approaches to budgeting?**

The most widely used budget format is the *traditional* or *fixed* budget. This is where all of your revenues and expenses are established and you measure the difference between these numbers and your actual results periodically using a variance analysis report. The benefit of this approach is everyone knows how to do it. The disadvantage is it is frequently inaccurate and the company doesn't even try to adjust it until the next budgeting period.

An excellent, but seldom-used, alternative to the traditional budget in selected cases is a *flexible* budget. The flexible budget allows you to establish "ranges" of volumes or costs that have a reasonable probability of occurring, so that the result is a budget that takes into account more than one potential outcome with the related values shown. It does require you to initially separate the fixed costs out, because these costs will not be affected by the flexible portion of the budget (see the example below). The advantage is a potentially more accurate budget. The disadvantages include a little more work to develop it and some senior managers incorrectly thinking it reduces accountability.

		Flexible Budget						
	Variable Cost	Unit Levels of Activity						
Cost Item	Per Unit	10,000	12,500	15,000	17,500	20,000	22,500	25,000
Direct Materials	$2.40	$24,000.00	$30,000.00	$36,000.00	$42,000.00	$48,000.00	$54,000.00	$60,000.00
Direct Labor	$3.90	$39,000.00	$48,750.00	$58,500.00	$68,250.00	$78,000.00	$87,750.00	$97,500.00
Variable Factory Overhead								
Indirect Materials	$0.60	$6,000.00	$7,500.00	$9,000.00	$10,500.00	$12,000.00	$13,500.00	$15,000.00
Indirect Labor	$0.80	$8,000.00	$10,000.00	$12,000.00	$14,000.00	$16,000.00	$18,000.00	$20,000.00
Utilities	$0.40	$4,000.00	$5,000.00	$6,000.00	$7,000.00	$8,000.00	$9,000.00	$10,000.00
Other	$0.50	$5,000.00	$6,250.00	$7,500.00	$8,750.00	$10,000.00	$11,250.00	$12,500.00
Total Variable Costs	$8.60	$86,000	$107,500	$129,000	$150,500	$172,000	$193,500	$215,000
Fixed Factory Overhead								
Supervisory Salaries		$19,000	$19,000	$19,000	$19,000	$19,000	$19,001	$19,002
Depreciation		15,000	15,000	15,000	15,000	15,000	15,000	15,000
Utilities		4,500	4,500	4,500	4,500	4,500	4,500	4,500
Other		10,900	10,900	10,900	10,900	10,900	10,900	10,900
Total Fixed Costs		$49,400	$49,400	$49,400	$49,400	$49,400	$49,401	$49,402
Total Costs		$135,400	$156,900	$178,400	$199,900	$221,400	$242,901	$264,402

The next budget model, used in certain industries, is the *rolling budget*. A rolling budget is used when you need to constantly adjust your budget to changing circumstances. You calculate your 12-month budget, obtain actual results from the next period (usually a month), calculate the variances, and recalculate your next 12-month budget. It certainly reduces the accountability, however, it does adjust to rapidly changing market conditions. This is why it is most frequently used in purely sales-oriented organizations.

The *zero-based* budget (ZBB) differs from the previous models in one major way: All values start out at zero, and must be thoroughly validated or they stay that way. It came to prominence in the Carter administration of the 1970's as a way to reduce governmental spending through automatic increases from already high numbers.

It is used in the corporate world as a periodic tool to challenge the status quo and to verify that increases in costs are justified. The advantage is obviously a reduction in unnecessary costs. The disadvantage is it adds time and work to an already tedious process.

The final budget model we will discuss is the *activity-based* budget (ABB). Developed as a part of activity-based management, activity-based budgeting turns the budgeting process on its head. At its core, activity-based budgeting begins by looking at the results *customers* want and will pay for, and the activities needed that create them. The activities are then linked to drivers that cause an activity to be required, and the related costs. All indirect costs are then identified within this process. Therefore, there are no more *overheads* to be allocated. All costs are now calculated for every product or service created and sold.

This is in dramatic contrast to the traditional cost-based approach, which often begins with sales, raw material and labor and then works forward. ABB can also help firms create more accurate budgets by aligning activities with objectives to improve strategic implementation.

So why doesn't everyone use ABB? The research needed to create an internal database of activities, drivers and costs to reverse the process would take so many hours, and the related cost of this time and effort is so great, that the vast majority of companies choose to use more traditional methods with less accuracy for a far more expeditious result.

9. What are the biggest problems with budgets?

The biggest problem with budgets is that most companies don't take the process seriously, because the budget is *always wrong*. You look at the previous budget, the results since then, the variance analysis report, which is seldom used properly, the requirements for next period and input whatever numbers you think you can get by the Board of Directors.

If you take the budgeting process seriously and research what has changed since the last budget, what you learned from the variance report and what resources you have available to meet the company goals, you might find the result more satisfying.

Budgets, properly developed and utilized, can help any company achieve better operational results than the alternative.

10. What is a budget variance and how can you benefit from it?

A *budget variance* is the difference between a line item's actual amount and that item's budgeted amount. These are most frequently discovered when you use the *variance analysis report* (VAR). The VAR is designed to give the user an instant view of what items on the budget are within an acceptable range (±) established by the company and which ones are outside. Those that are outside are then focused upon to determine the amount and the cause so that appropriate action can be taken.

A word of caution here: Too often this report is used to *blame* someone for the variance rather than its intended purpose, which to pinpoint problems and fix them.

Variance analysis report																
	This period		Difference		Cumulative		Cum diff				What is to	By	By	
Item	Budget	Actual	$	%	Units	Budget	Actual	$	%	Units	Cause	be done	whom	when	Metric

The proper use of a VAR is to:

a) Highlight the outliers
b) Determine the real cause of the variation
c) Decide what course of action should be taken so that future results will be closer to the budget
d) Determine who will spearhead the corrective action initiative
e) Commit to when this will be improved by
f) Measure the results to validate the action was taken and worked

When the VAR is used for its intended purpose, the end result is continual improvement in operating results, as compared to the budget, as well as an improved bottom line.

CHAPTER G - GENERATIONS IN THE WORKPLACE*

By Ivan M. Rosenberg

1. What does *generation* mean?

The term *generation*[3] refers to the aggregate of all people born over a specific 20-year span[4] who share:

- *A common location in history:* A common impact by historical events, such as wars, social unrest, technological advances, and accomplishments like the 1969 moon landing.
- *Common beliefs and behaviors*: At least a plurality of each generation share a common worldview about security, risk, money, marriage, and other concerns critical to shaping their progress from youth to old age.
- *Common perceived membership:* Self-identification with their generation gives members of the group a sense of their destiny and of what their work should be.

As verified by many independent surveys, most of the members of each generation have similar fundamental beliefs that guide how they behave and interact. This is not astrology. Rather, the distinctive behaviors of each generation are generated by:

- *Different child rearing approaches.* Every generation tries to correct the "mistakes" of the one that preceded them. In particular each one says, "I am going to be a better parent (whatever that means to them) than my parents," leading to different child-rearing approaches. For example, the children in some generations were left on their own when they came home from school; others came home every day to be greeted with milk and cookies from their stay-at-home mothers.
- *Events experienced during maturation.* For example, World War II and 9/11 were significant events during the formative years (ages 17-23) of different generations.

---

3   The modern concept of generations was described in Howe, Neil & William Strauss, *Generations: The History of America's Future, 1584 to 2069,* Quill, New York, 1991

4   Not all demographers and generation researchers agree on the exact start/stop dates for each generation, although they tend to be within 5 years of each other.

- *Different communication technologies.* The radio enabled one-to-many communications by businesses, but the Internet and social networks have enabled many-to-many and one individual-to-many communications.[5]

Each generation regards their own generation as the standard of comparison, and thus view both the preceding generation and the succeeding generation through negative eyes. You may have heard older folks skeptically speaking of the younger folks, *"these kids today..."*

2. What are the generations that may be currently in your workforce?

As mentioned above, each generation covers approximately a 20-year span, and there are typically five generations alive at the same time. The oldest is generally in or entering retirement, the youngest is just being born. In the current year (2011), the four generations impacting the American workplace[6] are:

- *Silent Generation: Born: 1925-1945*

    The youngest members of the Silent Generation just passed the typical retirement age of 65. They may be serving as consultants, lead training sessions, or be on the Boards of companies and not-for-profits.

- *Baby Boomer Generation*

    Born: 1946-1964 Baby Boomers, the largest generation until the "Millennials" (see below), were the result of the birth rate explosion after the end of World War II. Today, senior executives and managers are typically Baby Boomers. The oldest Baby Boomers are just entering the typical retirement age of 65. But many are continuing to work beyond retirement age, some because of the damage done to their retirement savings and pension accounts by the recession of 2008.

- *Generation X:*

    Born: 1965-1981 Typically middle managers are members of "Gen X."

---

5   The linkage of communication technology changes to generations was first articulated by Morley Winograd and Mike Hais. See Winograd, Morley & Michael Hais, *Millennial Makeover: MySpace, YouTube and the Future of American Politics*, Rutgers University Press, New Brunswick, NJ, 2008

6   The generations are different for different countries. Generational descriptions here apply to United States only.

- *Millennial Generation*

Born: 1982-2003 Those born in the Millennial Generation are just graduating from college, entering the workforce and occupying entry level positions. They are the largest generation ever, and will impact everything about our future.

3. Isn't this generation-stuff just a matter of age – won't they feel the same way you do when they are your age?

Making this assumption is a common error. The generational differences are as real and pronounced as the differences between people brought up in different countries. To effectively deal with the consequences of generational differences, it helps to understand that such differences are not personal, and have existed for centuries.

In *The Fourth Turning*[7] historians Strauss and Howe describe how, over the course of history, humans have shifted their view of time from a *chaotic* view, to a *cyclical* view, and to the current *linear* view. However, they make a strong case that the cyclical view more closely fits actual history. Many observers, in different time periods and in different nations and cultures, detected an 80-100 year repeating historical cycle, roughly equal to the maximum lifespan of an individual. Analogous to the four seasons of nature, within each cycle there were recognized four distinct 20-25 year historical periods[8]:

1. High (spring): a transition period of success and prosperity

2. Awakening (summer): a period of attention to spirituality

3. Unraveling (autumn): a transition period when international wars tend to occur

4. Crisis (winter): civil wars and revolutions tend to occur during this period[9]

Those born during each 20-25 year historical period tend to have common characteristics distinct from those born during the other three periods, leading to four distinct generational types. These types repeat in the same order each 85-100 year cycle, resulting in four archetypes, although different authors

---

7   Strauss, William and Neil Howe, *The Fourth Turning: What the Cycles of History Tell Us about America's Next Rendezvous with Destiny*, Broadway Books, New York, 1997

8   For a discussion of historical perspectives see Chapters 2 and 3 of Strauss, William and Neil Howe, *The Fourth Turning: What the Cycles of History Tell Us about America's Next Rendezvous with Destiny*, Broadway Books, New York, 1997.

9   According to Strauss and Howe, we are currently in a Crisis period.

propose different generational characteristics. Thus, the generation following the Millennials is likely to have the same generational characteristics as the Silent generation.

The salient shared experiences and the resulting broad characteristics of the four generations currently in the workplace are:[10]

- Silents

  o Child-rearing: Overprotected and smothered as children

  o Events: Korean War, Atomic Bomb, McCarthyism

  o Communications: Commercial Radio

  o As Adults: Risk adverse, conformist, and inclined toward compromise

- Baby Boomers

  o Child-rearing: Indulged as children

  o Events: Vietnam War, JFK/MLK/RFK Assassinations, Moon Landing, Civil Rights Protests

  o Communications: Network TV, Fax machines, Conference calls, Mainframe Computers

  o As Adults: Driven by deeply-held values

- Generation X

  o Child-rearing: Unprotected, criticized children

  o Events: End of Cold War, O.J. Simpson trial, Reagan's Shining City on the Hill, Clinton Impeachment, Feminist Revolution

  o Communications: Cable TV (CNN/ESPN/MTV), the Internet, email, PCs

  o As Adults: Alienated, risk-taking, entrepreneurial, pragmatic

- Millennials

  o Child-rearing: Protected and revered children

  o Events: 9/11, terrorism, Iraq War, Princess Di's death, Columbine and VA Tech school shootings, Oklahoma Bombing, Great Recession

---

10 Each of these generations represents a different generational archetype. Archetype characteristics include the child-rearing approach and the adult descriptors.

- ○ Communications: Social Networks (YouTube, Facebook, Twitter), Virtual Worlds, Multi-player Role Playing Games (RPGs), IM/Chat, Texting

- ○ As Adults: Group-oriented, problem solving, institution builders

4. **Why does every businessperson need to learn about the differences between generations?**

Your expectations about the world are derived from your beliefs. That is, you probably believe that *people should not steal*, and you are disappointed when someone you know does steal.

Your beliefs, and therefore your expectations, concerning how others should behave will likely not be fulfilled by the members of other generations, and the way you act and talk will not fit with their expectations. This can lead to conflict and have a negative impact on efficiency and effectiveness.

To be effective in impacting the behavior of others, managers and leaders need to see their own generational biases, see the generational biases of those who work for them, and have the skill to converse in a way that resolves the resulting conflicts.

For example, a Boomer manager observed that some of his Millennial employees were spending what he thought was too much time on social networking sites during work hours. He proposed implementing a new rule forbidding using such sites during work hours, consistent with his Boomer value that during work time people should be working and that being on social networking sites was not working. We suggested that group-oriented Millennials need almost continual connection with their peers, and that such a rule would probably result in their leaving his employ. In addition, it was likely that some of the social network interaction he observed was the workers asking their friends for help on a work problem with which they were dealing. Thus, he might consider that there were many people *working for him* that were not on his payroll. Instead of the proposed rule, we recommended that he focus on *results produced*, rather than *the time required to produce those results*, and that he ensure that all workers knew and respected the need for confidentiality in certain areas.

5. **There is such a wealth of information on the different generations; it's almost impossible to remember it all. What is the best way to easily remember the differences between generations?**

Our research shows that each generation's unique point of view can be represented by a single phrase. Thus, all a manager has to remember is one phrase for each generation, from which all generational attitudes impacting the workplace may be derived.

The four Generational Points-of-View are:

1. Silents: "Let's not get locked into extreme positions. Let's create a compromise that works for everyone." Silents avoid confrontation.

2. Baby Boomers: "What I believe is right is most important. I can't compromise on my values or principles."

3. Generation X: "I'm on my own. I don't trust what you are saying." Generation X members tend to reject anything that already exists, unless it comes from a trusted source.

4. Millennials: "The group is smarter than any one individual. Let's improve the world together." Millennials tend to be upbeat, optimistic, and group-oriented.

It is important to note that generational characteristics do not imply a particular set of political, religious, or societal views. For example, a values-oriented Boomer can be a conservative evangelical, a liberal atheist, or anything in between. The Generational Point-of-View is that Boomers consider their personal values to be fundamentally important.

6. **How do you use Generational Points-of-View to figure out and understand the different generational attitudes regarding the workplace?**

The use of the Generational Points-of-View can be illustrated by deriving each generation's different outlook on life.

1. Silents: "Let's create a compromise that works for everyone." Silents seek compromise and avoid conflict. As a result they are cautious, risk-adverse, dislike ambiguity, and prefer the status quo. Formality and conformity are their preferred methods for avoiding conflict and achieving success. A *Time* cover story described this generation as *withdrawn, cautious, unimaginative, indifferent, unadventurous and silent.*

2. Baby Boomers: "I can't compromise on my values or principles." Boomers tend to judge everything in life as right or wrong by the extent to which it conforms to their values. They rebelled against the Silents' conformity and attempted to have a perfectionist lifestyle based on personal values and spiritual growth. They were oriented to careers that reflect and influence culture, such as teaching, religion,

journalism, marketing and the arts.

3. Gen X: "I'm on my own." Gen X'rs are skeptical to the point of cynicism about most things in life except their families and friends. They depend on no institution or person outside of their inner circle. In contrast to Boomers' absolutist personal values, Gen X'rs consider nothing permanent or absolute. Unlike the Silents, they embrace risk, such as the dot-com ventures of the 1990s. They are entrepreneurial, starting about 70% of new businesses in the United States.

4. Millennials: "Let's improve the world together." Millennials have an optimistic view of what they and their friends can accomplish. This perspective helps them maintain their *can-do* attitude; particularly in the face of the many crises they have already faced. They may display a great deal of self confidence, to the point of appearing cocky or entitled, with optimism and a conviction that the future will indeed be better for all.

7. **How do you apply this knowledge to how your business operates internally?**

If you operate the business solely from your own Generational Point-of-View, you likely will encounter trouble with those of different generations, and your organization will not be as productive as if you took into account the different Generational Points-of-View.

Critical generational differences include the role of work in one's life, motivation, decision-making, training, reward and recognition, views of authority, and styles of working.

Using the same approach as in with the prior question, the generational attitudes toward decision-making can be derived as follows:

1. Silents: "Let's create a compromise that works for everyone." To avoid conflict, Silents act based on their positions within the organization. Bosses make the decisions for those lower in the hierarchy.

2. Baby Boomers: "I can't compromise on my values or principles." Boomers view the common values of their groups as right and any opposition as wrong. Believing that their values must prevail, they support group decision-making or decisions by a strong leader that enables their group (or team) to defeat the opposition.

3. Gen X: "I'm on my own." Gen X'rs don't trust anyone in authority; they rely only on themselves, individually, to make decisions.

4. Millennials: "Let's improve the world together." Consensus is the Millennials' preferred decision-making process. If a leader tries to impose their view without the consent of the team, Millennials will attempt to negotiate, viewing the decision as advisory-only.

8. How do you apply this knowledge to your business' interaction with the external environment?

The most important application of this information is to use it to speak appropriately to the Generational Point-of-View of those with whom you are communicating.

For example, let's see how the Generational Points-of-View might impact our first meeting with a prospect (or anyone with whom you are trying to establish a new relationship, e.g., a prospective employee, customer, investor, or Board member).

1. Silents: "Let's create a compromise that works for everyone." Given their age and diminishing role in the workplace, it is most likely that you will be proposing that the Silent make an investment or donation, volunteer, or join the Board of your organization. You would emphasize that your organization operates in a way that listens to all inputs and attempts to develop a compromise that serves everyone. Minimize any discussion of conflicts, although a Silent may help resolve such conflicts.

2. Baby Boomers: "I can't compromise on my values or principles." Emphasize that values guide the behavior of your organization. Describe those values and why they were chosen, even if they are likely different than those of the Boomer to whom you are presenting. The Boomer may not select you because of a difference in values (and you may not want them as a client for the same reason), but it is better to find out early rather than deep into the relationship. A Boomer may select you, even with different values, because of your values orientation.

3. Gen X: "I'm on my own." Generation X members want to hear how your offering will improve their life, or help them achieve their goals. If you are representing a firm, talk about the accomplishments of individuals within the firm, such as professional recognitions. The emphasis should be on the individual, not the firm.

4. Millennials: "Let's improve the world together." In contrast to Generation X, Millennials want to hear that your company operates in partnership, both internally and with its customers. They also want to hear what causes you are committed to and why, and in what way are you and/or your organization is changing the world.

Do not be deceptive – if your organization does not match the characteristics desired by a particular generation, consider not pursuing those individuals. Instead, look for generations that match how you operate (or consider changing the culture and style of your organization).

9. **How do you apply this knowledge when dealing with members of specific generations?**

Here are some guidelines that will improve your interactions with individuals from different generations to accomplish your intended goals.

- Be clear about your goal for the interaction. What are you trying to accomplish?
- To what extent does your own Generational Point-of-View determine that goal? For example, if you are a Boomer with a particular set of values, see if your goal is primarily derived from one of your values rather than from what will help the business. This might be the case where others are not behaving consistently with your values, although they might still be operating in service of the business.
- Frame your goal in terms of the common interests of you and the other party. As a Boomer, one of your values may be to earn more money so you can better provide for your family. The intention of the interaction might be to have others take action that will enable the business to make more money, and therefore you will make more money.

In speaking to a Generation X member, your goal should be shaped in terms of how in accepting your proposal they will earn more money or improve their skills.

Millennials may be more interested in how what you are proposing will help the organization change the world. Your goal would be to have them see that the proposed actions will help the organization be more profitable, and therefore it will have more resources to devote to such civic activities.

When speaking to members of another generation, (particularly since it is you who wants them to accept your proposal), it is preferable that you listen more than you speak, and ask questions more than you make statements. Find out the specifics of their Point-of-View as related to your proposal, and then shape your message to be appropriate.

10. How do you apply this knowledge when dealing with conflicts between generations?

People often complain using generalities rather than specificities. Have the parties identify the specific actions that are causing the conflict. For example, while Millennials might complain that their Boomer team leader is not a good team leader, the specific action is that the team leader does not support having a group discussion about decisions the leader has made. The Boomer team leader will likely complain that he has terrible team members who question his every decision.

Direct the parties from each generation to investigate the aspects of their Generational Points-of-View that are generating their relevant actions. In the above example, the Millennial Generational Point-of-View of *working together* might be driving their actions, and the Boomer leader's Generational Point-of-View is that bosses should make the decision and no one should question them (see question 7).

Then, have each group share what they learned – their relevant actions and their Generational Point-of-View. Perceptions of the other group will alter from "They are wrong!" to "Now I understand why they are acting the way they do, and I would take the same actions if I had that Point-of-View."

When the parties can see both Generational Points-of-View, resolutions to the conflict can be proposed that are consistent with both Points-of-View, and therefore are more likely to be accepted. For example, the Millennials might agree on decision areas or circumstances, e.g., urgency, when, in service of the team being successful, they will accept the team leader's decision. Other areas and circumstances would be identified as potential for group discussion, with the intention of coming up with a better decision than any one person could, thus serving the Boomer's desire to have their team win.

CHAPTER H – HUMAN RESOURCES

By Joe Herold

1. What are the elements of an effective Human Resources (HR) program?

Many organizations still look to their HR function to provide a base level of compliance and staffing. Getting people on board, trained, paid, and allowing the company to operate by staying in regulatory compliance are critical HR functions, and may be the only functions of the *personnel department* that appear important to the company's ultimate value creation. Human Resources professionals appropriately bristle at such a conclusion. Business leaders who've operated in highly successful companies (including notable examples like GE and Pepsi) know that the value contribution from HR can be exponentially higher than simple administration and compliance activities. So what is the right answer?

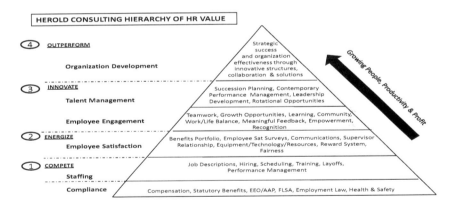

The most basic HR needs of any organization are compliance (meeting statutory thresholds in pay, benefits, employment law, etc.) and staffing (filling jobs, basic training, scheduling, etc.). If those needs aren't met, the organization can't survive, so leaders cannot begin to focus on value creation and growth opportunities. Once the needs at those levels are met, however, the organization can get comfortable exploring employee engagement, talent management and the innovative organization designs and solutions that mark highly successful companies.

A business is primarily about value creation. Human Resources professionals and their business partners, therefore, should map their choice of business strategy to the Hierarchy of HR value to determine the level and nature of HR investment and functionality they should focus on creating. If your business has chosen a high volume/low margin strategy, you may choose to focus your HR function on compliance and staffing. Executing flawlessly at those levels allows the business to survive and execute with minimal investment. With strong HR professionals, you may even get some focus on employee satisfaction, creating the ability to compete effectively. You may choose, however, to begin exploring the premium solutions, and benchmark returns that are achieved by companies that focus on climbing the value chain.

In summary, you can invest very little in your HR department when you don't need it to develop your staff. If and when you want HR to create more value for your company, you must investment more time and money in developing the employees who, in turn, should create more value (profit) for your company.

2. If you can't afford much of an investment in HR, what are the disciplines you must have in place to do business?

On the Human Resources front, the "survival" needs of a business are *Compliance* and *Staffing*. You need to comply with all applicable employment laws, or fines, sanctions and/or litigation can cripple your business. You must also be able to find and hire people efficiently and effectively to execute your business plan.

Compliance is a critical business survival need, and a precursor to starting down the path of hiring people. A variety of federal and state laws govern employment. Many organizations, including state Chambers of Commerce, market combined federal and state employment law posters that tell you what provisions you must comply with based on the size (number of employees) of your company. You're required to post those provisions in your workplace so your employees have access to them. If you have not done so already, ordering the required posters for your state will get you up to speed on compliance requirements and meet your posting obligation.

The most common risky compliance issues businesses must deal with include: classification of workers, overtime requirements, and wage and hour laws. Here is what is most important for you to know about these three important issues:

Independent Contractors vs. Employees

Many companies (particularly smaller, start-up businesses) attempt to limit payroll costs and liabilities by using independent contractors. Using "W-9" (or "1099") contractors allows the employer to avoid payroll taxes, workers' compensation costs and other obligations of a "W-2" employment relationship. However, if these relationships are classified improperly, they can violate federal law and create IRS violations and penalties. An independent contractor is only *independent* if he or she has specialized skills that require no training by you, has independent control over the methods of work, is not supervised by you or any of your employees, has his or her own company or tax identification, and invoices you for work performed. If any of those conditions are not met, seek counsel to avoid the costly mistake of misclassification.

Exempt vs. Non-Exempt Employees

Under the Fair Labor Standards Act (FLSA), employees may be classified as *exempt* or *non-exempt* from overtime requirements. Classifying employees incorrectly results in a violation of overtime requirements that can mount up to significant legal awards and penalties. Your safest default position is to classify employees as *non-exempt*, but that can be unnecessarily costly. Here are the three tests that must be met to classify a position as *exempt* from overtime requirements:

a) *Salary Level Test* - The government establishes a *floor* for the exempt test. Currently, employees earning less than $23,660 per year must always be classified as non-exempt. Employees earning more than $100k per year, on the other hand, are almost certainly *exempt*.

b) *Salary Basis Test* - The employee must be paid on a salaried basis (annual pay / number of pay periods), and his or her salary may not be reduced when absent or based on quality or quantity of work performed.

c) *Job Duties Test* (must meet one of these):
   - Exempt executive job duties – has management of people as his or her primary duty; is *in charge* of a group or department
   - Exempt professional duties – performs intellectual work, requiring specialized education and the exercise of discretion and judgment
   - Exempt administrative duties - positions that involve the exercise of discretion and judgment, with the authority to make

independent decisions *on matters which affect the business as a whole, or a significant part of it*

Wage and Hour

Both federal and state laws define a minimum wage that must be paid by employers. So your obligation is clear: Pay your employees a per hour rate that is at least the amount of the federal or state minimum wage, whichever is higher.

Federal and state laws also speak to the payment of overtime. Under federal law, you must pay non-exempt employees at a rate of time-and-one-half for all hours worked over 40 hours in a workweek. Some states, however, require overtime for hours worked over 8 hours in a day and/or 6th and 7th consecutive days worked in a workweek. Make sure you understand the overtime pay requirements *for the state(s) in which you do business*, and pay accordingly.

Other wage and hour laws, including those governing rest breaks, meal periods, etc. have been the source of significant claims, litigation and class action. Visit your state's website, contact your state's Chamber of Commerce or consult with an HR specialist to ensure you understand and comply with the wage and hours laws in the state(s) in which you do business.

3. **You want to make sure you're doing a good job of hiring the right people. What are the critical elements of a strong staffing process?**

A strong staffing process begins with a robust position description. A lot of time is wasted and poor hires made due to a lack of thought put into the position description. To write a position description that will increase the chances of finding and hiring the right employee for the job, you need to determine what type of skills, training, etc. you really need.

An effective position description should include:

- Primary purpose, function and responsibilities of the position
- Skills required to do the job well
- Attributes – talents/behaviors that are essential to success in this position
- Educational requirements

NOTE: Take the time to build this profile, and then update it regularly, based on those you see succeed in the position (or come up short) over time.

Once you have a strong position description, you're ready to find candidates. Depending on the nature of the position, you have several options here.

Online posting services, such as Craig's List, Hot-Ads, or other free posting sites available in your area provide job-listing services that are most effective for low to mid-level skill requirements. Electronic job boards like Monster.com, Jobs. com, TheLadders.com, etc. require a posting fee, but are less expensive than search partners (recruiters); job boards are effective for positions requiring specialized skills like engineering, accounting, etc. Highly specialized positions may require use of a search partner to tap hard-to-find talent. The talented people who can really help your business make strides are often not looking at job boards at all, and search partners can help you find them.

The final step in an effective staffing process is evaluating talent. Your evaluation process should be based on the skills and attributes in the position description, and should not wander off into non-essential or personal questions that have nothing to do with the challenges at hand. If, for example, the position you're filling requires the ability to manage complex projects, you might ask candidates, "Tell me about a situation in which you had to manage a complex project. Describe the project for me, tell me the specific role you played, and describe the templates, tools and processes you used to manage the project." After the candidate gives you that information, you might follow up with, "What results did you achieve? Did you meet all milestones and expectations? Were there any missed objectives or disappointments? If so, what did you learn from them?" Throughout the interview/evaluation process, be sure to avoid any interview questions that are related to a candidate's age; race, ethnicity, or color; gender or sex; country of national origin or birth place; religion; disability; marital or family status or pregnancy. Questions related to those or any other protected characteristics are illegal and not related to the critical matters at hand. Note that individual states may have added even more protected categories. Build a tight position "spec", and then focus your interview solely on those job requirements. You've heard the term talent management.

4. How does talent management differ from staffing?

Talent Management is higher up the hierarchy than staffing, and is a broader competency you must master if talent is a differentiator in your business strategy. A strategy reliant on speed-to-market with innovative applications is a key example in which talent would be a critical differentiator.

The central feature of a Talent Management process is a regular *Talent Review,* in which key leaders review the following:

- Business strategy and related current and emerging skills requirements
- Review of current talent – normally plotting key people on a grid, with results on one axis and success attributes on the other

Leadership Grid

	Results		
	Does Not Meet	Meets	Exceeds
Exceeds			
Meets			
Does Not Meet			

(vertical axis: Behaviors & Values / Personal Success Factors)

Leaders:
1.
2.
3.
4.
5.
6.
7.

- Action Plan – based on grid placement

Leadership Grid

	Results		
	Does Not Meet	Meets	Exceeds
Exceeds	TRAIN	MENTOR/ DEVELOP	REWARD AND/OR PROMOTE
Meets	PUSH	TRAIN/ DEVELOP	REWARD/ GROW
Does Not Meet	EXIT	EXIT	"CHANGE OR GO"

(vertical axis: Behaviors & Values / Personal Success Factors)

Leaders:
1.
2.
3.
4.
5.
6.
7.

- Succession Plan – If you don't have one or two candidates *ready now* to step into your key positions, you should accelerate development of internal candidates or start proactive identification of external candidates.

5. What is the difference between employee satisfaction and employee engagement?

Employee satisfaction is a focus of a *middle ground* HR strategy. Employee satisfaction concentrates on retention – keeping employees happy with the company and their jobs, so that they want to stay, refer friends and fulfill their responsibilities on a day-to-day basis.

Employee satisfaction most often relates to issues of competitive pay, clean and comfortable working conditions, adequate "work/life" balance, and fair treatment. Over time, research indicates that one of the most powerful drivers of employee satisfaction is a person's relationship with his or her immediate supervisor (the focal point and *facilitator* for many of the elements of day-to-day job satisfaction).

The core elements of a good employee satisfaction program include:

- A regular wage survey and pay adjustments, where indicated, to ensure employees are being paid competitively
- Attention to cleanliness, appropriate comfort, safety and health in the workplace
- Supervisor training
- A clear, communicated problem resolution process, including an *open door policy*
- Respect for employees' personal needs, within boundaries

Employee engagement, on the other hand, is a "high-end" strategy. Engagement includes, but also goes beyond, satisfaction. An engagement strategy is concerned with empowerment, and unleashing the company's talented people so they can contribute to their full potential. Employee engagement focuses on dynamics such as innovation practices, workflow, streamlined decision-making, collaboration and free flow of information.

6. What are the things you should consider in putting together an effective compensation plan?

As mentioned above, it is very important that you conduct a regular wage survey to understand the competitive market for talent and to make a decision about your own pay rates. If you're pursuing a low-cost strategy, set your mark at the 25th-50th percentile of the market. The closer your mark is to the 50th percentile, the lower your risk of rapid turnover. If, however, you're pursuing a high-value strategy, you should consider setting your rates nearer to the 75th percentile of the market, to increase the attractiveness of your business to talented people and to increase retention and satisfaction.

Many companies offer benefits plans, including health insurance, life insurance, savings programs, etc. Low-cost players and small companies should proceed cautiously with benefit programs – they can be costly, and are easier to add than to take away. If you'd like to offer some benefits, a simple HMO medical plan is a good, reasonably priced place to start. In addition, a 401k savings plan can be established at little cost to a company, and is often a popular feature. If you want to create a high-engagement/high-commitment culture, you should consult with a benefits broker to design a contemporary, effective benefits program.

Beyond base salary, incentive options are an effective way to create a focus on goals and success. The simplest form of incentive is a cash bonus program, normally presented as a percentage of salary or a lump sum amount. Tied closely to the behavior and results you most value, incentive programs can be a powerful addition to your total compensation program.

7. **How important are performance reviews and what should they focus on?**

There is some debate over the value of performance appraisals, but most leading thinkers still consider evaluations a critical element of building a high-performing organization.

To build an effective performance appraisal, be sure to incorporate these elements:

- Goals

    Start with a clear articulation of the goals to be accomplished, so that appraisal is meaningfully tied to success of the business. Goals should be *specific, measurable, attainable, relevant* and *timed*. (S.M.A.R.T.)

- Feedback on Skills and Attributes

    You can use a "check box" approach, but be careful not to make it read like a report card. Even though your employees are adults, a performance review that has a 1-5 type of rating scale has the effect of looking like an A-F report card, and can generate a corresponding set of reactions. Make your rating scale a *Needs Improvement, Meets* or *Exceeds* scale, or eliminate ratings altogether and just use your own words to describe the level of performance.

- Regular Feedback

    Don't leave performance discussions to a once-a-year review. If performance feedback is critical to organizational success, then it's certainly important to deliver the feedback regularly and consistently.

8. **You want to build a strong team of supervisors and managers. What are the critical features of a strong leadership development program?**

You should start with defining your leadership culture. What are the shared responsibilities, attributes and behaviors you want your leaders to embody and model? What does effective leadership look like?

Once you've defined and articulated the vision for your leadership culture, there are an abundance and variety of programs and options available to you. The key to a successful leadership development program is to fit learning options to the different challenges that leaders at various levels face. First-line supervisors should be given training in compliance with policies and employment law and problem solving, at a minimum. Mid-level managers need to add to their skills the capability of building and coaching teams and creating empowerment.

Training in situational leadership is essential in learning to diagnose one's team, given the tasks and goals at hand, and apply the most effective leadership style. More senior leaders are best served by learning via dialogue, case studies, simulation and/or immersion. Consultants are available to custom-design programs for your business, and many off-the-shelf options are available to meet your needs in a cost-effective manner.

9. **How do you decide on the best organization structure to implement for your business?**

Stiff, traditional "command and control" thinking leads many organizations to build organization structures that are costly, ineffective in achieving goals, and stifling to the talented people they employ. The right place to start designing is to build the structure around your business strategy.

Organizational units should be formed around key planks of your strategy, in most cases. If your business strategy is based on developing and introducing new technologies, for example, your organization should include units focused on specific technologies. If you're a service provider, you may want to consider building organization units around customer or industry clusters. If you're a manufacturer, you might be best served by an organization structure built around key manufacturing competencies or processes.

Within organizational units, work should be organized around goals and work process elements. Be careful to avoid thinking initially about *jobs*; rather, think about *chunks* of work. Once the *chunks* of work are identified, you can make decisions about outsourcing, combining and clustering that will drive efficiency and effectiveness.

10. **You hear other business leaders talk about a Human Resources *strategy*. What do you need to consider in creating an HR strategy for your business?**

Start by avoiding the pitfall of working forward from a traditional mindset. Human Resources is a large tent, and there are few – if any – cut-and dried "should do" scenarios when it comes to developing the HR strategy that will work best for your business. Instead, work backwards from your business strategy. Revisit the Hierarchy of HR Value model shown at the beginning of this chapter, and think about how it overlays your business strategy.

Are you a low-cost provider? Be great at compliance and staffing. Pay your employees competitively, and offer a low level of benefits. Limit training to critical skill requirements as they arise.

Is your business strategy run according to an innovator, high-value model? Make sure your compliance/staffing foundation is solid, then move onto innovative organization design and employee engagement. Pay your employees in the 50th-75th percentile of the market, and offer strong benefits tailored to their needs.

Your HR strategy should take into account people, process, communication, compensation and organizational interdependencies, and should spring from your vision and values.

CHAPTER I – INNOVATION

By Ted Whetstone

Innovation is the ability to see change as an opportunity—not a threat.
–Thomas Edison

"And now, it's my pleasure to introduce one of the *funniest* people I know…"

As I approached the podium, a muffled numbness fell over me. The bright lights glared in my face as the crowd, in anticipation, rose to their feet clapping enthusiastically. The subject I had come to speak about completely left me. After that introduction, all I could think of was one thing: "Be funny." I froze.

Have you ever been in a meeting where an urgent strategic problem is presented and everyone in the room turns to you for the solution? All eyes are on you: the cameras, the lights, the pens in hand—and all you can hear in your head is "Think of something, fast man! Innovate!"

But innovation isn't something you simply pull out of a hat. Innovation is as much about discipline as it is inspiration. It's something that you build into the fabric of *who* you are and *how* you operate. In this chapter, we'll review the basic tenets of innovation and clear up some of the questions and myths surrounding the subject.

Tip: Relax. There are no right answers. There are only best guesses.

1. What is innovation?

An innovation is one of those things that society looks at and says, if we make this part of the way we live and work, it will change the way we live and work.
–Dean Kamen

Innovation, defined by Webster's as *the introduction of something new or a new idea, method, or device,* is most commonly confused with invention, which is described as a *discovery, finding or something invented.* While invention stresses something *new* or *discovered* (like the idea of the first light bulb), innovation tends to build off that discovery, bring it to market, and give it *value,* because it means something to the world.

Innovation is any novel or beneficial change that adds value and impacts how the world works. It's sometimes an elusive term that can refer to something potentially tangible and measurable, as well as something that can only be understood via a visceral experience. For instance, I'd describe the video game Angry Birds as fundamentally innovative, because of its comical simplicity and addictive user engagement.

Of course, not all innovations pan out (I'm thinking of the water-powered car, the floating human gym, and the fifteen-year-old light bulb). Just because something's *innovative* doesn't necessarily make it an ideal solution!

Tip: Trust your gut. But also test your ideas. Rarely is innovation successful on the first attempt.

2. Why innovate?

The enterprise that does not innovate ages and declines. And in a period of rapid change such as the present, the decline will be fast. —Peter Drucker

Why innovate? Some might argue, "If it ain't broke, don't fix it." In a vacuum-like existence, that's a perfectly reasonable strategy. But in the *real* world, it usually isn't. The reason is *change*. Change happens, it's part of life, and it's not about to stop. The way you react to change or, in fact, *cause* it, may dictate your very success in the market. There are a host of business reasons to innovate, including increased revenues/profit margins and competitive advantage. But there are less obvious reasons, too. Some are selfish to the organization, while others are altruistic such as inspiring people and introducing ideas/products that make the planet better.

Innovation is invigorating. It makes what we do exciting. It makes working somewhere worth giving it our best. Nothing feels more alive and inspiring than an organization brimming with creativity, ideas for improvement, and a sense of collective enthusiasm. The reason we're attracted to innovation is that it's new, fresh, and in some way creative. And whether you think you're creative or not, it's still a fundamental human calling that deeply resonates.

No matter how innovative you are it's not a panacea; there will always be challenges to overcome. Either it will lead you into unfamiliar business areas where you have to learn and acquire new proficiencies, or it will give you growing pains as you work to keep up-to-date with your processes. It's always better, however, to cannibalize your old products or services with new and better ones… than have a competitor do it for you. The question really isn't whether to innovate or not, but to what extent you're willing to embrace innovation as central to your business strategy.

Tip: Remember, in a dog sled the *lead* dog has the best view!

3. What are the different types of innovation?

Innovation distinguishes between a leader and a follower. –Steve Jobs

Because innovation takes many forms, it can be segmented and classified in a myriad of ways. Here are a few core types:

Disruptive innovation
This generally involves the introduction of a new technology or process that the existing market didn't expect and so it shifts accordingly, sometimes radically. The iPhone, for example, generated a disruptive change in the telephone (smartphone) market. In contrast, incremental or sustained innovations can create competitive advantage but not in a way that transforms the market landscape itself.

Product innovation
This refers largely to the product development cycle. An extensive array of tools and methodologies help guide the process from idea generation to idea selection, concept prototyping, test marketing, production, marketing, and sales. Up to half of the product development process can be dedicated to the *front-end* ideation stage.

Process innovation
This is about implementing a new or significantly improved production or delivery method. Its purpose is usually to achieve cost-saving efficiencies, increased speed-to-market, and/or improved quality.

Market innovation
This embodies the customer interaction experience, typically during the purchasing process. Positioning according to specific market segments can be a great differentiating strategy for many companies. So can customer experience. (Apple retail stores are an excellent example.)

Companies can choose to innovate internally, applying R&D resources, operational best practices, and marketing muscle. But they can also innovate externally by engaging their customers and supplier stakeholders to identify innovation opportunities. This is also referred to as crowdsourcing, user innovation, distributed innovation, open innovation, or other terms. However you slice it, innovation shows up in unexpected ways but the net effect is always recognizable: There's some beneficial change in a product, practice, or model that adds value.

Tip: Challenges are *ideal* playgrounds for practicing resourcefulness. Embrace them.

4. Do small vs. big companies approach innovation differently?

Innovation is creativity with a job to do. –John Emmerling

Each organization naturally exploits innovation opportunities differently based on their unique strengths. Typically, the bigger the company, the slower it adapts to change in the marketplace. Conversely, smaller companies don't have the operating inertia caused by large staff, so they can more rapidly identify and mine new market opportunities.

Big companies have to bet on products and programs with billions of dollars in market potential. They can't afford to develop markets that represent a mere $10 million in annual sales. There's high risk associated with innovative development, because it translates into huge losses if they fail. To mitigate that risk, larger companies tend to follow more formalized innovation initiatives— some exploit all stages equally, while others focus more intensely on one area. Small firms, however, have the advantage of swiftly reorganizing around changes in the marketplace. Their modest size allows them to follow a more organic innovation path, morphing as necessary to execute effectively.

But these generalizations don't apply to everyone. First, big companies register more patents than small firms. Second, smaller teams in a large company with direct access to decision makers can be just as effective and nimble as the smaller guys. Third, there's very little data on small-firm innovation so accurate, direct comparison is difficult.

Yes, size matters when it comes to breadth of choices and depth of spending. But sometimes—speed counts more!

Tip: Focus on your unique strengths and characteristics. If you can't fix them, *feature them!*

5. How do you measure innovation?

There are two worlds: The world we can measure with line and rule, and the world that we feel with our hearts and imagination. –Leigh Hunt

They say that you can't improve what you can't measure. True enough. Measures, however, aren't always available or effective in quantitative terms; they can also be qualitative. Innovation, accordingly, is expressed in many different dimensions. You need to understand which ones are important to you before you run off to measure everything. Measuring the innovation itself doesn't necessarily give you insight into its value.

One natural inclination is to compare the innovation costs against increased sales, profits, and time to market. But with this approach, alone, you may be overlooking valuable soft intangibles that matter. It all depends on how you want to position your company. If your strategy is to attract the best employees, then measure that. If it's to create brand loyalty, then measure that.

How you measure depends on *what* you measure...and vice versa. One way to measure contributions to innovation is to count the number of ideas- or patents-per-employee. Impacts can be measured, such as the costs attributed to an idea's development and the revenues associated. You can also measure new products' percentage of sales and profit, the sustainability of revenue from a new product or service line, product quality and reliability, customer satisfaction and loyalty, the number of customers from new market segments, reputation, and brand image.

Consider the main stages of a product or service life cycle: ideation, design, production, distribution, and sales. Where in the marketplace do you want to be strongest? What are the qualities that differentiate you most from the competition? How has that shifted over the years? What is it about your organizational DNA that makes it unique and how can this help you leverage maximum perceived impact? Go there. Develop measures that give you insight into whether you're improving or stagnating in that area.

Maintaining a clear innovation strategy will help provide the context for your investment decisions, as well as what you choose to actually measure.

Tip: Stay focused on the end goal: sustainable competitive advantage.

6. What innovation strategy is right for you?

We cannot solve our problems with the same thinking we used when we created them. –Albert Einstein

It all starts with your vision. What is it your firm seeks to achieve? What's unique about your culture, people, and products? In what way are the passions of your founder(s) or leadership special or irrefutable? Where do you want to make your mark? Find your North Star. With the ever-rapidly changing marketplace, long-term strategic planning is getting tougher all the time. What you *can* plan for is how you're going to handle change. In the end, innovation comes down to choices in the moment, which in turn, flow forth from your operating principles.

Consider the companies you admire. Who would you like to emulate? Do you have the resources or capacities to do what they do? Can you see your business mastering the front end of innovation, i.e., coming up with novel products and services? Are you better or more agile at responding to change in the marketplace? Are you looking to create a game-changing shift in the way a particular market segment operates? Are your people more inclined to be intensely creative and independent or are they more pragmatic and process driven? If you've never profiled your organization in terms of character traits, you should start. The strategy you ultimately choose will be closely related to the culture you wish to create and vice versa.

Tip: Listen to your (company's) heart.

7. What will innovation cost you?

Money is not real. It is a conscious agreement on measuring value. –John Ralston Saul

It's tempting to look at innovation from a *cost* perspective. Yet, in the context of doing business it should be seen as an *investment*. Investment decisions balance a calculated risk with potential payoff. The payoff could be, of course, measured in terms of sales and profits, but could also just as easily be measured in terms of strategic know-how or intellectual property that provides unique capabilities in the marketplace. Conversely, you might consider the costs to your business if you *don't* innovate. Then the investment decisions almost come from the perspective of necessity versus curiosity. Ultimately, you will want to track or measure cost *and* payoff.

A good way to determine the intangible value of an innovation initiative is to consider what is *the product of the product?* In other words, the product (a/k/a the innovation) in itself isn't the important part. It's about the purpose for doing it. Starbucks didn't innovate coffee but perfected the coffee experience. What customers are buying, in effect, when they walk into a Starbucks is the product of the product: They're usually unconsciously buying into a club, a feeling of belonging, and ultimately a relationship. The coffee is just the vehicle. Innovating that experience (at some cost) was executed with the outcome in mind. The cost of their stores is measured in dollars—but the value to their customers to gain *membership* to the club? Priceless!

Tip: Innovation is a means to an end. As long as the end is worth it, cost becomes a well-made investment.

8. What are some of the best innovation tools and techniques?

There are no dreams too large, no innovation unimaginable, and no frontiers beyond our reach. –John S. Herrington

The best innovation practices involve harnessing human creativity and applying solid process methodology including:

- Using creative brainstorming techniques to elicit ideas
- Using filtering and selection techniques to combine or cull them
- Prototyping best concepts
- Testing the market, iterating, and rolling out

Let's focus on the first two points: brainstorming and filtering. There are hundreds of creativity and brainstorming techniques, particularly for groups. The key to successfully generating ideas is to remove thought obstacles. This is best accomplished by assigning one person to facilitate a group. The purpose is to ensure the free flow and capture of ideas without stopping to evaluate. Later, you can categorize, filter, and analyze but never up-front.

Note: The facilitator doesn't participate. He or she simply assists and captures ideas.

Some suggestions:

- Change location. Ideally get away from your normal work spot...but occupy a dedicated space or room for the practice.

THE BOOK ON...BUSINESS FROM A TO Z

- Turn off ALL sources of distraction (minimum one hour).
- Involve others. Most often, one person's suggestions will trigger ideas in another. The best group size is 8–10 people.
- Get a cross section of people with different viewpoints and experiences.
- Inspire and encourage playfulness!
- Don't judge. There are no bad ideas in brainstorming!
- The goal is to generate as many ideas as possible in an hour.
- Have each person develop his or her own ideas on paper first, then share openly. This ensures maximum participation.
- Don't get distracted evaluating the merit or potential of ideas.

After you've gathered a host of ideas, you'll need help filtering them. There are many effective techniques but consider the following:

- Make your final list of ideas.
- Select HALF of them (this is important) that are likely to have a high impact (mark them with an H) and half that look to be low impact (mark with an L).
- Now go through the same list and indicate which half are easy (E) and which are difficult (D). You should now have four sets of possibilities.
- The ones that are easy (E) with high impact (H) are clearly the ones you want to do first! If you do nothing else, do these.
- Take the difficult (D) but high-impact (H) items and brainstorm ways to make them easier.
- Don't spend time with the easy, low-impact (E, L) items. This doesn't mean you shouldn't do them. Instead, you might consider outsourcing them to a lower-cost provider.
- Take the difficult, low-impact (D, L) items and either agree to throw them out (recommended) or look for ways to make them easier or of higher impact.

Tip: Get witty. Playful banter will exercise everyone's brainstorming muscles. It helps you get out of *stuck* thinking and keeps you lighter on your toes.

9. What's the best way to develop and sustain an innovation culture?

Innovation has nothing to do with how many R&D dollars you have...it's not about money. It's about the people you have, how you're led, and how much you get it. –Steve Jobs

Developing an award-winning culture doesn't require a PhD in organizational development. It simply requires an understanding of people. Fundamentally, people just want to contribute and make a difference. It might sound cliché—but they really *do*. People are smart, and if you treat them that way, they might just deliver the solution you'd never come up with in a hundred years. So go and empower them! Engage them in creating solutions that astound, surprise, and tantalize.

Innovation is about leadership. Creating an innovation culture starts and ends with the context that management provides to its team. If there's an operating environment of fear and blame, you'll most certainly discourage risk-taking. If employees are given a sense of ownership and empowerment, along with appropriate responsibilities, they'll step up to the challenge and frequently surprise the heck out of you. To successfully foster and sustain an innovation culture, you must:

- Stay committed and focused
  Particularly in turbulent or volatile market conditions, it's imperative that management provides consistent, clear leadership.
- Communicate, communicate, communicate!
  You must create an inspiring vision and consistently reinforce it.
- Define success criteria and reward accordingly
  It's human nature to avoid risk and stick with the known. Use failures as learning lessons versus excuses for blame.
- Set goals, deadlines, and measurements for innovation
  Steady progress and achievement are important to maintain confidence.
- Empower people and foster creativity, yet manage according to your core principles
  Unbridled creativity can be exciting, but it can also end in anarchy if guiding principles aren't set as the foundation.

Tip: You have two ears and one mouth, so use them in that proportion!

10. What immediate actions can you take toward innovation?

You see things; and you say, "Why?" But I dream things that never were; and I say, "Why not?" –George Bernard Shaw

Ask questions and listen. Listen fully. Listen to your instincts. Listen to your peers. Listen to the competitors. Listen to the marketplace. Be sure, however, to ask the kind of questions that inspire breakthrough thinking. Stretch them toward the audacious, if necessary. Break out of habitual thinking patterns. Challenge yourself.

Spend some time brainstorming the following with your coworkers:

- What would be ideal?
- What would really excite us?
- What would our customers say they'd ideally like?
- What would our customers have us eliminate or stop doing?
- What assumptions are we holding onto? What if we remove them?
- What could surprise us?
- What ideas, services, or products could we combine to create something new or different?

To foster innovation, here are some suggestions:

- Be curious. Be inquisitive as to why things are the way they are or aren't.
- Put yourself in your customers' shoes. Really.
- Read from disparate sources and borrow ideas from completely unrelated industries.
- Google your topic in images and let the pictures trigger ideas.
- Set impossible goals with "failure is not an option" as a mindset. Even if you only achieve 60 percent of your most audacious goals, it will force you to act differently than if you follow the safe and known path.
- Hire people who are driven to be the best.

Tip: Organize a small innovation-minded team to champion company initiatives. You don't have to be the *chief plate spinner!*

CHAPTER J - JURISPRUDENCE

By Bruce Dizenfeld, Esq.

1. When do you need to hire an attorney?

When you have a legal question or problem, you should look for an introduction to an attorney. Attorney time can be expensive, so you should not engage an attorney until you at least have an idea of what you want to accomplish. However, once you can express what you have in mind as a business objective, it may be beneficial to speak with several attorneys. Use this interview process to get feedback on your plans, as well as to evaluate whether you want to work with the attorney you are interviewing.

If you speak with an attorney prematurely, they may appear to be disinterested. This may be due to your lack of preparation. You want your prospective counsel to be as excited about your project as you are, so prepare as you would for any business meeting.

From a timing standpoint, early stage discussions with an attorney are primarily to obtain an attorney's perspective rather than have them complete a particular task. This time should be limited and conceptual; its purpose is to provide initial guidance only, and to lay a foundation with your counsel on which you will build momentum at the same pace as your proposed project gains traction. This early stage discussion will also enable your legal counsel to help you identify stages at which certain tasks or documentation should be completed.

Early stage discussions are for direction only; do not use your counsel as a crutch to second-guess your early business decisions or as a sounding board – that is what your other business partners, consultants and counselors are for.

If your project has evolved to the stage that you are aware of certain specific tasks that need to be completed by an attorney, it should be obvious by now that attorneys use existing document and agreement templates as a starting point. Ask your legal counsel if you can get a copy of the template they are likely to start from, so that you may use it to become familiar with the issues it prompts. This way, you can ask counsel for clarification in advance of the project being initiated (in the event it might effect the input you are being asked to provide). The template will also provide you with the means of organizing the information required by counsel to complete the document. If the attorney wants to charge you for the receipt of the template, that may be an indication of what you can expect in the future. The value of the attorney's time is not taking the information you provide to input it into the template. The value of the attorney's time is determining which template to use, answering your questions regarding the relevance of certain provisions, and supplementing the template to address unique issues where they apply.

2. **When should you look for a professional other than an attorney?**

The goal is to use your partners, consultants and counselors to their highest and best use. You are likely best served speaking with legal counsel only after initial conversations on the issue(s) with whatever other advisors you rely upon. Although legal counsel may have a solid accounting, tax, finance, or industry background, they will:

- Not be as qualified or focused on any one of these subjects as those advisors you may have in these areas;
- Charge attorney rates for non-legal consultations, and;
- Be addressing a topic for which you will not be asking the attorney ultimately to take ownership.

Experienced advisors will have overlapping input in areas outside of their specific training, but use this overlap to help you evaluate and question your specialists and not in lieu of their input.

3. **Where do you find the right attorney?**

Once it is time to begin interviewing counsel, the question is often where do you find the *right* person. The process is not unlike dating; the right attorney for someone else may not be at all the right attorney for you.

There are several places to begin your search. Asking people who you believe reflect your values for references is a good place to start. They may refer you initially to an attorney they respect but who practices in an unrelated specialty; this is still a worthwhile referral. Although that attorney may not be able to help you, he is in a better position to assess who may best address your needs, and if they reflect a personality characteristic that others you trust think is worthy, they in turn will likely provide a referral to someone similar in style to their own.

Another place to check would be with others in the industry. An out-of-area contact may be just as valuable to obtain a referral chain back to your own geographic area as a local one. Depending on your needs, legal counsel on business transactions need not always be local, given the ease of electronic communications these days.

When you are seeking legal counsel to handle a litigation matter, your business lawyer is the first place to start, assuming you have one. Your business lawyer wants to preserve your resources and is more focused on the big picture outcome vs. the type of success that might be obtained in litigation. Litigation is a form of competition, and it may be difficult and not always desirable to temper your litigation attorney's enthusiasm. Let your business lawyer monitor the process on your behalf and absorb some of that litigation angst.

4. Should you go with a sole practitioner, a small firm, or larger firm…and why?

Selecting the individual attorney is more important than using a pre-selection process based upon the size of the firm. As a practical matter, the nature of your legal need will end up defining the resources that need to be available to the lawyer you select. The size of the firm simply determines what resources may be immediately available. In this era of outsourcing, supplemental/resources are available to all – although smaller firms may not be in the habit of using a big budget approach to solving problems.

There are instances where a law firm's name provides a certain degree of credibility, which in turn will reflect your commitment to a project. In general, this often reflects more your financial commitment to the process. However, there may be sole practitioners with stand out reputations in your industry that may accomplish the same result.

Bottom line: If you find the right individual lawyer for you, the rest will take care of itself.

5. Do you need a generalist or a specialist?

This question requires further definition. If by reference to *generalist* you think of an attorney that does both business transactional work and litigation, and might throw in an occasional estate plan, bankruptcy and marital dissolution case, then consider the following point. Although the attorney is obviously well rounded, such counsel is likely more appropriate as a general advisor (if you believe their perspective and judgment is comparable to your own way of thinking). She may also be useful to you in handling smaller matters. The danger is that their level of sophistication and knowledge with regard to a particular industry or area of law may be insufficient to anticipate pitfalls that may arise on more sophisticated transactions. You can use the generalist as an advisor to interact with your specialist. Just make sure you are using each to his or her highest and best use.

If you are sophisticated enough to be a purchaser of legal services, you are likely sophisticated enough to go directly to the interview and engagement of a specialist, based on which area of the law with which you need assistance: A litigator for handling a dispute, a business lawyer to handle a contract, business formation, or transaction, or a bankruptcy or family lawyer to handle a business of family dissolution. Certainly tertiary specialists, such as intellectual property or securities counsel may be better accessed through lesser-specialized counsel, such as a business lawyer, litigation counsel, or real estate lawyer. Doing this can narrow the issue and involvement of these specialists to the issues on which they can provide their highest and best input without too much overlap and duplication of effort. Although these tertiary specialists may undertake the more mundane services, their services are more efficiently purchased and synthesized through your business, estate planning, or family law counselor.

Another definition of specialist would be any attorney specialist within one of the practice areas, i.e., business, litigation, real estate, etc., but who also has specific knowledge in the industry in which your business is involved, e.g., healthcare, government contracting, construction, etc. Seeking someone with industry specialization can be an added benefit, as it lessens the learning curve to understand your issue and with industry specific laws, regulations, customs and terminology. This is not necessary, but it is a benefit. The perfect attorney without specialty industry knowledge can be better than a qualified industry specialist with whom you do not have the same compatibility (see discussion of compatibility, below). Often you and your other trusted advisors are sufficient specialists in the applicable industry to bridge the knowledge gap of a non-industry specialist in litigation, business, real estate, etc.

6. What questions should you ask?

Do you charge for an initial discussion?
Don't refer to this as a consultation, as you are not seeking answers. You are exploring your compatibility with the lawyer, whether you feel like you can trust his knowledge and judgment, and only indirectly receiving feedback on your issue as may be offered. Sometimes the admission of uncertainty and need for further research is a better measure of knowledge and reliability than a quick answer.

If I engage your services, will the first meeting be included in the charges?
Although the attorney may not charge up front for an initial meeting, once engaged, that meeting may become the beginning of the engagement.

Does the attorney require an upfront deposit?

If the attorney does require this, you should further determine whether the deposit applied in whole or in part to the first charges, or if it is held as a security deposit to be applied to the last invoice on the project.

Depending on the nature of the work, can I get a fixed fee commitment on certain tasks so that I can budget my expenditures and, if necessary, receive notice if there is some reason the charges will exceed the budget?

The fee structure with an attorney is simply a matter of negotiation. The use of hourly rates is not required by anything other than it is the fee structure with which attorneys are most comfortable. Services have historically been billed on an hourly rate, and this is still, far and away, the most predominant fee structure. However, this does not mean that a fair fixed fee engagement may not be possible. Since attorneys will continue to think in terms of hourly rates, the fixed fee will either result in the lawyer being paid more for the project than the hourly rate would justify, or if the project on an hourly basis would have cost more than the fixed fee charged the attorney will feel they are giving time away. An alternative fee structure should take this mindset into consideration.

Can I arrange for an alternate payment plan; e.g. a fixed monthly amount with a periodic true-up, and can I get a rate break if we use a fixed monthly payment paid on time, since it is likely to reduce the hassles and uncertainties of the billing process for the attorney?

Unlike the fixed fee structure referred to above, this alternative fee engagement is based upon the timing of payment and not how the services are valued. This changes the focus from either party getting the benefit or the bargain of a negotiated fixed fee, and simply focuses on budget processes and cash flow management. There is generally much more flexibility among attorneys adopting an alternate fee arrangement along these lines.

Do you offer value discounts? For example, if my total charges exceed certain threshold amounts, can I get a discount on the rate?

Note: Institutional clients tend to get discounts due to the volume of work anticipated and the efficiencies it provides to the practice. Non-institutional clients are not in the same bargaining position if there is no history of continued legal service requirements. But if the relationship does develop into an extended and continuing relationship, a *look-back* discount may be appropriate.

When will you be using others to perform some of the work, and what criteria will be used when making such an assignment?

A response that leads you to believe that assignments are made when the lawyer is too busy, or that these assignments are made when there is a desire to train and educate an associate, would not be the kind of conclusion you want to draw from the answers given. You want to know how the lawyer's *team* works, and if you can communicate directly with the other *team* members to avoid paying for inter-attorney discussion time. This also gives you the opportunity to determine if you trust the judgment and services of the *associate* or *paralegal* as much as the lawyer you hired. Most of the time they reflect the lawyer's own approach, but that may not always be the case.

7. **How do you know the attorney is qualified to handle your case?**

Selecting an attorney is less about your evaluation of his or her qualifications, and more about whether you are compatible. Your attorney is your representative. You need to be able to answer the following questions in the affirmative:

- *Does the attorney seem to understand and appreciate your goals or does he have his own agenda?*
- *Is the attorney* engaged, *i.e., does she seem interested in your project or is this just more billable hours to her?*
- *Does the attorney reflect your style and demeanor?* It is a mistake to hire an attorney that you perceive to be extremely aggressive and mistake that for being *engaged*. If *aggressive* is not your dominant personality trait, your attorney is not representing your approach to problem solving. The consequences of a personality mismatch is that opportunities for settlement of a dispute or negotiation could be lost if your attorney's approach to problem solving is different that your own.

Through the referral process and initial attorney interviews, it is likely that all of the candidates are *qualified* to do the work. At this point, their ability to *represent* you is likely more important.

8. **What is an engagement letter, and what should be included in this document?**

An engagement letter is an agreement that defines the terms and conditions on which your attorney will render services on your behalf. This includes things such as: The method and rate to be charged for the services, e.g., the attorney bills in $1/10^{th}$ of an hour increments at a specified hourly rate. The engagement letter should also include the disclosure of any conflicts of interest your attorney may have. In California, and in other states, attorneys are required to obtain a written engagement letter as a condition of their right to enforce their claim for payment for their professional services at their established rate.

Be aware that in connection with the engagement of legal services for the formation of a new business entity, the attorney will often disclose, and require a conflict of interest waiver in connection with legal counsel formally representing the entity and *not* the individual principals of the entity. Be aware that legal counsel under such circumstances may be a bit more reserved about addressing issues of individual or personal concern and, as such, recommend that each of the principal's obtain their own legal counsel for such individual issues. It is a delicate balance for legal counsel to provide useful input to avoid the additional cost of separate legal counsel for each of the principals, and to reserve their focus solely upon matters applicable to the entity and its formation.

9. **How do you decide what form your business should take?**

There is a review elsewhere in this book regarding the advantages and disadvantages of a few different forms of entity. For purposes of this chapter, we want to review how legal counsel may look at this choice of entity decision and the kind of input legal counsel will need from you to aid in this process.

The goal of the choice of type of entity to form is driven by its intended function. For example, will the business operate for the goal of generating current distributions of profits or managed primarily to build appreciation with an anticipated reinvestment of cash and profits back into the business. Also, will the business need to borrow to make capital investments or is borrowing primarily just for working capital? (See Chapter D – Debt for more information). These questions may suggest a tax pass through entity, or the use of a standard subchapter C Corporation to absorb the tax on profits at the corporate level.

Other questions may involve whether there will be any foreign investors that would disqualify forming as a corporation in reliance upon a subchapter S election.

Additionally, legal counsel should ask if the business is state specific or national in nature for purposes of determining the benefit and ability to take full advantage of forming the entity in Delaware or Nevada. The reasons for this relate to tax, flexibility with corporate governance, sophisticated business courts to interpret and to enforce a more complex business structure, or other attributes unique to formation in a remote jurisdiction.

Finally, there are certain professional or industry limitations on the use of certain forms of entity. For example, licensed professionals may not form as a limited liability company in California.

10. How do you know if your case is worthwhile?

Let's assume for the context of this book that the "case" involves a contract breach (money claim or violation of contractual covenant), a business related tort (i.e. tortious interference with contract), or the protection of a property interest (i.e. infringement claim regarding copyright, trademark or trade secrets).

Business claims generally do not lend themselves well to engaging a lawyer on a contingency fee basis, i.e. having the lawyer assume the risk of success in consideration of a percentage of the anticipated settlement or award). Business cases on the plaintiff side of the claim tend not to include claims that involve a high risk to the defendant of a punitive damage claim (upside potential and leverage for settlement). This forces the businessperson to perform a risk to benefit analysis that can vary greatly based upon the nature of the claim and the amount at issue.

Another immediate factor in evaluating the value of a case is to determine, if that action arises out of a contract, whether or not the contract provides for the prevailing party to be entitled to recover their legal fees. This provision can work as both a sword and a shield, depending on the likelihood of success in the action. If you are confident in the likelihood of success, the threat of adding to the defendant's cost, the obligation to reimburse the legal fees, creates further settlement leverage. Keep in mind, however, that the actual ability to recover the legal fees is often at the discretion of the court, which is often reluctant to grant this additional award if they believe there was a legitimate dispute that should have been settled, not required so much court time, and does not have a compelling public policy to be upheld. Additionally, the right to recover legal fee may get factored into insignificance in connection with the negotiation of a settlement, which tends to be a global compromise number without regard to the respective costs incurred by the parties.

Starting a discussion regarding the value of a case with the legal fees is often the ultimate factor in determining whether to proceed with an action and when it should be settled. Unfortunately, *justice* is expensive, and being aware of this fact should impact your focus on the terms of any transaction. Do not trust enforcement of an agreement to the courts; try to build into every transaction a sufficient degree of mutual dependence and reliance that will require the parties to need to work together. A final note: When dealing with the courts, there are no guarantees. Even *if* you win a judgment in court, you may never realize any money. Even if you prevail and obtain an agreement for payment, this does not fully guarantee you will ever receive the money. Therefore, based on this, it's vital that you protect your assets (physical and intellectual) as if you will not be able to get compensation for their being breached.

CHAPTER K – KNOWLEDGE MANAGEMENT

By Jerald M. Savin

Everyday businesses generate vast amounts of data. The subject of this chapter is turning that data into useable *knowledge*.

1. **What is knowledge? What are its basic elements? Why is this important?**
    Often, the terms *data*, *information* and *knowledge* are used interchangeably. To truly understand the elements of knowledge, I want to first distinguish these three terms from each other:

    - *Data* are the basic facts and figures that describe a business transaction.
    - *Information* refers to the meaning and significance attached to *Data*.
    - *Knowledge* is the accumulation of this information into an organized, coherent whole.

    To illustrate these distinctions, consider a customer purchasing merchandise from a supplier. The *data* are the specifics of the sale: who purchased what items, in what quantities, at what prices, etc. *Information* is the business implications of the order, i.e. the picking, packing and shipping of product, creating and billing the customer, determining how much replacement merchandise to acquire.
    In one sense, the *Information* is the "So what?" What should the business do in response to the order? *Knowledge* is the accumulation of orders and what they say about customers, products, business operations, finances and so on.
    Data is transformed into *information* and *knowledge* when it is captured, stored, organized, classified, cross-referenced, analyzed and used by the business. What differentiates *knowledge* from *data* are the implications, ramifications, consequences, inferences and decisions associated with the accumulated *data*. The order is part of a much larger universe of sales information and knowledge, which ultimately leads to insights.
    This data-information-knowledge continuum exists in a combination of oral, written and electronic forms. Much of the data is stored in sophisticated

computer systems; however, a remarkable amount of data is handwritten, and much resides as "tribal knowledge" in employees minds. So, these types of data reside outside the automated systems. The trick is to get that data into the automated systems, where it can be preserved and organized alongside the data already in the system, making it readily available for research. Take the example of sales prospects. Much of this information may reside in the minds of the salespeople. Implementing a CRM system allows this information to get out of people's heads into an automated system where it becomes the property and knowledge of the Company.

Along this path, we are so accustomed to thinking in terms of electronic data that we often forget about the information that resides outside of our systems. We will come back to this topic in question 8.

Why are data, information and knowledge so important? In a word, *knowledge is power* (Sir Francis Bacon).

A basic tenet of Knowledge Management is:
- Getting the Right Information…
  - To the Right Person…
    - In the Right Form…
      - At the Right Time.

We will explore these four ideas in the remainder of this chapter.

2. What information does the Company require to operate effectively?

The place to begin thinking about Knowledge Management is the basic information needed to operate a company effectively. There are certain common threads and distinctive elements depending upon the company and the industry it is in. Some of the common threads to consider in our recurring illustration, Order Processing, are the following:
- Customer information
- Product information

Customer information typically includes names, billing and shipping addresses, telephone numbers, customer categories, pricing and discounting schemes and so on. Product information generally includes product names, product categories, pricing schemes, discounting schemes and particularly quantity by location. These are examples of commonly maintained data elements.

An individual Company may require additional or different data elements. For example, sales commission structures vary widely, requiring different underlying data. Sales rebates occur in some industries but not in many others. Where sales rebates apply, additional or different data elements may be needed.

To highlight industry differences consider gross margin for manufacturers vs. distributors vs. professional service companies vs. asset intensive industries. Gross profit for manufacturers takes direct and indirect manufacturing costs into account. Gross profit for distributors considers inventory acquisition costs, and maybe some carrying costs. For a professional services business, gross profit depends upon keeping its service professionals chargeable. For an asset intensive company, gross profit is determined by the spread between what the capital earns and what it costs. These four industries have gross profit in common, but the calculations are quite different requiring different data elements.

What information does a business need to operate effectively? The answer to this question involves the data elements that businesses share in common with each other and data elements that reflect the Company and its business processes.

3. **What do the owners or C-Suite members of the Company need?**

Moving from operations to executive decision-making shifts focus from data elements to the knowledge that senior executives and owners need to make good executive decisions. Here too, there are certain common elements and other items that are executive and company specific.

Common data elements may include sales statistics, material costs, labor costs, inventory turnover, fixed asset requirements, factory capacity, capital costs and so on. Executives look at the relationships among these items and their trends over time.

Not only do specifics vary by industry, they also vary by the executive's responsibilities, temperament and approach to management. For example, a CEO may be focused on strategic issues and direction, while the COO is focused on operational effectiveness, and the CFO is focused on finances and accounting. Each is a senior executive. Each has his or her individual responsibilities, which mandate different information. Thinking in terms of style and approach, does the executive manage by intuition or by facts and figures? Is the executive a decision-maker or a coach that empowers his/her staff?

Getting the right information to the right person means identifying the information that a company needs to operate effectively and make wise decisions. Clearly there are common universal elements of data and differences among companies and their executives.

Once identified, where will this information come from? Which gets us to our next question.

4. How is this knowledge managed?

It is hard to imagine a company today that isn't dependent upon sophisticated computerized information systems. Typically these are ERP systems, where ERP stands for Enterprise Resource Planning. They capture, store, organize and process much of a company's business information. These systems were designed with two ideas in mind:

- To handle a company's business processes from start to finish, from cradle to grave, from beginning to end
- To span the entire enterprise from sales, to manufacturing, to warehousing, to human resources, to accounting, and beyond

These sophisticated information systems were designed to manage the typical business processes, including selling goods or services, purchasing goods or services, manufacturing goods, maintaining financial records, tracking customer interactions, etc. They were designed to keep a complete record of everything that happens to a transaction along the way. For example, they capture and store the order processing data, from the receipt of the initial order to its ultimate payment; including picking, packing, shipping, billing, recognizing receivables and recording payments.

Because these systems are transactional, their information is organized around the process, not necessarily organized for management reporting. Recalling the distinction between data and knowledge, these systems are strongest with respect to data, and weakest from the knowledge management perspective. To compensate for this weakness, data warehouses or data marts are often added to these systems, either internally within the system or externally outside of the system. The primary purpose of these data warehouses is to re-organize the business data in ways that facilitate management reporting.

The answer to the question of how this information is managed: ERP systems supplemented with reporting databases normally manage this information.

5. What is required to ensure accurate, reliable and timely information?

Decisions are only as good as the information they are based upon. In IT, there is the familiar expression: *Garbage In, Garbage Out.* Put in different words, bad data begets bad decisions. This idea underscores the need for accurate data. Accuracy, reliability and timeliness are essential qualities of useable data. Data that exhibits these qualities is said to have *data integrity*. When any of these qualities is compromised or lost, the usefulness of the information is severely degraded.

Without going into great detail, let me suggest some of the common problems that compromise data integrity: Outright erroneous data, missing or incomplete data, orphan data, or late, stale or tardy data. Orphan data refers to missing cross-references; for example, this could be an order with a customer number that does not link with a specific customer. The typical cause is the deletion of the customer without deleting the associated customer transactions. This leaves customer transactions without a customer.

Similarly, reports may be misleading or incorrect, because the data upon which the reports are based are incorrect, or the selection criteria used to populate them is incorrect. For example, a sales report may include only a portion of sales, but this is not obvious looking at the report.

These problems can occur anywhere along the data-information-knowledge spectrum. *Data* level errors may include the wrong customer, the wrong items, the wrong quantities, the wrong unit of measure conversions, and so on. *Information* level errors may include shipping damaged or obsolete items, missing promised shipped dates and backorders that are never shipped. *Knowledge* level errors may involve misunderstandings about sales trends and inventory stocking levels.

Data integrity is present when the underlying information systems enforce data integrity through effective validation and quarantine procedures, and when these systems are surrounded by effective internal control procedures. The typical objectives of internal controls are to prevent, detect and correct errors, to flag missing data elements, and to confirm the datasets and selection criteria used to generate reports.

Two techniques worth a brief mention are *timeliness* and *quarantine*. Timeliness stresses the element of time. When data is late, stale or delayed, it isn't timely. Quarantine is a technique whereby data that is incomplete, potentially incorrect or outside of normal limits is set aside for further review before it is processed.

One of the reasons companies spend the "big bucks" for ERP systems is for reliability as well as the vast array of features and functions they provide.

6. **How are exceptions, patterns and trends called to a business owner's or business executive's attention?**

The real power of information systems is their ability to identify exceptions, patterns and trends in large volumes of data. Some simple examples include: Finding unusual orders, finding orders delayed by shortages, understanding changes in order volume and sales mix, understanding fluctuating gross profit, understanding relationships between staffing, and various business metrics, such as sales and understanding the relationships between marketing and sales campaigns and sales activity.

Understanding these exceptions, trends and relationships lays the foundation for valuable *insights* that enable exceptional decision-making. The task is ferreting useful information out of the ERP treasure troves, being able to find the proverbial "needle in the haystack".

Ferreting out useful information is a two-part problem. First, the data warehouse needs to contain relevant information, and the information needs to be organized in such a manner that it can be located. The second part of the problem is having business intelligence (BI) tools that facilitate this process.

Besides digging through large volumes of data to locate exceptions and trends, competitive enterprises need forward looking data. Predictive Analytics is the sub-discipline within Business Intelligence that focuses on inference and prediction. Its objective is to identify future business opportunities, such as knowing which customers are more likely to switch to a competitor and why. For example, in the case of wireless carriers, customer churn (switching carriers) is a major cost. Knowing why customers switch carriers and how to reduce this turnover is priceless.

7. How is information disseminated and protected in a business?

Getting the right information to the right people in the right form at the right time is all about distributing information. The flip side of the coin is protecting that information from inappropriate distribution.

The *right form* used to be limited to reports, sometimes nothing more than long lists of data that people would pour over trying to make sense of the business. Today, executives yearn for reports that cut through the large volumes of data and focus on matters requiring attention particularly where business performance metrics exist.

Mobile technology is profoundly changing both the mechanism and timing of information distribution. In our 24/7 world, executives expect to be able to access their information from anywhere, anytime, and on any device. For a long time, this meant being able to login into the company network from remote locations. The advent of smartphones and tablet devices, such as the iPad®, has expanded the alternatives in ways still being developed. Messages, alerts and dashboards can be "pushed" to these mobile devices, making information readily available anywhere, at anytime.

With these capabilities comes heightened concern about protecting company knowledge, especially information related to proprietary intellectual property. The first line of defense is access control, limiting user access to prescribed information. There are a whole host of concerns beyond access. Suffice it to say that controlling the distribution of information is becoming increasingly worrisome and difficult.

Various regulations impose additional burdens to protect certain information. In healthcare, the government enacted HIPAA to protect patient information. Various states and government agencies have enacted laws regarding the retention and distribution of personal financial information. The Payment Card Industry (PCI) established Data Security Standards (DSS) to control personal financial information.

A well-designed automated information system needs to distribute information to authorized users, needs to have adequate controls to protect essential business information, and, in the case of a breach, needs to promptly notify management.

The motto for knowledge: *Collect it and protect it.*

8. What roles may information outside of the Company's automated systems play?

No discussion of Knowledge Management today is complete without a discussion of the vast array of information available on the Internet. This resource cannot be ignored, but it comes with two big challenges. The first challenge is linking knowledge on the Internet with its corresponding entities in our in-house systems. The second challenge is understanding the information itself. This problem can be summed up in one single word: *unstructured.*

The data in an information system is, by the very nature of the system, structured. For example, knowing a customer number, a user can dig out all of the information in a company's systems related to a specific customer or a group of customers. The information on the Internet is structured completely differently. The information of interest may be in plain sight on Facebook or Twitter, but identifying the customer and determining the content can be a challenge. How does one link the Facebook or Twitter post to a customer or prospect? Is a name sufficient to ensure an accurate link? Second, what is the individual saying? It is positive or negative? What is the specific meaning of the post? This involves interpreting human language.

The emergence of social media is expanding the realm of knowledge management and the tools required to manage it. New disciplines are emerging that address some of these issues, including business intelligence, predictive analytics and sentiment analytics. The crux of the problem comes down to managing unstructured or *semi-structured* data.

Parenthetically, there are now entire businesses that are completely knowledge based. Take Google, Facebook and Twitter, for example. Their products are entirely informational. The term "information age" aptly describes this environment and our dependence on information.

9. **What are the emerging trends in Knowledge Management?**

The volume of data businesses generate is voluminous and growing exponentially. This is readily apparent on so many levels: Larger databases, more data elements, and more complex systems encompassing more aspects of the enterprise. Our storage vocabulary moved from kilobytes, to megabytes, to gigabytes, to terabytes, to petabytes (= 1,000,000,000,000,000 bytes = 10^{15} bytes). What's next? Exabytes = 10^{18}. Yikes, that's a *lot* of data. Companies need to develop strategies to cope with this even increasing resource.

Business Intelligence software is becoming more prevalent. Every ERP package has an integrated reporting package. Excel® and Crystal Reports® are the most common options and they are being continually enhanced. Take Crystal Reports®, for example. A simplified version of Xcelsius, BusinessObjects' high-end dashboarding tool, was added to Crystal Reports® to enhance the product. Messaging, alerting and dashboard capabilities have been added to most ERP systems, reducing the need for additional software.

As previously mentioned, the pervasive use of mobile devices is changing the Knowledge Management landscape. Owners and executives expect to be able to connect to their office systems when they are out of the office. They expect to have important information pushed to them on their mobile devices.

The net result of all of these advances is that business is now a 24/7 game in which owners and executives are in constant communication with their businesses whether in or out of the office.

10. **With all of this in mind, what should a business owner or company executive do to effectively maximize knowledge?**

These things stand out:

a) Develop a plan that identifies the knowledge that needs to be captured, organized and managed. Know where this information resides internally and externally.

b) Design and implement a Knowledge Management environment that aggregates this data in sufficient granularity to allow real in-depth analysis. Include mechanisms to transfer data between applications and data marts. Include databases within which to manage and appropriately analyze the data. Implement alerting and reporting tools to effectively disseminate this data. Include mechanisms to capture and incorporate Internet data.

c) Establish procedures and controls to ensure data quality. Remember bad data leads to ill informed decisions.

d) Experiment with your data. Look for the hidden nuggets that are outside your normal view and suggest new opportunities.

e) Finally, continually revise and refine your Knowledge Management environment to make it more effective.

Concluding thoughts

The most exciting aspect of Knowledge Management, and of Business Intelligence, is finding new "insights" that improve your business. These insights may improve your products or services. They may allow you to better serve your customers. They may enable you to build better products and services, and ultimately allow you to be more profitable and successful.

CHAPTER L – LEADERSHIP

By Barry Pogorel

The questions and answers that follow echo back and forth, leaving you standing in the domain of leadership. What we offer is *asymptotic* in nature. *Asymptote* is a term in mathematics exemplified by a line approaching another line infinitely, always getting closer, but never actually touching the second line. Leadership is not something to be or do perfectly, but rather an asymptotic developmental space in which to endlessly grow in mastery. Because it happens in real life, working with other people in changing situations with high stakes, what I propose is not meant as a set of rules to conform to, but more as guidelines for *living-learning* – learning in real life in the midst of action.

1. **What are common myths about leadership?**

   A recent search of amazon.com for *leadership* yields 78,656 hits. Joseph Rost, in his book *Leadership for the Twenty-First Century,* wrote:

   > *Indeed, with few exceptions there is little that can be said to be a science of leadership...The facts are that...the concept of leadership does not add up because leadership scholars and practitioners have no definition of leadership to hold on to. The scholars do not know what it is that they are studying, and the practitioners do not know what it is that they are doing.*

   Before we propose anything about leadership, let's identify some of the most prevalent *myths* surrounding it. When you are wearing tinted sunglasses, it is difficult to see the true color of things. Myths – especially those that fall in the category of *common sense* and *obvious* – are often the most pernicious in coloring our perceptions and thinking. These taken-for-granted notions are pitfalls to a leader, and misdirect her as to who she needs to be and what she needs to do. The following are some ubiquitous myths:

   - A leader is always, or most of the time, *decisive.*
   - She always *knows what to do*, though others are not sure.

- The leader has *charisma*: some intangible quality that attracts people to her, to her words, to her plans and goals.
- A real leader has a different kind of *personality* from other people, gifted with a unique intelligence, way of speaking, and attitude.
- A leader inherently has a *talent* for leading others.
- Leaders are mostly *born with* the ability, although some people are lucky to *have had the right experiences* that made them leaders.
- True leaders *don't make mistakes*, or at worst make forgivable ones.
- Leaders are *without fear and uncertainty.*
- A real leader must be *ruthless and uncaring* - the job, the goal, the mission comes first.
- A leader is a *tower of strength* to all around her when others falter.
- A leader is *super-human.*
- Leadership is a *role, position, or title* which, when one has been so designated, is then a *leader.*
- A leader's *power corrupts.*
- A leader is *alone.*
- The job of leadership is *burdensome (heavy hangs the head that wears the crown).*
- Leadership comes from the *top down.*
- Leaders are *hard to find*, rare, one out of many.

And how about two completely contradictory myths:

- A real leader's *personal life works* on all fronts: health, family, financial—and
- A leader *has no personal life.*

What makes these myths insidious is that they don't sound like myths—they sound like *the truth*...and they add up to one conclusion: The real leader is, basically, *someone else* (not you).

Where do these myths come from? Some are *idealizations*, formed around well-known leaders. Synonyms for *idealize* are: *admire, dream, glorify, put on a pedestal, or rhapsodize.* Why are we seduced by these illusions? Business can be challenging, uncertain, and overwhelming. We want someone we can look to for the path, the answer; we want someone to bring with them the solution. There must be *someone* who knows the answer! The truth is, there isn't. *Leadership is a creative act, an act of self-expression, without a single right answer, path, style, or form.*

2. **What is the job of leadership and how is it distinct from management?**

The smaller the organization, the more you are doing everything. As the organization grows in size and dimension, a differentiation of accountabilities becomes necessary, since one person cannot do it all. Leadership begins to arise as distinct. *Dictionary.com* has this to say about leadership:

a: To go before or with to show the way; conduct or escort

b: To conduct by holding and guiding

c: To influence or induce; cause

A leader is committed to some vision that does not yet exist in reality. Again, borrowing from the same dictionary, about vision:

a: The act or power of anticipating that which will or may come to be prophetic vision; the vision of an entrepreneur

b: An experience in which a personage, thing, or event appears vividly or credibly to the mind, although not actually present

c: Something seen or otherwise perceived during such an experience: "*The vision revealed its message*"

The leader keeps her vision present and in the awareness of the people of her organization. Although we think of *organizations*, really no such *thing* exists—only people working together in a particular relationship with each other to achieve some end. Leaders, as part of that structure, are people who have a particular perspective and function: they look from the end point, the future, the vision, and they have that perspective inform their choices, actions, and communications. Everything they do is in service of realizing that future.

When I became a father with the birth of my first child, I found that a father wasn't only a new role or title: it was a *perspective* that colored everything I saw and thought about. It was a point of view that colored everything else in my life— my work, my other relationships, my health, and my finances. Everything was considered in light of the good for my new child. Similarly, a leader is affected by the future she is focused on: it becomes a perspective on everything her organization must do. One could say that a leader is *single-minded* in service of that future, that vision.

By contrast, management's accountability is to make the vision, the future, happen in reality. Management sets goals and makes plans to reach those goals, builds organizational structures, delegates accountabilities, allocates resources, solves problems, monitors progress. Managers work to minimize risk, reduce the unknown, and increase predictability. Managers spend most of their time in the day-to-day of running the business, focused on the short term. Any leader is certainly engaged in some management as well. However, leadership is the keeper of the vision and intends something big, something not yet existing, something exciting, something challenging, and something of value that makes a difference. Therefore, leaders deal with the longer term. By its nature, this is more uncertain, and riskier than what the manager deals with.

3. **What is the personality or set of essential characteristics of a powerful leader?**

Actually, asking this question is useless and will have you looking in the wrong direction. Here's why:

Leaders must be malleable and flexible, like a sailor steering towards a certain point on the shore: Given the tides, winds and weather, the sailor tacks back and forth, shifting direction and style to get to the desired point. One leader may be loud, another soft-spoken. One leader may be energetic, another thoughtful and slow to act. One leader may be comfortable in front of a group, another may not be. Leaders are women and men, young and old, experienced and not. The one element all leaders share is that they are dedicated to make something happen that doesn't yet exist. Big visions create big leaders (a reversal of usual thinking). Great purposes create great leaders.

Because we are part of a universe that operates according to physical laws, there are certain laws that constitute effective leadership. These laws are transcendent to personality, style or characteristics, and even circumstances. There are three fundamental *Operating Principles* that maximize performance and, when fully embraced and lived, lead to breakthroughs:

Your word is your bond

People in an organization must collaborate, coordinate their actions and count on each other. They must operate beyond excuses, reasons, and justifications for why something did or did not happen. When people relate to their word as their bond, then they do what they said they would do and they insist on the same from others. Relating to word-as-bond builds trust and deeper relationships. The deeper the trust between people, the bigger the challenges they can take on, and the bigger the problems they can tackle successfully.

Honesty

This is the absence of deception and falsity. In speech, it means saying it the way it is. In action, it means being genuine: the way you present yourself is the way you actually are. Honesty includes openness—there is nothing hidden. In a relationship, if you are open and honest in your communications, it leaves no room for others to make up what you are thinking or meaning. A contemporary business term for this is *transparency*.

112

Your word is your bond plus *honesty* embodies the two essential elements to creating trusting relationships: you mean what you say, and you say what you mean. When these two Organizing Principles are operative, things become clear and simple. What is not working is obvious and correctable. What works is equally clear.

A passion for something big

Another way to say this is: *having a large purpose.* It is another Principle of powerful leadership. The dictionary provides these definitions for *purpose*:

a: The reason for which something exists, or is done, made, used, etc.
b: An intended or desired result; end; aim; goal
c: Determination; resoluteness

The leader refuses to let anything get in the way of realizing her purpose.

People tend to think that a leader is special because she has something special *inside* her: some emotional, psychological, intellectual quality or state within. I propose that a leader is someone who has something special *outside* her: A vision or a purpose that inspires her and makes demands on her as to who she must be, and what she must do that she would otherwise never have been or done. This vision is not simply a goal, as in some finite, quantifiable result. In the achieving of the vision, there is something larger available—an opportunity for personal growth, a chance to break-through historical constraints or barriers, a contribution to society and added value to life, an achievement which inspires others to act on something arduous – even seemingly impossible. In the realization of the purpose, other opportunities become available, and the character of leadership comes into existence.

So if you are a leader, what is your Everest? What is your Apollo 11?

Since the leader is up to a noble calling, others' passion is kindled as well. As the leader stands for something big, challenging, or difference making, others become inspired. Inspire means *to breathe life into*. When a leader is inspired, others around her are inspired. Because the vision is big, the leader must make big demands of those around her—bigger than those people would ordinarily make of themselves (and bigger than the leader, as an ordinary citizen, would make). Like a great coach demanding of an athlete, a leader demands. The more she has *compassion* for what it takes for others to perform, and yet does not back away from the high level demanded, the more people feel moved to act, achieve extraordinary outcomes, and grow.

"If I were to wish for anything, I should not wish for wealth and power, but for the passionate sense of the potential, for the eye which, ever young and ardent, sees the possible. Pleasure disappoints, possibility never. And what wine is so sparkling, what so fragrant, what so intoxicating as possibility!" – Soren Kierkegaard (1813-1885)

The three fundamental Organizing Principles implicitly lead to several more sub-principles:

Act from love (more popularly known as relatedness or affinity or respect) not from anger or fear.

When people are respected, appreciated, and acknowledged, they feel drawn to act, even in the face of enormous demands and difficulties. This creates a culture of trust and collaboration, responsibility, creativity, appropriate risk-taking, and a sense that the work people do matters. Cultures lacking in respect, appreciation, and acknowledgement produce isolation and territorialism, leading to the urge to operate on "survival tactics" mode. These tactics include: Sticking to formulas and safety, distrust, futility, fear-based risk avoidance, dog-eat-dog competitiveness, and other counter-productive behaviors.

Courage

Helen Keller said it all: "Security is mostly a superstition. It does not exist in nature, nor do the children of men as a whole experience it. Avoiding danger is no safer in the long run than outright exposure. Life is either a daring adventure or nothing."

Responsibility

The buck always stops with the leader.

Being human

You can only be as big as you can be small—don't pretend you are not petty. On the contrary, honesty requires not hiding that you are sometimes small or petty, and gives others the breathing room to be real themselves. This includes fear, selfishness, concern with irrelevancies, and emotional reactivity. The illusions we harbor about Lincoln or Gandhi mislead us from the trivial and even contradictory aspects of how they were—their greatness was no less for it. True leadership includes forgiveness – not in the religious sense, but rather in having room for the smallness of oneself and others. Forgiveness is not an excuse or justification for anything, just some space to get on with it.

A leader embodies these Operating Principles. Leaders shape culture by modeling ways of being and functioning that teach and influence. The more widespread these Principles are in a workforce, the more effectively goals and visions are realized.

4. **The medium of an artist is paint; what is the medium of a leader?**

Simply put, leaders work with the medium of *words*. A leader realizes her vision by creating an image of it for others through words. The strategic plan of the organization is simply words, and action begins with words. What a leader says has enormous impact. For example, it is very different when a leader says, "We are going to put a man on the moon and safely return him to earth by the end of this decade," as opposed to "We're going to give it our best attempt." The latter statement already has excuses built into it for why it may not be done, and the former is a clear, fully responsible commitment, free of reasons why it won't happen. Which way of speaking is more likely to yield the desired outcome? Which inspires others?

Perhaps even more impactful, however, is how a leader hears.

"There is an art of listening. To be able to listen, one should abandon or put aside all prejudices, pre-formulations and daily activities. When you are in a receptive state of mind, things can be easily understood; you are listening when your real attention is given to something. But unfortunately most of us listen through a screen of resistance. We are screened with prejudices, whether religious or spiritual, psychological or scientific; or with our daily worries, desires and fears, and with these for a screen, we listen. Therefore, we listen really to our own noise, to our own sound, not to what is being said. It is extremely difficult to put aside our training, our prejudices, our inclination, our resistance, and, reaching beyond verbal expression, to listen so that we understand instantaneously." – Jiddu Krishnamurti (1895-1996)

A leader practices the *art of listening* as an ongoing discipline. There are many benefits of powerful listening. The person attempting to communicate has a sense of being heard. In what they say, you will hear ideas, opportunities, and conceptions beyond what you would have come up with on your own. Also, you can speak to what they *actually* said rather than what you *thought* they said which allows for resolution of issues, moves conversations (and projects) forward, and deepens relatedness.

The philosopher Martin Heidegger said, "Language is the house of Being. In its home, man dwells. Those who think and those who create with words are the guardians of this home." What your organization is, how you and others view yourselves and each other, is made real by how you and they speak. The bricks and mortar of your organization is language.

5. **Can you develop or learn leadership, and if so, how?**

> "I investigate myself. A man's character is his fate."
> – Heraclitus (c. 540-470 BC)

Most books and teaching about leadership are *descriptive* and *prescriptive*. Describing how to dance doesn't make a good dancer. Describing how to lead doesn't make a good leader. It gives no *portal* into being a leader. Most of us didn't listen to what our mother told us to do (had we, it would have saved a lot of time). Why? *Our actions don't come from what we have been told, read, or know, but from what we are committed to.* This is simple, but profound: To develop power as a leader, get committed to something that requires this.

Take on something big. Put your stake in the ground for what others (and perhaps you) have said is impossible, and find a way to do it. Heraclitus said, "Your character is your fate." Conversely, your fate, or future, is your character. I don't mean the future *when* it happens (certainly this will affect you)—I mean *right now, what is your future?* It shapes and defines you and what you must do. A leader develops her character by taking on something big, seeing what is needed to accomplish it, and letting it form the person she must be.

In this light, it is understandable that at the birth of the United States, many extraordinary leaders stepped forward, including Washington, Adams, Jefferson and Madison. What they imagined, what they committed to, demanded greatness.

A second aspect of developing leadership has to do with failure. As in mastering any discipline, failure is the greatest opportunity someone has to learn. Rather than it being a stopping or quitting point, or invalidation, train yourself to think of failure as a lesson, an insight, an occasion for growth and development.

A third critical aspect of leadership is causing leadership in others, so a leader asks the same of those around her: take on big objectives, honor their word as their bond, and be honest/real.

6. **What are the primary constraints or obstacles to handle to be an effective leader?**

Any kind of automatic reactivity is counterproductive to leadership. The human brain is a survival mechanism. It does this in two ways: *mechanistically responding to threats,* and *mechanistically planning the future.*

Amygdala hijack is a term coined by Daniel Goleman to describe disproportionate emotional responses. *Perceived threats* (real or imaginary) can bypass our neocortex (the *thinking brain*) and go directly to the amygdala, which is the trigger point for the primitive *fight-or-flight response.* When the amygdala feels threatened, it reacts irrationally and destructively. We become mad, righteous, invalidate others, justify ourselves, stop listening, get forceful, attempt to control or avoid being controlled, act impulsively, and later often regret our response and feel we were temporarily *taken over* by something. In fact, we were.

The brain is also a *predictive machine* designed to apply past experiences, decisions, and learning like formulas to the future. The limitation with any formula is its mechanicalness. There is a saying: *To a man with a hammer, everything looks like a nail.* The brain-as-predictive-machine not only gives us an automatic response; it also filters and shapes what we perceive.

The antidote is self-awareness, including recognition of one's patterns of reactions and formulas. Leaders must see reality, what is, and respond appropriately. Since situations are always changing, a leader must see what is *now* and have her responses correspond to what is *now.* Neuroscience has borrowed a term from Buddhism: mindfulness. A leader cultivates mindfulness, non-reactivity, being in the here and now.

7. **How does a leader turn vision into reality?**

When a leader puts her stake in the ground for a vision, operates as word-is-bond, and communicates and relates honestly, others are touched and inspired. They experience the leader speaking to and for them, for what they most want to be and do. A leader continually engages them, articulating and reifying the vision, while listening to them to modify and extend it. The leader is a collaborator, in a dialogue with her associates, so the vision becomes theirs. The workforce is included as much as possible in the formulation of strategy and plans, so execution and planning end up being the same thing. No *buy-in* is necessary. They own plans, objectives and accountabilities, because they participated in creating them. They are aligned in a shared vision.

8. **What can be learned from neuroscience about brain function that can make you a more effective leader?**

Human brains are wired for our survival, such that they are either *attracted/rewarded* or *repelled/rejected* by people and situations. This manifests in five ways: a concern for *status, relationship, fairness, autonomy,* and *certainty* (per research and writings by Jeffrey Schwartz and David Rock). Here are a few thoughts on how leaders might be responsive to these:

- *Status* is fulfilled through appreciation and recognition.
- *Certainty* is accomplished through operating as word-is-bond and honesty.
- *Relationship* is built by both listening to and loving people.
- *Autonomy* is granted when people have the freedom to act appropriately to their level of competence/responsibility, and when it's safe for them to risk and even fail.
- *Fairness* is satisfied when rewards match performance and when everyone's voice is heard.

9. **With so much to do, how does a leader prioritize?**

As a student, I was privileged to participate in a series of discussions with the great abstract-expressionist painter Richard Diebenkorn. I was struck by his single-mindedness and total obsession with painting. Everything fit inside this sole fascination for him. It gave a context, a perspective, *in which* he thought, and *from which* he viewed everything. A leader's vision is her perspective. Strategies, problems, opportunities, personnel issues, etc. are all viewed through the lens of the vision. If they assist in fulfilling the vision, or they get in the way, they are dealt with. If they do not, they are ignored. *The leader knows what is most important to do by letting the future she is committed to, inform her, and speak to her.* Athletes and musicians talk about being in the zone, about themselves disappearing and being a channel for something else to act through them; the leader disappears into the vision and leads the organization from there.

10. **How does a leader deal with problems?**

It is a platitude to say that problems are really opportunities. What's more, the word *challenge* is often a euphemism for our more authentic reaction to a problem, which is something like "!#%^&!" Looking deeper, we can see that a problem is simply an obstacle that got in the way of making something happen that we were committed to. An effective way to deal with problems is to:

1. *Know that there will always be problems* and that this is part of making something happen—accept it, welcome it, rather than resisting it.
2. *Take effective action* in dealing with a problem:
   - *Put aside your strategies and recipes* (which includes both the mechanistic reaction of negative judgments of you and others, the organization, the industry, the world; *plus* put aside all formulaic solutions).
   - *Determine what happened*: Get clear on what exactly happened versus all the points of view, opinions, perceptions, and reactions from what really happened.
   - *Ask what's next* and take whatever actions are appropriate.

A leader is – most of all – a combination of intense factualism and groundedness in reality, and at the same time future-based vision and unbounded creativity.

CHAPTER M – MARKETING

By Jennifer Beever

1. What is marketing?

A great way to begin to answer the question, "What is marketing?" is to ask, "What is marketing *not?*" First of all, marketing is not sales. A good distinction between marketing and sales is that marketing makes your phone ring, fills up your email inbox, and helps engage customers in the buying cycle. Sales close the deal. Other things marketing is not include: graphic design, advertising, or public relations (PR).

Done well, marketing can impact not only new customer sales, but also existing customer sales, wallet share (the amount of revenue you get from each customer), employee attitude and retention rate. According to Philip Kotler,

"Marketing is the business function that identifies unfulfilled needs and wants, defines and measures their magnitude, determines which target markets the organization can best serve, decides on appropriate products, services, and programs to serve these markets, and calls upon everyone in the organization to 'think and serve the customer.'"[11]

Mike Schultz and John Doerr state that marketing has the ability to:

"...engage potential customers, increase the close rate, increase revenue and increase affinity with employees."[12]

Marketing has changed a great deal due to the disruptive innovation called the Internet. Because the Internet has changed the way people buy, marketers have to change the way they market. Buyers don't want to be bothered by the interruption of ads or telemarketing calls. Buyers want information about products and services when they want or need to buy something. Buyers are in control.

Because of the focus on the buyer, a new term has emerged in marketing today – *lead nurturing*. Lead nurturing is how marketing supports the buyer through the buy cycle and the stages of awareness, information, assurance, and

11 Kotler, Philip, *Marketing Management: Analysis, Planning, Implementation and Control*, Sixth Edition. Prentice Hall, New Jersey, 1988.
12 Schultz, Mike and Doerr, John, *Professional Services Marketing*, Wiley, New Jersey, 2009, p. 2.

loyalty. According to Brian Carroll, it is marketing's job to engage buyers and provide relevant and consistent dialog with viable prospects regardless of timing to buy.[13]

2. How do you price your products and services?

Pricing must take into consideration customer demand, price sensitivity and elasticity, the competition, and market conditions. Customers will be more sensitive to prices if they know there are substitutes, or if they think your product lacks differentiation. The demand for your product will be less elastic in response to a price increase if customers know that there is little competition out there, if customers are not apt to change suppliers often, or if it appears that your product has a competitive advantage.

Many businesses price on a cost-basis, which includes fixed overhead costs, such as utilities, salaries, rent and other costs that do not vary; as well as variable costs, such as labor and materials. (See Chapter C – Cash Flow for more information).

A value-based pricing model that has proven to be a real differentiator in today's value-oriented culture is detailed in the book, *Value Merchants*[14]. This model includes calculating the actual bottom-line improvement your service/product creates for your customer and demonstrating that value to them.

Be careful about reducing prices as a promotional effort to increase sales. In some industries a price drop indicates a decline in value or in quality and may be a detriment to sales. Instead, price increases can be used to close more sales before an increase is in effect. However, they will not be effective if demand for your product is elastic due to lots of competition, ability of buyers to change vendors easily, and lack of differentiation.

Some of the problems with pricing include: Too much emphasis on cost and not enough on profit, failure to change prices with a changing market, prices that are not tied to positioning which affects the perception of the product, and lack of customizing prices to markets and product variables. When a company determines its pricing strategy, it is essential to communicate that clearly to marketing and sales as well as other departments.

3. What's the best strategy for marketing your product/service?

Today's best marketing strategies focus on knowing your customer, your competition, and industry dynamics equally well. A strategy based on customers is forward thinking, as opposed to a strategy based on what competitors are already

13 Carroll, Brian, "Inbound Lead Nurturing," Inbound Marketing University webinar, Hubspot, Inc., 2009.
14 Value Merchants: Demonstrating and Documenting Superior Value in Business Markets,
James C. Anderson, Nirmalya Kumar, James A. Narus, Harvard Business School Publishing, 2007

doing, which has business owners looking laterally. (See Chapter I – Innovation for more information.) There are several tools that are helpful in analyzing your situation to come up with the best strategy for marketing.

Voice of the Customer (VOC) is a popular strategic planning marketing tool, and is defined as the process of capturing customers' expectations, preferences and aversions. One drawback of VOC is that customers may not know what they don't know; so external knowledge is often required to identify opportunities for innovation, new products and services.

You can use "marketing personas" to understand customers, and to communicate that understanding to employees and other stakeholders. A marketing persona is a story written about each customer segment your company serves. The persona in the story is given a person's name, and the story describes the customer type's attitudes, likes, dislikes and needs. Creating and sharing marketing personas makes it easier for everyone to understand, empathize with, and make better decisions about the customers you serve.

The SWOT (Strengths, Weaknesses, Opportunities and Threats) analysis is well known and easy to understand. The SWOT analysis below incorporates action items with the analysis, making the tool more action-oriented.

SWOT Assessment with Actions!

Translating SWOT into Action!	Strengths • Breakthrough product formula • Seasoned sales consultants • Agility, flexibility in R&D	Weaknesses • Lack of cash • Legal legacy • Stakeholder communications • Fledgling distribution • Marketing/sales alignment
Opportunities • Cost of diesel fuel • Increasing emissions regulations • Focus on sustainability	*Maximize strengths to take advantage of opportunities* • Continue solution selling • Brand and position well • Awareness campaigns	*Resolve weaknesses to take advantage of opportunities* • Resolve legal issues • Increase sales, raise capital • Improve communications • Increase quality distribution
Threats • Cost of diesel fuel • Sell cycle variability • Low barrier to entry	*Maximize strengths to mitigate threats* • Focus on cost savings *and* eco-friendly benefits • I.D. and communicate sales cycle and ideal prospect • Protect I.P.	*Minimize weaknesses to reduce threats* • Generate positive publicity • Sales training for distributors • Increase market share

Blue Ocean Strategy[15] is an approach in which businesses create *blue oceans* of uncontested market opportunity rather than compete in the existing bloody *red ocean* market space. A good example is Southwest Airlines recognizing regional, low-cost air travel as its blue ocean - an untapped market with growth potential.

4. How much should you spend on marketing?

When you calculate your marketing budget, you need to consider your conversion rate of buyers and average sales prices. If you know this information, as well as your forecasted sales revenues, you can build backwards into your required number of leads that will generate the sales you require.

What you spend on marketing also depends upon where you are in your product lifecycle. When a product is new in an industry, marketers need to educate the marketplace about its benefits and invest in brand creation and awareness campaigns. When a market heats up, competitors need to aggressively market to grab market share, which may require more funding. In a mature market, marketers can look for niche specialties to attract more demand and reduce marketing spend. In a declining market, marketers can treat a product or service like a *cash cow*, and cut marketing costs to ensure a profit.

---

15 Kim, W. Chan and Mauborgne, Renee, *Blue Ocean Strategy*, Harvard Business School Publishing Corporation, 2005.

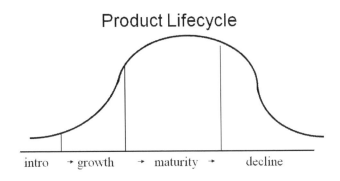

Product Lifecycle

intro → growth → maturity → decline

Marketing Strategy

educate → compete → niche → harvest/exit

5. What marketing tactics produce the best results?

Marketing tactics depend upon who your buyers are (your marketing personas) and your budget. If your marketing persona is a story about a young person who prefers to shop online and shares information on Facebook a lot, you may choose to invest in online marketing tactics such as social media, websites, email and video. If your marketing persona is about a baby boomer who uses the Internet reluctantly and prefers print materials and shopping in brick and mortar stores, then other marketing tactics such as direct mail and trade shows may be more effective. (See Chapter G – Generational Issues for more information).

Marketing tactics that are integrated produce the best results. Integrated marketing means that your marketing tactics work together to reinforce and increase prospect and customer response rate.

Integrated Marketing Creates Response Compression

Don't evaluate marketing tactics solely on cost. Some of the more expensive marketing tactics may yield the best results. Trade shows are an example. It can be quite expensive to ship your products, equipment and staff to a trade show. Yet, if the leads generated from the show have a high conversion rate to sales, the expense may be justified.

If you have no performance history for a marketing tactic, you can still estimate results to project your return on investment (ROI). For example, if you expect 100 leads from a trade show and you have a 10% prospect to customer conversion rate, you might net 10 new customers. Multiply your 10 new customers by your average sales per customer and you have your expected additional revenue. Divide this number by the cost of the tactic and you have your ROI.

Take some risks. Doing something different in your marketing – especially if you have been in the same space for a long time and your competitors execute the same marketing tactics – gets the attention of the marketplace. Make sure you track your results, including cost per lead, lead conversion rate and ROI.

6. What results should you expect from your marketing efforts?

The real test for business marketing results is whether or not there is a positive ROI. The results you track will vary on the objectives of your marketing, which might include: Build brand awareness, become an industry thought-leader, increase qualified website traffic, increase customer loyalty, or generate leads for sales.

Measuring results varies by objective. If your objective is to build awareness or become a thought-leader – both difficult to quantify – you might need to do surveys, focus groups or informational interviewing to measure results.

If your objective is generating leads for sales, some of the important data you should capture includes number of leads generated, source of leads, cost per lead, lead conversion rate, and sales revenue generated.

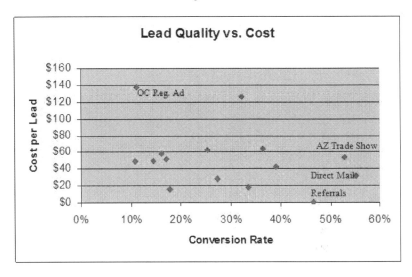

Measure quality as well as quantity. For example, in the illustration above, you may spend equal amounts to advertise in a newspaper and to exhibit at an industry trade show. The ad cost per lead is $138 and 12% of the leads from the ad convert to sales. The trade show cost per lead is much lower ($57 per lead) and the conversion rate is 54% (See our Chapter Q – Quality for more information).

Don't get emotional about your marketing. It may feel good for your ego to have an ad running in your city's paper or to see your company name and logo on the billboard, but those good feelings may not translate to top line sales revenue. Kevin Clancy and Peter Krieg wrote an excellent book on this topic, called *Counterintuitive Marketing*.[16] (See Chapter X – X-ray for more information)

7. **Are you marketing through the right channels?**

Business owners have many options when it comes to choosing the right channel through which to market products and services. The decision should start with the customer. Start by asking how your target customers purchase similar products. Is it through a direct sales force or agents, resellers or retailers? If a product is complex, or if there is a high need to control the sales process to ensure quality, direct sales might be the best choice.

---

16 Clancy, Kevin J. and Krieg, Peter, *Counterintuitive Marketing: Achieve Great Results Using Uncommon Sense*, The Free Press, New York, 2000.

If you do go direct, can you sell through inside sales people or do you need sales people who travel to the customer? Many companies today are hiring more inside sales reps who use technology like webinars and video teleconference calls to conduct sales meetings. Other methods of direct sales include catalog or online sales.

- **Resellers** usually have a need to bundle your product or service with something else they offer. Examples are IT service providers who resell software and equipment, engineers, and consultants.

- **Sales agents** are often people who know an industry or who have a relationship with the customers you want to reach. They receive a commission for each sale.

- **Wholesalers** buy your product in bulk, requiring little or no sales and marketing support from you. Your cost is much lower but they expect a hefty discount in return.

- **Retail outlets** work for those who need to reach consumers.

If you end up with multiple channels through which you market, remember that resellers, agents, wholesalers and retailers are also your customers. Keep channel conflict to a minimum, and market creatively to them to build and retain mindshare about your brand, your products and services.

8. Are you targeting the right customers?

Knowing your customers is critical. What are their demographics and psychographics? If you don't know, you can survey your customer list to get some answers. To uncover potential target markets, you can look vertically and map your supply chain. Which companies above or below you on the supply chain can refer you to their customers? Can you bring them in as partners – in the form of referrers, resellers or agents?

Niche marketing has served many companies well. Claiming you are the vendor in a specialized market is not easy to forget – niche marketing makes it easier for referral sources and others in your industry supply chain to remember.

Understanding profitability and lifetime value can help you determine the best customers for your business. Do you know which customers are profitable? With which customers you lose money or receive a smaller profit margin? Do you know the lifetime value of a customer?

9. How do you get your customers to buy more?

It is seven times more expensive to get a new customer rather than to sell products and services to an existing customer. Customer marketing and retention programs require (again – I'm starting to sound like a broken record, but it's important!) that you know your customers. What is your customer defection rate? Why do your customers leave?

When evaluating how to market to existing customers, consider the lifetime value of each customer-marketing persona. Domino's looked at the cost per slice that a customer may buy when they came into a store – under $5 dollars. But, that same customer over ten years is worth $5,000.[17] With a lifetime customer value in mind, you can make better marketing decisions.

Unfortunately, many businesses are more focused on getting new business than retaining existing customers. Try not to fall into this trap. Create a plan for marketing to existing customers. With your marketing personas in hand, identify the best ways to communicate to your customers, utilizing different media so that no matter how a customer likes to receive information, you have covered the bases: video, graphics and photos, audio, print materials, etc.

Today's technology supports easier ways to sell more to customers. Online shopping carts alert shoppers to *items others bought* that are related to an item being purchased, taking advantage of what Robert Cialdini calls the Principle of Consensus, which posits that the testimonials of others have a very important effect on people's buying decisions.[18]

10. Should you hire marketing staff or outsource?

Because of higher employee costs, including mandatory health insurance and other costs, companies are increasingly limiting their hired employees to "mission critical" and core competencies, often outsourcing functions such as accounting and finance, HR, legal counsel, and marketing. Some of the benefits of outsourcing marketing include:

- Eliminating the costs associated with employing marketing personnel

- Taking away the burden of managing marketing staff from busy business owners

- Giving the company a senior-level, outside viewpoint

---

17 Reichheld, Frederick, and Sasser, Earl Jr., "Zero Defections: Quality Comes to Services," Harvard Business Review, (September/October 1990), pp. 105-111.
18 Cialdini, Robert B., *Influence: Science and Practice*, Allyn and Bacon, Needham, Massachusetts, 2001.

If we conservatively estimate benefits at 35% of salary and a 30% bonus, costs are as follows:

Experience	Salary	Benefits (35%)	Bonus (20%)	Annual Total
Entry	$40,000	$14,000	$8,000	$62,000
Middle	$75,000	$26,250	$15,000	$116,250
Senior	$120,000	$42,000	$24,000	$186,000

A cost scenario for working with an outsource marketing firm might be as follows:

Senior-Level Pro.	Monthly Fee	Months	Annual Total
Hourly, Retainer, or % of Project	$2,000 – $8,000	12	$24,000 – $96,000

Marketing is a dynamic and exciting discipline that has become an increasingly important business function. Today marketing must emphasize the *relationship* between the company (provider of goods and services) and the customer (consumer of same) to build real long-term value. The company must not only satisfy the customers' actual needs via fit, form, and function; it must also meet their *perceived* needs, while at the same time working toward and achieving its own goals.

Managers must continuously adjust their marketing plans to a constantly shifting marketplace. Changes in technology, as well as social and economic demands, require you to be part magician, part futurist and part pragmatist... while acting locally and thinking globally.

CHAPTER N – NETWORKING

By Ivan Misner, PhD and Paula Frazier

1. Just how many referrals per month can you expect to get from your networking efforts?

The number of referrals you should expect to receive is dependent on the type of business you're in and the effort you exert to develop your network. Some professions receive more referrals than others. For example, a florist is going to get many more referrals than a real estate agent.

However, the florist will have to sell a lot of flowers to make up for one real estate sale. Hence, the type of profession can somewhat determine a range in the quantity of referrals. Having said that, however, the actual number that someone in a specific profession can get varies dramatically depending on their efforts to develop those referrals.

In general, the number of referrals you can expect will vary depending on your profession and your efforts in the networking process. However, on average, we've found that many businesspeople can generate more than 50 referrals per year via their participation in a single networking organization. What makes this number truly significant is that most people would agree that a referred contact is much easier to close into business than other types of contacts. We believe this is the reason that so many business owners say they generate most of their business through networking.

2. What are the stages of networking relationships, and which one(s) should you focus on?

When our colleagues at The Referral Institute train people to network, one of the first things we teach them is The VCP Process®:

- *Visibility (V)* - This is the point in the relationship at which individuals first meet. They have a conversation, trade contact information, and move on. This might happen several times. At this stage, individuals merely have to remember one another and have some basic knowledge of the other.

- *Credibility (C)* - This is the second phase of the relationship. In this phase, two individuals have interacted several times and trust one another. The longer they know, work with, and support each other, the deeper their credibility and trust. At this phase of the relationship, the two networking partners begin to trust and help each other — and the relationship continues to grow.
- *Profitability (P)* - This is the third phase of the relationship. At this point, two networking partners completely trust each other, open their networks and customer databases to each other, and proactively help each other. Each has a deeper understanding of the other's business and knows how to develop referrals and connections as well as open doors.

Once you are comfortable with these terms, stop networking for a few moments. Stand still, look at what you have, prioritize it, database it, and cull it, rather than continue to work on only the Visibility part of process. Instead, devote more time to the "C" and the "P." Credibility comes with a closer, deeper relationship, and profitability is the goal that can be maintained only through constant nurturing of that relationship for mutual benefit. It's not "Nice to meet you; now I've got to go talk to someone over there." It's "How are you doing, and how can I help you achieve your goals?"

3. **How can you use networking to get others to promote your business?**

How many times have friends, family and associates said, "If there's anything I can do to help you, let me know"? How often have you said, "Well, now that you mention it, there are a few things you could do"? If you're like most people, you aren't prepared to accept help at the moment it's offered. You let opportunity slip by because you haven't given enough thought to the kinds of help you need. You haven't made the connection between specific items or services you need and the people who can supply them. But when help is offered, it's to your advantage to be prepared and to respond by stating a specific need.

Don't let the next opportunity for others to help slip through your fingers! Being prepared with some simple requests can make a real difference in the success of your business. Systematic referral marketing requires that you determine, as precisely as possible, the type of help you want and need. There are many ways your sources can help you promote yourself and your business:

a) They can provide you with referrals. The kind of support you'd most like to get from your contacts is referrals--the names of specific individuals who need your products and services. They can also give prospects your name and number. As the number of referrals you receive increases, so does your potential for increasing the percentage of your business generated through referrals.

b) They can introduce you to prospects. Your contacts can help you build new relationships faster by introducing you in person to people they think need your products and services. Furthermore, they can provide you with key information about the prospect. They can also tell the prospect a few things about you, your business, how the two of you met, some of the things you and the prospect have in common, and the value of your products and services.

c) They can endorse your products and services. By telling others what they've gained from using your products or services in presentations or informal conversations, your sources can encourage others to use your products or services.

d) They can display your literature and products in their offices and homes. If these items are displayed well – such as on a counter or bulletin board in a waiting room – visitors will ask questions or read the information. Some may take your promotional materials and display them in other places, increasing your visibility.

e) They can distribute your information. Your contacts can help you distribute marketing materials. For instance, a dry cleaner might attach a coupon from the hair salon next door to each plastic bag he/she uses to cover customers' clothes. Including your flier in the middle of their newsletter is another idea.

f) They can publish information for you. Your contacts may be able to get information about you and your business printed in publications they subscribe to and in which they have some input or influence. For example, a source belonging to an association that publishes a newsletter might help you get an article published or persuade the editor to run a story about you.

4. What is the best way to create an effective personal introduction to people at networking events?

The primary goal of networking is to meet the right people, with whom you can give and receive information, support and referrals. To do this, one of the things you must do is, make meaningful contact with other business professionals who can use your services, refer someone else who can use your services, or both. And one of the fundamental elements of this process is making effective introductions. The ideal introduction is *brief* and *memorable*. It has to provide enough impact to arouse the interest of those to whom you're introducing yourself.

Whether you're introducing yourself to an individual or a group, you have a choice of how you deliver your message. The primary vehicle for your introduction is your verbal presentation.

Does your introduction work? People will judge not only the message, but also the messenger. How you look, carry yourself and listen will affect what others do with the message you've delivered. As you network, your underlying hope is that people will use your products or services and pass your message on to others who will also use your products or services.

When participating (even as a guest) in various business organizations, you may be asked to introduce yourself. Preparing a script for this process will improve your results. One of your scripts should be an overview of what you do. Other presentations can address various aspects of your product or service.

Here is a recommended sequence for your brief introduction:

- Your name
- The name and a brief description of your business or profession
- A "memory hook" that includes quick, ear-catching phrases
- A benefit statement of one particular product or service you offer – what you do that helps others

5. Networking involves a good deal of public speaking – how can you overcome a fear of this?

It's definitely a fact that you don't have to be a great public speaker to be a great networker, as a lot of networking takes place in one-to-one or small group situations. However, one of the major components of networking is joining a networking group. In most – if not all – of these groups, the time will come when you will be asked to get up in front of the other members and tell them about your business. Many people who are great in one-on-one situations are literally paralyzed by standing up in front of a group to speak. In fact, in the many surveys we've seen over the years, people have ranked the fear of public speaking higher than the fear of dying! Standing and talking to an audience can be frightening, especially if it's for more than a couple of minutes.

Here are five suggestions for people who are nervous doing presentations at their networking groups:

a) Prepare, prepare, prepare! Don't wing it! Prepare an outline of what you want to say and practice it.

b) Be specific and talk about the things you know best. Don't try to teach people everything you do. Focus on no more than two or three areas of what you want them to learn about. Most importantly, cover the topics you feel you understand the best. This will reduce some of your stress

c) Use handouts, visuals or PowerPoint slides to support your presentation. For people who are worried about stage fright, these props can help carry them through the talk.

d) Remember, you're the expert. Think about ways that help show that and are not threatening for you.

e) Be creative. Think of some way to communicate the information in a way you feel comfortable.

Think creatively about what you know and what you feel comfortable doing to express that knowledge. You'll discover that you don't have to pass up an opportunity to talk a little longer to the networking groups you belong to.

6. What's the best way to network in a large group?

Networking with a large group is both good and bad. It's good because there are many people that your members can meet. However, it can also be a problem because it's very easy to get lost in the crowd with so many people involved.

There are several things you can do to make a large group's networking efforts more effective. If everyone is seated at tables around the room, make sure that before the official meeting begins, you give your introduction to everyone at your table.

It's important, whenever possible, to sit at tables where you don't already know the majority of other people. That helps to ensure that you are really networking, rather than simply sitting with your friends.

The bottom line: Don't let the fact that you are only one of many people at a large event keep you from a successful networking experience. We have found that people, like water, tend to seek the path of least resistance. Without some structured activities at networking events, they will often do what is easiest, not what's best. Don't be one of these people! Remember: It's not called "netSIT" or "netEAT"; it's called "netWORK," and in order to have a successful networking event, you need to "work" the network.

7. Why is it so important to continue to network with your *clients* after they are no longer just *prospects*?

Your business thrives on you making contacts and getting new business. What happens after you've made the sale and your "hot prospect" is now a client? How often should you be in touch with that person? What are some rules of thumb for keeping in touch and nurturing your relationship? Staying in touch is an important part of the networking process. Here are several tips for keeping in touch and strengthening your business relationships:

a) Spread out your contact opportunities. Regardless of the type of relationship with your clients, regular contact is generally good. Each meeting becomes an opportunity to strengthen the relationship and to enhance your visibility and recognition.

b) Schedule predictably. Stay in touch with your clients regularly. Train them to expect to hear from you at certain times. For example, if you usually contact certain customers during the first week of every quarter, they will come to expect it. If they don't hear from you, they may actually call to see how you are doing on their own.

c) Make each contact lead to the next. Before concluding a meeting or telephone conversation, schedule the date of your next contact. In written correspondence, close by stating the date your customer should expect to hear from you again: "I'll send you a note or e-mail by the end of the quarter." Having made the commitment, you're more likely to follow through.

d) Assume responsibility for making contact. You can't control whether clients will contact you, but you can control when you contact them. Take the initiative; stay in touch with your customers. This is especially important for your most important clients. When clients or customers do not feel cared for, they are more likely to try someone else.

e) Invite them to networking events. One way of making sure to stay in contact with your customers is to invite select ones to some of the networking events that you go to.

f) Stick to your plan. As you achieve success in establishing routines with your sources, some of them may begin taking initiative with contact. Don't let this interfere with your contact schedule; that is, when they initiate the call, don't count it as one of the contacts you've scheduled.

8. Why should you resist the urge to "sell" to your network?

Most business owners who believe in "networking" belong to networking groups, including Business Network International (BNI, the networking organization Ivan founded in 1985). Educating the members of this type of group about the type of referrals you want – up to and including specific individuals you would like to meet – is much more important to the success of your efforts than just "selling" what you offer to them. This demands a shift in how you see your networking partners. They're not the clients; they are, in effect, your sales force. And for your sales force to sell you effectively, they have to know who to sell you to and how to sell you.

Here are four tips for incorporating this educational style into your networking meetings:

a) Teach your network members what your "dream referral" looks like. If you could go to your next networking meeting with a walking, talking dream referral in tow, what would he or she be like? Describe this person in detail to your networking partners. The more details you can provide, the greater the chance that your partners will recognize that person when they come across him or her outside the meeting.

b) Share customer profiles and case studies of current customers. This is a highly effective way to educate your networking partners about what it is you're looking for in a new client. By sharing the qualities of your current clientele, you're illuminating the canvas for the rest of the group so they can see the picture you're painting for them.

c) Break your business down into its lowest common denominators. It's very tempting to start your personal introduction with a statement like: "We're a full-service XYZ." Resist this urge! Get detailed! Educate your networking partners at every meeting about the specific things you provide. Bring support material to provide a visual. Do demonstrations, when possible.

d) Ask specifically for the referral you want. We often hear members of networking groups say things like "Anyone who needs…" or "Everyone who's looking …" Usually, when we hear "anyone" or "everyone," we tune out, because we know so many "anyones" and "everyones" that we end up referring no one! When you're asking for a specific type of business referral, your request from your networking partners should be specific. Using a broad, generic catchphrase will limit the effectiveness of your results.

By keeping your focus on educating your networking partners about what type of referrals you wish to receive, you'll find that the referrals you begin to get will be of a higher caliber and offer more chances of becoming closed sales than if you try to sell the members on what you're offering.

9. What are some common "networking faux pas" you should avoid?

Faux Pas #1: Not responding quickly to referral partners

There are countless examples of people receiving referrals at networking groups and then contacting the referral a few days later. The old phrase, "If you snooze, you lose," is apropos here. If the referral knows you had her name and number on Monday and took your time calling, this sends a negative message about your business.

Faux Pas #2: Confusing networking with direct selling

A business owner once said, "I'm really good at networking. I've been doing it for a long, long time." A colleague of Ivan's asked her, "So what's your secret?" said, "Well, a friend and I enter a room together. We imagine drawing a line down the middle. She takes the left side; I take the right side. We agree to meet at a certain time to see who collected the most cards. The loser buys the other one lunch."

When asked what she did with all those cards, the business owner said, "I enter them into my distribution list and begin to send them information about my services. Since I have all their information, they're all good prospects, right?"

This is a classic example of an entrepreneur not understanding that networking isn't about simply gathering contact information and following up on it later. That's nothing more than glorified cold calling. It gives us the chills. Ivan used to teach cold calling techniques to business people – and he did it enough to know that he didn't want to ever do it again! For this reason, he has devoted his entire professional life to teaching the business community that networking, done well, is a much better way to build long-term business.

Faux Pas #3: Abusing the relationship

There are many ways we've seen networking partners abuse relationships, but the following story is one of the most glaring examples.

A woman was invited to attend a 50th birthday party of an associate who used to belong to a networking group in which she also participated. They once had a long-term working relationship, and, out of respect, she decided to attend. When she got there, it was very obvious the partygoers were being recruited for a business opportunity. The only refreshment served was the recruiting company's diet shake! Never mislead your networking partners. For that matter, never mislead anyone. Trust is everything when you're talking about relationship networking. Inviting people to a business opportunity pitch disguised as a "birthday party" isn't being honest with the very people with whom you want to build a trusting relationship.

All these faux pas directly relate to good people skills. The prevailing theme of all three is to treat your referral partners and potential referral partners with professionalism and care.

10. What is a "contact sphere" and how can it help you in your networking efforts?

Contact spheres are a great way to start building your professional network. A contact sphere is a group of business professionals who have a symbiotic relationship. They are in compatible, noncompetitive professions, such as a lawyer, a CPA, a financial planner and a banker. If you put those four people in a room for an hour, they're going to do business together. Each one is working with clients that have similar needs but require different services.

Hence, they're working that symbiotic relationship.

One of the best examples of a contact sphere is a caterer, a florist, a photographer and a travel agent. We call this the "wedding mafia"! If one gets a referral to a wedding, then they all get a referral to the wedding. These professions, more than most, have truly learned how to work their contact sphere.

Here are some other examples of contact spheres:

- Business services: printers, graphic artists, specialty advertising agents and marketing consultants
- Real estate services: residential and commercial agents, escrow companies, title companies and mortgage brokers
- Contractors: painters, carpenters, plumbers, landscapers, electricians and interior designers
- Health care: chiropractors, physical therapists, acupuncturists and nutritionists

CHAPTER O – OPERATIONS

By Lee Schwartz

1. How does operations inter-relate with the other functional areas of your company, including sales, marketing and finance?

Have you ever really noticed how a stool is built? Whether three-legged or four, when built correctly the legs are proportionally spaced and balanced. Damage a leg and the stool wobbles; remove or significantly cripple a leg and the stool topples over. Businesses are similar in nature. They are not one-dimensional. A single area of a company, for instance operations, cannot by itself keep an organization afloat.

Departments within organizations are as reliant upon their counterparts as they are dependent upon the team within the department. Just think of the dysfunction that would ensue if the sales team didn't supply operations with forecasts. Consider the financial ramifications of shipping orders without credit controls sanctioned by the finance people. Consider a world where sales and marketing are blind to what's sitting on the warehouse shelf or the factory floor; salespeople would be a bit challenged knowing what to sell. Imagine the customer dissatisfaction created if orders received were full of backorders.

Unfortunately, it's more common than not in every industry to have functional areas in conflict with their counterparts: sales vs. marketing...sales vs. operations...finance vs. sales... HR vs. legal. Those companies who have forged strong ties within the organization through open communication and bonding toward a common purpose, and who also do not view the workplace as an "us vs. them" environment, will achieve greater success. Shatter the paradigm of department independence at the cost of internal relationships, and become a facilitator for interactive discourse and communication within your organization. Then watch the bottom line grow.

2. What is the difference between operating results and operating success?

Let's assume that you're responsible for getting customer orders out the door. Let's further assume that once an order is received, it takes five days for processing and shipping. Now let's look at a key metric: The percentage of the items ordered that actually shipped. For purposes of this illustration, let's say that out of 100 items orders, only 87 left the building and 13 were backordered. That's an 87% service level. Is this success?

Certainly we have results. But are these successful results? Place yourself in the shoes of a customer. In a world where instantaneous gratification is more the norm than not, will your customer be happy knowing that their order will take five days before shipping? And when the order is received, how happy will they be when over 10% of what they ordered didn't arrive? To be clear, the average (from 2006 to 2010) for industry leading companies when it comes to delivering their orders complete and on-time is 95.8%+ of the time[19].

The first step is to measure activity. Establish key performance indicators (KPIs) that quantifiably assess performance. *Average days outstanding, scrap rate percentage, service level, inventory turnover,* and *dollars shipped per sales representative* are all examples of metrics that can be tracked and are critical to your success. And by tracking these kinds of metrics, you can also plan. If, to be profitable, the company must achieve $1,000,000 in sales per month, then the goal is $50,000 per business day.

Once measured, what do these numbers mean? The above-mentioned 87% service level, based on best practice norms of 96%, renders that activity sub-standard. So it's important that you, your department, and the company set objectives that, when realized, achieve success…not only in your eyes, but also in the eyes of the customer, whether internal or external. What you want in the end are not just results but *successful results.*

3. **How do you budget for operational success?**

Operational success cannot be achieved without a guiding budget.

So where to begin? First, you need a strategy, a plan of action. What do you (or your department or company) wish to accomplish? Once known and agreed to, from champion to users, it's time to understand all the tasks and steps required to achieve results. Of course this list must include the necessary resources, including materials and equipment (see Chapter S – Strategy for more information).

Start by assigning true costs to these identified activities. Against the costs, it's imperative to budget sales that are realistic. Don't simply accept historical results; include seasonality and cyclical trends. Separate fixed costs (those that are not volume dependent) from variable costs (those that *do* vary directly with volume changes). With the help of your sales and marketing teams (covered in question 1 of this chapter), predict revenues as reliably as possible (see Chapter F – Forecasting and Budgeting for more information).

19 IndustryWeek's Continuous Improvement newsletter; August 2, 2011

Once the numbers have been agreed upon, be sure to measure continuously. Set KPIs (Key Performance Indicators) and link the numbers to them. Create dashboards. Review reports. True operational success is realized when there's functional achievement within the financial constraints established by a budget.

4. **Do operations differ depending on the type of industry?**

Have you ever heard of the Pareto Principle, otherwise known as the 80/20 rule? When first put to the test, Pareto noticed that 80% of Italy's land was owned by 20% of the population. In 1992, the United Nations released a study that showed the richest 20% of the world's population controlled 82.7% of the world's income.

In the business world, the 80/20 rule would predict that 80% of your company's sales/revenues come from 20% of your customers/clients. Or, 20% of the inventory items stocked represents 80% of total dollars sold. Or, in a service business, 80% of your clients may account for only 20% of your profits. So what does this all mean when it comes to answering this question?

Operations are operations. It doesn't matter what industry you work in... brick and mortar manufacturing/distribution or service providers like law or CPA firms...the approach with operations is greatly consistent across the board.

Years ago, I was competing for an engagement with a biotech company. Their processes required the refrigeration of their products. I had never worked in a refrigerated environment...and told them so. They replied, "Not a problem. 80% of our operational processes are no different whether in a climate controlled or ambient environment." This was certainly music to my ears.

Whether you work in the factory, the distribution center or the corporate office, the process of operations will be consistent. You still need to define the workflow, map out the steps necessary to complete the task, install procedures, document the process, measure the outcomes...and continue to improve.

5. **Does corporate culture, and the way you communicate, have a bearing on successful operations?**

Research and practical observations of successful companies have established a direct link between strong corporate cultures and high performance. In a firm with a strong culture, employees tend to march to the same, productive drummer. Companies with strong cultures tend to have shared values. Shared values and behaviors make people feel good about working for a firm; that feeling of commitment or loyalty is said to make people try harder. One CEO of a medium-sized organization shared the following: "I cannot imagine trying to run a business today with a weak or non-existent culture; why, people would be going off in a hundred different directions."

Proper communication contributes mightily to achieving a strong corporate culture and shared values. There's no debate. From day-to-day activity to the more strategic discussions, open, candid dialogue is a must. But how does that occur?

Today's world is one defined by technology. Emails, blogs and Tweets are more and more the tools of choice. And they all have a rightful place. But in their midst, direct, face-to-face communication is becoming almost passé. *Don't let this happen at your company.* Make sure that you meet regularly with those above, below and along side, in the other room and on the floor above, within or outside your department. Whether through one-on-ones, daily stand-up meetings or traditional around-the-conference-room-table gatherings, personal interaction is a gateway to operational success.

Developing the right organizational culture is the responsibility of top managers of every organization. Corporate culture can and will have a major impact on employee morale and productivity. It's not about just being a good employer, but about having employees committed to the vision and strategy of the organization (see Chapter S – Strategy for more information).

6. Are policies and procedures necessary for successful operations?

Most everyone has cooked a meal at some point or another. What's your approach? Do you pull out all the ingredients and have at it, especially the first time? Or do you consult a cookbook first? I'm guessing it's the latter. Why? Because you want that special dish to be perfect...the first time and every time.

Isn't that your objective at work as well? You want the outcome to be consistently the best it can be. And you want that to be the case whether it's you rolling up your sleeves, or one of your counterparts or – my favorite – the new hire. And you want that result repeatedly, because while it's acceptable for a basketball player to make 50% of their shots, in your business world that's just not going to cut it.

What better test of a policy or procedure's effectiveness than to turn to the novice employee, give them the SOP (Standard Operating Procedures) and watch them complete the task correctly and within the expected timeframe. If the newbie can make that happen, so will the more seasoned employees.

Writing policies and procedures is tedious work, no doubt about it. Because it's tedious and consumes valuable time, management won't necessarily be a consistent champion of this cause. But you can be; and you should. Whether you are a business owner or you merely supervise other employees, carve out the time. Memorialize (write them down) the steps necessary to complete the tasks you're responsible for. Operational success is far more achievable to those who make this commitment and complete it. An Aberdeen Group report entitled *Achieving Operational Excellence in Wholesale Distribution* states that leaders standardize business processes 33% more frequently than followers do. Be a leader!

7. **Can you optimize operations without leveraging technology?**

What is the purpose of optimizing operations? It is to remove the waste out of our activities. Can technology contribute? It sure can. Imagine how many steps (and, therefore, time) you save when your Warehouse Management System (WMS) directs the sequence of pulling an order. How much more productive and efficient is the manufacturing process when robotics are used? Do conveyors and sortation equipment optimize the effort to move raw goods/finished inventory from point A to point B? Of course they do!

The easy answer to the question above is no. But is that the reality? Is a Kanban scheduling system that guides the user towards what, when, and how much to produce rooted in technology? It's not. A manufacturing cell is designed to enable increased production velocity and flexibility. Many times technology has nothing to do with the improvements achieved.

Look around. We're personally tied to our technology…our PDAs, iPads, our laptops. What company today operates without some form of technology? I dare say virtually none do. But yet all we do cannot be mechanized. A human touch is still required. So the real answer to this question is – yes and no. Technology is just one arrow in our quiver of tools necessary to achieve operational optimization. The science is determining the necessary technology to use. The artistry is balancing the use of technology with the human contributions. Proper balance of the two is what you want to achieve.

8. **Must you choose between efficiency and effectiveness?**

A track and field sprinter has one – and only one – goal in mind: To get to the finish line as quickly as possible. At the other end of the spectrum, a bomb disposal expert diffusing live munitions must take all the time they need to do the job right. The heart surgeon, however, must walk a fine line between speed and outcome. The heart can only be on the heart machine for so long, yet one slip and the patient's life is in jeopardy.

The heart surgeon is balancing efficiency with effectiveness. In operations the two are also inseparable. They're joined at the hip. Consult your dictionary and you'll see the following definitions –

- Efficiency - *accomplishment of or ability to accomplish a job with a minimum expenditure of time and effort*
- Effectiveness - *adequate to accomplish a purpose; producing the intended or expected result*

Or, as Peter Drucker put it, *effective* is doing the right thing, while *efficient* is doing things right.

Let's move from the operating room to your office, factory floor or warehouse. No matter what the task, isn't the goal to perform the activity as quickly and accurately as possible? Whether it's the manufacture of the widget, the shipping of an order or the deposit of cash, the faster the task is completed the less it costs the company. Lower costs translate to greater profitability. And more profits could mean bonuses or increased salaries.

But: Does doing the work at top speed mean that the task was done correctly; that it achieved the desired results? No. The typists who type at 80 words per minute but make a dozen mistakes won't keep their job very long, nor will the order-entry assistant who enters the most orders in the department but also makes the most errors. The production manager who produces a record amount of widgets per hour, but must scrap 20% of the finished goods will also soon be looking for another job.

Your responsibility is to balance efficiency with effectiveness. One without the other will prevent you from achieving operational success.

9. Is it critical to continuously improve your processes?

By the time this book hits the streets, it's quite possible that Apple will have introduced to the marketplace their next generation iPad. If the rumors are true, the "iPad3" will have even more than its predecessors. The launch of the original iPad was enormously successful. So why the need to unveil generation 2? G3?

This is because the goal of any company should be constant improvement. Intel knows that as they introduce their latest chip it will be replaced soon; the next generation is already beyond the drawing board. Therefore, they want to be the ones who make their own chip obsolete because if they don't, someone else will. Continuous Process Improvement (CPI) is an ongoing effort aimed at improving current business processes used to provide goods or services. It's an ongoing effort to incrementally improve how products and services are provided and internal operations are conducted. The implementation is tactical, but the concept is strategic.

CPI activities target process simplification and reduction to elimination of process waste. Think about the tasks you perform. Can they be completed in fewer steps than what it takes currently? How much time would that relieve for you to focus on other activities? And how many dollars would that save the company/your department?

CPI is not just a managerial approach; it helps develop a culture of innovation and constant improvement within the company. It focuses on improving the bottom line, by saving money through increasing efficiency and raising sales through enhancing quality. I highly suggest you become a champion of CPI (see Chapter P – Process Improvement for more information).

10. Is it true that you must "Evolve or die?" (Eckhart Tolle)

"Borders is Liquidating!" read the headline. "National book store chain Borders *'botched its move into the digital age'",* said its critics. Over 200 stores closed, and 6,000 people out of work...just because the company didn't evolve.

There's a famous quote by Sir Winston Churchill, "If you're standing still you're falling behind." Think about the implication of that statement. It's not hard to know when a company is suffering. The signs are evident: Sales are in decline; it's hard to pay the bills; the company can't move enough inventory out the door; income statements are bleeding red. But even in the world of status quo (where sales are flat lined; you may be able to pay your bills, but can't get approval to buy that needed piece of equipment, etc.), it's important to be able to see when your company is treading water...with the shore looking more and more distant as your competition leaves you farther and farther behind.

Even before the economic recession that began in 2008, the landscape was littered with companies – including Tower Records, Musicland, and Linens 'n Things – that didn't evolve. And because they didn't evolve, they're no longer with us.

Can you, in whatever capacity you hold, make a difference? Of course you can. You can read, research, investigate, discuss. You can try new things, on a continual lookout for industry best practices. Thanks to the constant advances in technology, the world of information is within your grasp. Seize the opportunity: Advocate for change, for continuous process improvement, for evolution. *Make* things happen; don't just *let* them happen.

CHAPTER P – PROCESS IMPROVEMENT

By Lee Schwartz and Daniel Feiman

1. **What is a *process*?**

   A process is a sequence of interrelated steps that achieve a specific and planned result for the customer of the process.

   OK, so what does this *really* mean? Broken down, it means: *a process is a sequence (series) of interrelated (interconnected) steps (stages) that achieve (accomplish) a specific (precise) and planned (scheduled) result (outcome) for a customer (internal or external).* This result must be individually identifiable and quantifiable. So you need to create a plan to achieve a goal that regularly and measurably satisfies your customer.

   Further, in saying that the process steps must relate to each other, this means the completion of one step leads to (flows into) the initiation of the next step in sequence.

   As to the *customer* of the process, a customer receives the result or is the beneficiary of the process. The customer can be a person or department – within the company or outside of it – that can be identified and can place judgment on the result and process.

   Examples of process include: Unlocking a door, answering the telephone, following a written procedure, setting up a machine, taking a customer order, ordering inventory, delivering a presentation, booking travel, landing an airplane, administering medicine, etc. Some of these processes are rather simple and routine, while others are complex and critical. Yet they are all processes.

2. **What does it mean to *improve* a process?**

   Change is the only constant. – Heraclitus, Greek philosopher

   Improving a process is to make it better than it is or was. It means not just fighting fires created by doing what you do, but preventing them before they ignite. Process improvement means changing the mindset within the company, from the common practice of blaming someone or something for problems or failures to proactively making the needed changes to improve. It is a different way of thinking and acting. Actual process improvement involves following a specific process to achieve change, which we will delineate later in this chapter.

When you actively participate in real process improvement, you look for the causes of the problems or wastes in a process and use that information to reduce the variation (which in itself creates waste), remove non value-added activities and have the planned result of improving customer satisfaction.

The most common, and best, approach today is to *Lean Out* the process, or change it to eliminate the waste permanently. In our experience, we have found that in virtually all process (and there are hundreds in the typical company), waste exists. And this waste costs the company money. By improving a process, you can reduce the unnecessary waste, while still accomplishing the intended goal(s) of the process. Less waste equals less cost. Less cost equals higher profits. It's simple mathematics.

3. **What is waste, exactly?**

Waste is what you do or use that is excess or unnecessary. It slows down the process or increases its cost. There are several critical areas of waste. They include:

a) *Transport* – moving products that are not actually required to perform the process

b) *Inventory* – any amount of inventory at each stage (raw material, work-in-process and finished goods) not being currently used in the process

c) *Motion* - people or equipment moving or walking more than is required to perform the process

d) *Waiting* - waiting for the next step in the production process

e) *Over Production* – producing more than is required to meet demand

f) *Over Processing* – using more processing than is required, usually resulting from poor tooling or product design

g) *Defects* - the effort involved in inspecting for and fixing defects

h) *Unused creativity* – people doing what they are told, rather than being engaged and encouraged to come up with better ways of doing things and solving problems

4. **How do you improve a process?**

You start with how your process is today, or the *as-is state*. This demonstrates exactly how the process is performed currently. Document this in two ways. First, you simply write down all the steps in the process from beginning to end. This can be either in a narrative form, phrases, or using some dedicated tool or a process form. This is usually more challenging than it sounds. Why? Because most people do not realize the number of individual steps involved in even the simplest of tasks. You really have to take some time to think about what actually starts the process and how it actually ends. Then you have to add step(s) in-between the two.

Second, you draw a flow chart of this process. Flow charts use standard symbols to indicate the beginning of a process, process steps, decision points, action items, etc., along the path. Flow chart software can be found in the Microsoft Office suite, as well as several specialized software products. Here are a few of the typical symbols you would use to develop your flowchart:

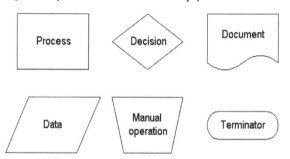

Once the process is documented in the *as-is* state, you determine what changes need to be made to optimize the process, and then draw the *future- or ideal-state* using the same tools you used when developing the *as-is state*.

Comparing these two documents, you can then determine the steps needed to transform the company from the *as-is* to the *future-state*. Then you document an action plan showing how the company is going to get from one state to the other. Once this action plan is documented, develop a training program to teach everyone involved in the process exactly how it is to be performed from this point forward.

Once everyone who uses the process is trained to perform the process the new way, you should conduct a periodic audit of the process, to determine what adjustments need to be made to continue the improvement. Additionally, it must be regularly measured against a standard (either internal or external) to assure that progress is being made through reduced waste.

5. **What are the actual steps to go from the *as-is* to the *future-state* in a process?**
Here is a list of the basic steps that help facilitate the transition from *as-is* to *future-state*:

a) Take a dedicated process improvement form (as mentioned in question 4, above) or a blank sheet or paper
b) Choose a process and write it down on the form
c) Identify the beginning and end of the process on the form
d) Write down the steps of the process, in sequence, as it currently exists (*as-is state*)
e) Draw a flow chart of the *as-is* process
f) Identify the Suppliers (internal and/or external) to the process
g) Interview the Suppliers to align what they deliver to what the process needs
h) Identify the Customers (internal and/or external) of the process
i) Interview the Customers to align what the process delivers to what *they* need
j) Eliminate any unnecessary steps in the process and/or add in new ones
k) Modify the existing steps in the process to create the *future-state*
l) Update the process form to reflect the desired *future-state*
m) Update the flow chart accordingly
n) Document how the process is to be measured
o) Develop training materials based on the newly designed process and flowchart
p) Train all process users on the *new* process
q) Measure the process on a regular basis
r) Adjust as needed

6. **Why do you need to document the process?**

People feel more responsibility to conform to a process that is written down. It is also easier to standardize and to measure progress when a process is documented. Additionally, as you document the existing process, each team member contributes his or her sense or understanding of how it is performed. As the document is developed, showing the individual steps, they can discuss how they each see it to make sure all of the steps are included.

The old expression, "We are all smarter than one of us is smart," applies here perfectly. As the team reviews the existing document together, they can see opportunities for refinements and improvements that are relatively easy and obvious. Further study will reveal more room for improvement.

Another benefit of documenting the process is to enable the team to standardize it. This is the first waste reduction opportunity. Why standardize the process? Because when everyone performs a process the same way, and that way is deemed to be the best, it then has to be more efficient. When a process is more efficient it uses fewer resources. When a process uses fewer resources it costs less… so it saves money.

When a process is documented, everyone can be trained to perform it the same way. And everyone can refer to this document in the future should there be a need or a question. The training relates directly back to the standardization, which is accomplished through training. Then the training can teach everyone the *right* way to perform the process moving forward.

Lastly, you now have a measurement baseline against which to calculate improvement. The *as-is* document is your starting point, while the *future-state* becomes your goal. Incremental measurements on a regular basis are critical to recognizing success with your improvements and identifying areas where adjustments might be needed.

7. **When is the best time to start to improve a process?**

Start today. Begin by choosing those processes that are either obviously "broken", or have the biggest impact on your operations. The sooner you start, the sooner your efforts will begin to reflect positively on the bottom line.

Easier said than done, you may say. Yes, it always is. And you feel you don't have time to take on one more task that doesn't immediately hit the bottom line? Well, take heart; this is an example of the difference between an expense and an investment. An *expense*, as you may know, is money spent with no expectation of a return (e.g. rent for facilities). However, an *investment* is money spent *with* an expectation of a return (e.g. a mortgage payment).

We know that as processes are improved, waste is reduced (and eventually eliminated) from them. When waste is reduced so is the related expense. So it logically follows that as you improve processes you drive down the cost of them and therefore, improve the bottom line. The increase in the bottom line is the *return on investment* or *ROI*.

8. **Who is involved in the improvement?**

For process improvement to be successful, you need a team approach. A team is defined by BusinessDictionary.com as *a group of people with a full set of complementary skills required to complete a task, job, or project. Team members (1) operate with a high degree of interdependence, (2) share authority and responsibility for self-management, (3) are accountable for the collective performance, and (4) work toward a common goal and shared rewards. A team becomes more than just a collection of people when a strong sense of mutual commitment creates synergy, thus generating performance greater than the sum of the performance of its individual members.*

That is a team. And a team is required to properly and consistently implement process improvement so that it *sticks*. The team should include the following:

a) *Process Owner*

This is the person who chooses to spearhead the initiative, keep it going and keeps the users focused on improving the process as he performs it. The process owner works closely with the *Process Champion* and her team.

b) *Process Champion*

This person should be more senior than the process owner, as part of their responsibility is to remove roadblocks that might prevent the process owner from improving the process. Typically, a process champion will oversee several processes simultaneously with common or related purposes. The process champion supports the process owners in prioritizing improvement and developing improvement teams.

c) *Process Users*

These are the people who actually use the process being improved.

d) *Process Team Members*

These are the individuals who participate in the improvement initiative and work with the process owner to divide the work involved.

e) *Process Suppliers*

These are those who provide what is needed to properly carry out the process. They may be either internal or external...and they may be either a "person" or a "department".

f) *Process Customers*

These are internal or external, and may be certain people, a department, or a company that receives benefit from the output of a process, or uses the output of a process.

g) *Subject Matter Expert*

This is a person who has significant experience and/or expertise in the process that is to be improved, and is willing to act as a resource to the *master trainer*. This person may or may not be directly involved in the process on a regular basis.

h) *Master Trainer*

This person is trained specifically to train others. She reviews the documented process, and develops training material and resources for those who will work with the process. Frequently, the master trainer also verifies that the process users can perform the work as documented.

9. **How do you measure improvement?**

You measure the improvement of any process by starting at the beginning. That is, measure where the process is now. Outputs, quality, time, through put, errors, mean time between failures (MTBF), etc. are all potential measurements.

Once you decide what to measure, you have to establish a baseline; i.e., what is (are) the value(s) now? Then you determine what you would like them to be. This becomes the target (or targets).

Many companies start by finding and reviewing their industry numbers. Every industry produces its own set of statistics. Frequently you can find the mean (average), upper quartile (best 25%) and lower quartile (bottom 25%) for most ratios and performance metrics you might be interested in. These are usually available at no charge from your trade association as one of the benefits of your membership.

Other sources include *Standard & Poor's, Dunn & Bradstreet* and *Risk Management Association*. Each of these resources regularly produces reports, for a fee, that go into great detail on every industry's ratios and statistics. Major universities' research libraries will also carry volumes containing this information.

Most operating and accounting systems today have the ability to capture the data that is needed. Regardless of whether you are using Quick Books, Excel, SAP, or anything in between, you need to measure where the process is today. The progress you are making against your goals will guide you toward the adjustments needed to achieve, sustain and further improve the process over your time horizon. The results you calculate will determine what actions you take.

10. **How do you ensure the improvements stick?**

Ah, the million dollar question. There are a few elements you must combine to ensure these improvements *stick*. Let's back up a bit. You start by

a) Documenting the process as it is and how you want it to be
b) Using this as the basis of your improvement plan
c) Establishing a training program as part of your action plan
d) Regularly, objectively measuring the results of the process
e) Comparing to a benchmark (either internal or external)

Success can be celebrated; declines can be investigated, and adjustments can be made.

Measuring the effectiveness of the process versus the expected outcomes is critical to achieving these targets. "What gets measured gets done" is an old adage, but still true today. The process must be measured against an objective, accurate standard. This way you will know whether the process is working or not, and whether it is improving or not.

By reinforcing the behavior you want (following the process) and deterring the behavior you don't (ad hoc), you will form new habits. Habits are what you do without having to think about it. These new, *improved* habits will ensure the improvements stick and your bottom line will improve.

A landmark article by John Kotter delineates the primary, and repeating, reasons major initiatives fail in companies[20]. They are listed below:

a) Allowing too much complacency
b) Failing to create a sufficiently powerful guiding coalition
c) Underestimating the power of vision
d) Under communicating the vision by a factor of 10 (or 100 or even 1,000)
e) Permitting obstacles to block the new vision
f) Failing to create short-term wins
g) Declaring victory too soon
h) Neglecting to anchor changes firmly in the corporate culture (until new behaviors are rooted in social norms and shared values, they are always subject to degradation as soon as the pressures associated with a change effort are removed)

Considering the above-listed obstacles that can cause a process improvement initiative to fail, what should you do to combat them? Below we have listed a solution to overcoming each of the reasons for failure above.

a) Establish a sense of immediacy and get to work.
b) Create a team of real leaders and get out of their way.
c) Develop a vision, mission and strategy.
d) Have the champions communicate regularly using multiple media and require feedback.
e) Encourage risk taking and authorize the champions the latitude to do what is necessary, including changing systems or structures to get things done.
f) Measure regularly and celebrate every sustainable success.
g) Realize that because process improvement should be continuous, you are never done - just better.
h) This is the tough one. Cultural changes take time. To be self-sustaining

---

20 "Leading Change: Why Transformation Efforts Fail" by John Kotter. Harvard Business Review, March-April 1995.

you must incorporate what we have said here and constantly reinforce what works, adjust what doesn't, measure and repeat.

Continuous process improvement is not easy; however, the gains are well worth the journey. Do it because it is the right thing to do; do it because it you want to do things better; or do it to improve the bottom line. Just do it.

CHAPTER Q – QUALITY

By Andy Pattantyus and Lee Schwartz

1. How is quality defined?

You must have heard this adage: *Beauty is in the eye of the beholder.* Where one looks at their office neighbor with just a casual glance, someone else is staring at his or her "perfect ten". Have you ever strolled through a museum and asked yourself, "That's *art*?" It must have been considered so by the curator, otherwise it wouldn't be hanging from the wall.

So, is there *one* definition of beauty? Hardly. It's so subjective. Can the same be said about quality? Is it equally as subjective? If you decide to take a peek at www.Merriam-Webster.com, here's some of the definitions of *quality* you'll find: *Degree of excellence…Superiority in kind…Peculiar and essential character.* We don't know about you, but we're hard pressed to find an absolute definition.

Quality is a much more complicated concept than it appears. Even experts in the field have offered different definitions.

- Dr. W. Edwards Deming – *Quality is predictability.*
- Phillip B. Crosby – *Quality is the conformance to requirements.*
- Dr. Joseph M. Juran – *Quality is a fitness for use.*

Defining quality is elusive. It's abstract. Some have found a one-word answer – WOW! If you're provoked to such an outburst, then by default the product or service must be of quality, right? Others defining quality have been more wordy. Robert M. Pirsig, author and philosopher, offered a more philosophical explanation: "Quality is neither mind nor matter, but a third entity independent of the two, even though Quality cannot be defined, you know what it is."[21] What's your answer? For the purposes of this chapter, we will use the relatively simple definition of quality as: *producing a result that meets or exceeds the customers' requirements or needs, as they perceive them.*

---

21 Cameron, Kim and Sine, Wesley, "A Framework for Organizational Quality Culture," American Society for Quality, 1999. http://webuser.bus.umich.edu/cameronk/PDFs/Organizational%20Culture/FrameworkOrg-QualCulture.pdf

2. Why spend so much time and effort producing a quality product/service?

This may sound like rather a silly question on the surface, but there are two implied concepts here. One is the question of whether *the goal of business is to produce a quality outcome*. Our answer is an emphatic *yes*. After all, isn't quality a significant differentiator between the average struggling company and the few that excel? The second concept may be bit more obscure: *Is it fair to say that to produce something of quality, whether a service or a tangible widget, more time is required to do so than to produce something of lesser quality?* Is there a direct correlation between the time spent and quality achieved? As we examine the question, these answers are not intuitively obvious.

Let's consider an imaginary company, The Acme Widget Works. Acme is a functioning business today. And it's quite likely that the ownership wishes that to be the case for years and years to come. Why else be in business, right? Then the owners of Acme should spend the time and effort necessary to ensure that the consumers of their product are happy campers (a tease to the answer for question 9 below), because they want to remain in business. And there is an assumption here that in order to stay in business any company must meet the *customers' expectation* of quality. If you don't consistently meet expectations, you won't be able to stay in business very long. This is the simple answer to the "why" portion of the question.

But there's more to the answer. The second implied concept above is that in order to achieve a quality product or service, you have to spend a significant amount of time, well beyond that of lesser quality output. If this is true, aren't you increasing the cost for the sake of quality? There's really no direct connection between the time spent and the degree of quality produced. If you're a parent, you probably know about the concept of spending *quality time* with your kids. The implication is that the amount of time spent is not always the best indicator of achieving the desired outcome.

And so it is with the production of quality services and products. The amount of time applied is not always directly proportional to the level of quality produced. Working *smarter* is much more important than working *harder*. Don't take shortcuts when it comes to quality. Incorporating Lean principles will remove many wastes (See Chapter P – Process for more information). The quest for consistent quality comes down to balance. There's no exact formula that ties amount of time spent with level of quality, but it is clear that doing things right the first time definitely eliminates the costs of doing them a second time.

3. Do quality initiatives require full organizational support?

Quality is an attitude as much as it is a quantifiable element; it has to be part of the company culture. Company leaders set the tone that permeates throughout the organization and down to every worker in the company. Achieving quality may be hard work at first, but can be ultimately very rewarding. But *is* it worth the effort? If quality is demanded of some, and not of others, then cultural strife will erupt in pockets throughout the organization. This will create a race to the bottom, and poor quality is the result. Either the entire company cares about quality, or it doesn't.

Achieving, sustaining, and improving quality is a process. Like any process, systems are needed to enable people to work consistently with each other and to support the process. While individual effort and commitment is essential, establishing and maintaining *systems* is always the responsibility of the organization.

A system is a set of connected things or parts, working together, forming a complex whole. Systems have structure, are defined by components and their composition. Systems have behavior, which involves inputs, processing and outputs of material, energy, information, or data. It also has a set of rules that governs structure and/or behavior.

It is the organization that must decide to invest in the systems that support the quality goals. Without full organizational support, systems cannot come to life, and cannot survive. Quality systems and concepts are abstractions to most workers, so quality systems are among the most vulnerable systems in a company.

A good way to get the entire organization on board is to commit the company to seeking ISO 9001[22] certification. For those not familiar with ISO 9001, it is one of a family of internationally recognized quality management standards that define systems and methods designed to help organizations. By setting up quality systems conforming to ISO 9001, companies can ensure they meet the needs of customers and other stakeholders.

The realities of everyday life tend to introduce variability into every process. Employees and suppliers come and go. Natural disasters disrupt the established supply chain, necessitating substitutions. The recent earthquake and resulting tsunami in Japan affected supply chains for companies around the world, resulting in many quality consequences. Disruptions tend to reduce quality, so quality improvement must be a continuous endeavor, a process that never ends.

---

22 ISO 9001. http://en.wikipedia.org/wiki/ISO_9001#Contents_of_ISO_9001

4. What does it take to be a quality producer?

To be a quality producer requires two things: 1) an understanding of what the customer wants, and 2) the organizational commitment to deliver. A strong organizational desire for quality (the will) is extraordinarily important, because without it, quality is not possible. Every person working for the company must have the same attitude and commitment for producing high quality (see question 3). The customer defines quality, because they directly experience the product or service, which either meets their expectations, or does not. Generally, the more the customer must pay, the greater expectation of quality they have. Today's customers expect good fit, finish, functionality and reliability as a *given*, because anything less wastes their time. Because time is valuable, reliability and product support enter the quality equation. Does the product require occasional service? If so, then what is the quality of the service experience?

The methods for achieving quality are summarized in question 5, below. Controlling quality starts with measurements and process control. Consistent quality requires a consistent process, run in a very stable fashion. High yield (low defects) at every step leads to a high quality final result (see Chapter Y – Yield for more information). The same methods can be used to control processes for assembly, transaction, service and administration. A company with the ability to control their Quality Control processes will also be able to control all the other processes within the company. Being a quality producer always comes down to process control.

5. Is there more than one approach to achieving quality?

There are many models with many names, but the essential elements for improving quality are always the same. Achieving an initial standard of quality, improving upon it, and then sustaining the improvements is also a process... known widely as continuous process improvement. (See Chapter P – Process Improvement for more information.)

All methods to achieve quality follow roughly the same pattern: *Plan, Do, Check, Act* (PDCA)[23], *Define, Measure, Analyze, Improve, Control* (DMAIC)[24], and *Define, Measure, Analyze, Design, Verify* (DMADV)[25][26]. These approaches embody the following principles:

23 American Society for Quality, "Plan-Do-Check-Act Cycle," 2011. http://asq.org/learn-about-quality/project-planning-tools/overview/pdcacycle.html

24 American Society for Quality, "The DMAIC Methodology," 2011. http://asq.org/learn-about-quality/six-sigma/overview/dmaic.html

25 "DMAIC vs. DMADV" http://www.isixsigma.com/index.php?option=com_k2&view=item&id=1252:&Item id=111

26 "The DMADV Methodology" Six Sigma Online, Aveta Business Institute, http://www.sixsigmaonline.org/six-sigma-training-certification-information/articles/the-dmadv-methodology.html

a) Establishing objective criteria for defining "acceptable" vs. "defective"
b) Applying metrics to identify defective units, transactions or processes
c) Identifying the root causes for the defects
d) Eliminating the root cause of a defect
e) Refining product design and process design to eliminate the root cause(s)
f) Closing the loop by verification
g) Implementing process controls to sustain the improvement

PDCA[23] is also called the Deming Cycle or the Shewhart Cycle, named after quality pioneers W. Edward Deming and Walter Shewhart. Have you ever heard of the concept of A3 sheets[27]? Pioneered by Toyota and one of the problem solving methods used in the PDCA, A3 is a practice of getting the problem, the corrective actions, and the action plan down on a single sheet of large paper. (A3 paper is the international term for a large sheet of paper, roughly equivalent to the 11-by-17 inch U.S. sheet). PDCA establishes a producer-coach accountability relationship, develops a quality attitude within workers and management, and forms the foundation for a learning organization.

DMAIC[24] is the essence of Six-Sigma[28], the quality improvement method originally conceived by Joseph M. Juran[27] and popularized by Motorola in the 1980s. The basic principle is to reduce variability by finding and eliminating root causes for variations. Since becoming popular, Six-Sigma has grown to be a well-established practice throughout industry for producing quality products and services.

While systems, methods, practices, and principals are all necessary components, only people can improve quality. All viable quality improvement methods must include management methods, as Deming defined[29], to instill long lasting quality behavior.

Call it what you will, the principles of quality are really very much the same. Juran[29], Deming[30], and Shewhart[31] gave birth to the essential methods for achieving quality over 50 years ago, with Crosby[32] and Duncan[33] enhancing quality practices decades later.

27 Shook, John, "Managing to Learn: Using the A3 Management Process," 1st Edition, Lean Enterprise Institute, 2008.
28 American Society for Quality, "Six Sigma," 2011. http://asq.org/learn-about-quality/six-sigma/overview/overview.html
29 The W. Edwards Deming Institute, "The Deming System of Profound Knowledge," excerpt from Chapter 4 of "The New Economics," 2nd Edition by W. Edwards Deming, http://deming.org/index.cfm?content=66
30 American Society for Quality, "W. Edwards Deming," 2011. http://asq.org/about-asq/who-we-are/bio_deming.html
31 American Society for Quality, "Walter A. Shewhart," 2011. http://asq.org/about-asq/who-we-are/bio_shewhart.html
32 American Society for Quality, "Philip B. Crosby," 2011. http://asq.org/about-asq/who-we-are/bio_crosby.html
33 Duncan, Acheson J., "Quality Control and Industrial Statistics," 5th Edition, Irwin, 1986

The appetite for achieving quality output has been universally applied over the years. The Japanese were the first to wholeheartedly embrace the practice. James P. Womack[34], management expert and founder of the Lean Enterprise Institute, Inc., explains how the Japanese heartily embraced the emerging quality and productivity methods. Did you ever question why, for years and years, the Japanese automobile industry, as typified by Toyota, achieved greater success than their American counterparts? They were the first out of the gate.

The USA was slow to catch on – not just in the automotive industry, but also more broadly. American manufacturers and producers continued operating by old principles. Only when U.S. producers recognized the verifiable benefits of quality methods did it begin to see an uptick in quality. So yes, there are various quality improvement methods. But more importantly than the fact that multiple methods exist is to acknowledge that to be competitive in today's global economy, it's necessary to employ some form of quality practices.

6. Should quality be measured? If so, then how?

Dr. W. Edwards Deming, regarded by many as the leading quality guru of his time, once uttered, "In God we trust, all others bring data." To achieve quality, whether product or process, requires measurements, data and analysis. How else does a company know whether they've achieved their quality objectives?

Sometimes the feedback is as eye-popping as a slap in the face. Walk into a store with posted signs saying, *"Everything must go! Closing our doors!"* What prompted such finality? It could have been disgruntled, dissatisfied customers voting with their feet, caused by poor product quality or less-than-adequate quality of service. Other times more quantitative assessments are necessary, measuring such factors as: defective rates, or the number of returns per day. H. James Harrington, noted performance improvement author and consultant, proclaimed:

"Measurement is the first step that leads to control and eventually to improvement. If you can't measure something, you can't understand it. If you can't understand it, you can't control it. If you can't control it, you can't improve it."

Harrington was a key player in adding reliability[35] as a factor in the definition of quality, which consumers do intuitively. This initiative has subsequently been expanded to the formal practice of RAMS, or Reliability,

---

34 Womack, James P. et.al, "The Machine That Changed the World: The Story of Lean Production, How Japan's Secret Weapon in the Global Auto Wars will Revolutionize Western Industry," Harper Perennial, 1991.
35 Harrington, H. James and Anderson, Leslie C., "Reliability Simplified: Going Beyond Quality to Keep Customers for Life," McGraw-Hill, 1999.

Availability, Maintainability, and Safety. These are all quality factors in complex systems such as automobiles, trains, planes, power plants and heavy machinery.

Several popular business quality measurement tools are widely used to measure quality:

a) *Balanced Scorecards*[36] – a management tool linking strategy directly to measurable goals that is used to keep track of the execution of activities and to monitor the consequences arising from these actions.

b) *Flow Charting*[36] – the visual representations of production processes that help companies see what areas need improvement, usually through an *as-is vs. to-be* comparison.

c) *Key Performance Indicators (KPIs)* [36] – are selected measures specifically chosen to objectively assess the company's operations, indicating progress toward achieving its stated goals and activities.

d) *ISO and ISO-type certification programs*[36] – these are a family of standards designed to help organizations ensure they meet the needs of customers and other stakeholders through standardization and documentation of procedures.

e) *Survey Research*[36] – these include various methods for collecting quantitative (data) and qualitative (opinions) information considered to be representative of a whole. Such information, which a company cannot obtain except by using a survey method, answers critical questions.

The only hope a company has to achieve and sustain a quality output is to measure what is created. Measuring objectively, regularly and systematically is a must to achieve and sustain quality. Measure the right items that tell you what you want, and need, to know. As leadership trainer John E. Jones declared, "What gets measured gets done; what gets measured and fed back gets done well; what gets rewarded gets repeated."

7. Is there a cost to achieving quality?

This question could be better stated this way: *What's the cost of not achieving quality or producing poor quality goods or services?* Certainly there's a cost to manufacture/deliver a product or service, regardless of its level of quality. The higher the quality of raw materials used, or the less efficient the worker/employee doing the work, the higher the raw cost to deliver. So, from this perspective, quality does have its costs.

---

36 APICS Dictionary, 13th Edition, 2011

But those raw production costs can be reduced. Processes such as Lean or Six-Sigma can drive down the expense of production through reducing waste or unnecessary costs, whether in the factory or law office. In 1995, Motorola Communications embarked on a Six-Sigma initiative to drive waste out of their manufacturing processes. In a period of four years, Motorola was able to save $2.2 billion while retaining their high quality standards.

Management theorist Phillip B. Crosby, in his book *Quality is Free*[37], defined the cost of quality as having two main components: the cost of good quality and the cost of poor quality. For the purposes of this question, let's stay focused on the latter, because they're certainly the more elusive contributors.

Internal failure costs triggered by errors in products and inefficiencies in processes manifest themselves in rework, delays, shortages and re-testing. External failure costs reveal themselves after delivery of products and services, when customers: 1) complain, 2) try to extract fee concessions or 3) exercise warranty claims. Valuable labor and materials are consumed in the transactions with the unhappy customer and the reworking of the returned good or service.

So, yes, there is a cost to achieving quality! There is an even *greater cost of failing to achieve quality*, which in the end may become the demise of the company.

8. Quantity vs. quality – which wins?

Quality and quantity are not adversaries, so one does not have to be sacrificed for the other. Indeed, as quantities grow, a company needs reliable high-speed production processes, which require higher quality raw materials and repeatable processes. Thus, the internal need for quality improvements increases. High quality becomes essential to production. Many products, parts, and services involving massive quantities (billions) require near perfection in every part of a transaction, supported by reliable processes. Think bank transactions, or rivets attaching the skin of an airplane. You, the consumer, want every transaction or part to be perfect. The lowest cost production process is also the one with the fewest defects. High-speed machinery demands extremely consistent parts that are free of defects – in other words, high quality. Defects require extra effort to correct. Defective parts, which cannot be sold, must be handled and disposed. Thus, defects consume labor and money without bringing additional revenue.

---

37 Crosby, Philip B., "Quality is Free: The Art of Making Quality Certain," Mentor Books, 1992

9. Who's the ultimate arbiter of quality – the producer or the user?

Given all that's been said in answering the first eight questions, can the answer to this question be in doubt? Simply refer to www.qualitydigest.com and search for the definition of quality. There's overwhelming and consistent feedback from their followers that should lead any of our readers to the following conclusion – quality is in the eyes of the consumer/customer/client/user. Here are some examples we extracted:

"Quality is the customers' perception of the value of the suppliers' work."

"…when you have produced a product that brings smiles to your customers, then you have achieved Quality."

"The word *Quality* represents the properties of products and/or services that are valued by the customer."

"The degree to which something meets or exceeds the expectations of its consumers."

Let's not ignore nor understate the contribution of the provider. For there to be any chance that the user will be satisfied, what comes from the office, factory and/ or warehouse must be thought to be the best that can be produced. But in the end, the customer is the final arbiter. Armand Feigenbaum, the father of Total Quality Management (TQM)[36], summed it up succinctly: "Quality is the customer's opinion."

10. Can you take quality to the bank?

Most people think that better quality costs more money. However, in operations, better quality *saves* money because 1) fewer resources are needed to create the product/service in the first place and 2) fewer resources are expended to correct defects in the field and service warranty claims and to compensate for unreliable outcomes.

Initiatives to improve quality should show a return. If the quality improvement ROI calculation does not show a return, then likely the true cost of bad quality IS reflected in the poor numbers. The costs of poor quality include not only wasted materials, but also wasted labor, cost of extra inventory in Raw Materials (RM), Work-In-Process (WIP) and Finished Goods (FG), cost of returns, cost of warranties, etc. Rework is extremely disruptive to workflow, compounding the difficulty of planning capacity and raw material orders *plus* the extra cost of doing so with no offsetting revenue. Rework reduces margins.

A higher quality product is more reliable than the alternative, thus pleasing the customer by actually meeting or exceeding their expectations and needs. A higher quality process will run smoothly and predictably, lowering production costs. You can take quality improvements to the bank in the form of reduced costs, which result in higher profits!

So, what is the key to achieving optimal ROI on quality? We say it is balancing effectiveness with efficiency both strategically and tactically (see Chapter O – Operations for more information).

CHAPTER R – RISK

By Patricia A. Kotze-Ramos

1. **What is risk (or crisis) management?**

Risk (Crisis) management is the process by which an organization deals with a major event that threatens to harm the organization, its stakeholders, employees, customers, clients or the general public. Three elements are common to most definitions of crisis: A threat to the overall organization, the element of surprise, and a short decision time in which to determine how to handle the crisis effectively.

Unfortunately, *risk* is a normal part of operating a business. However, it is how the risk or the crisis is dealt with at the time of its occurrence or following a risk management plan that is the key to a successful or positive outcome. Contingency plans should always be a part of the overall risk management plan. Adding a security system or updating a current in-place system is a good start to a potential theft of property or product; however, it is not the solution to all inherent risks.

A yearly review of your risk plan is recommended for all business owners; consider also bringing in a security or risk management professional to provide recommendations or conduct a security survey to cover all the vulnerabilities to which your operation may be exposed. This review should also include the security, disaster or management team members assigned to be responsible in the time of a crisis or risk of profitability.

In review, remember: *Reckless business owners take reckless risks, cautious owners take calculated risks, and taking a calculated risk is better than taking no action at all.*

2. **Considering the above, what exactly is risk management?**

Risk management is the identification, assessment, and prioritization of risk (whether positive or negative) followed by the coordinated and economical application of resources to minimize, monitor, and control the probability and/or impact of unfortunate events or to maximize the realization of opportunities. Risk can come from uncertainty in financial markets, project failures, legal liabilities, credit risk, accidents, natural causes and emergency planning.

The strategies to manage risk include transferring the risk to another party, avoiding the risk, reducing the negative effect(s) of the risk, and accepting some or all of the consequences of a particular risk.

The International Organization for Standardization (IOS) identifies the principles of risk management as an integral part of organizational processes. Your risk management principles should be continuously improved upon to keep up with the evolution of technology, as well as the evolution of your business.

3. **How should a business identify, assess and mitigate risk?**

Risk Management, at its essence includes identifying, assessing and mitigating risk. The following represents the steps that should be taken when initializing risk management:

a) Identify, characterize, and assess threats pertaining to your business
b) Assess the vulnerability of critical assets to specific threats
c) Determine the risk (i.e. the expected consequences of specific types of attacks on specific assets) to the company products, information or concepts
d) Identify ways to reduce those risks (from A to Z)
e) Prioritize risk reduction measures based on a strategy and depending on the risk involved

Examples of risk sources include stakeholders of a new business project, employees of a company and clients and/or customers of whom the business depends upon. The chosen method of identifying risks may depend on culture, industry practice and lawful compliance.

In several industries, written lists composed of known risks are available. Each risk on such a list can be checked for application to a particular situation specific to your business, or can be tailored by an outside source or consultant to meet your proposed strategy for implementation at the time necessary. Based on my experience, companies face the following pure risks, in no order of importance: war, natural catastrophe, industrial disaster, civil disturbance, crime, conflicts of interest, workplace violence, terrorism (including kidnapping), legal risk, and others (such as personnel piracy, traffic accidents, or disturbed persons).

Assessment for Risk Management and potential risk treatments

Once risks have been identified, they must then be assessed as to their potential severity of loss and to their probability of occurrence. During the assessment process, it is critical to properly prioritize the implementation of the risk management plan based on the threat each risk represents. Once risks have been identified and assessed, all techniques to manage the risk fall into one or more of these major categories (from ASIS.org):

a) Avoidance (eliminate from the start, withdraw from particular cause or not become involved)
b) Reduction (optimize – mitigate the risk)
c) Sharing (transfer the risk to the original source if possible to assume or to insurance)
d) Retention (accept the risk and put it in the budget)

4. Why is it important for your business to have insurance?

There are several major reasons why insurance is a necessity for all businesses. The following points detail the importance of keeping your business properly insured:

- Insurance is often a statutory requirement. Workers compensation and business auto insurance are operational requirements in most states. A big advantage of business insurance is that it can reduce the liability of your business in case of an accident.
- Purchasing business insurance transfers catastrophic risk to the insurance company (e.g. a $1,000,000 Business Liability limit costs $3,000 per year). Businesses can buy coverage to transfer the $1,000,000 to the insurance company because an uninsured $1,000,000 loss can often put a company out of business.
- Theft, damaged goods, vandalism, and even natural disasters can all result in financial losses for your business.
- Insurance is often purchased to comply with contractual requirements, such as when a lessor requires a lessee to provide proof of liability as a requirement to do business or for a RFP contract. Lenders who provide uninsured loans charge inflated interest rates to make up for the additional risk of lending to an uninsured business.
- Insurance is often required to obtain a loan (banks require proof of insurance).
- Insurance provides protection of personal assets.
- Being insured shows a potential customer and existing clients that your business is protected from sudden loss and is stable. This can lead to an increase in business and greater income,

because clients and customers will select your business over competitors who aren't insured.

- Depending on what type of business you operate, you may also want to consider additional coverage via Employment Practices Liability Insurance (EPLI). EPLI is a stand-alone policy that protects against claims made by past, current and prospective employees against your company, its directors and officers, and its other employees. Some of the common employment practices violations include discrimination (based on sex, age, race, religion or other factors); sexual harassment (including *quid pro quo* harassment claims); wrongful termination; and a variety of other claims that include violating employees' civil rights or their ability to perform their jobs in an acceptable and fair work environment. These types of claims can be very expensive to defend against, even if the court finds in favor of the employer. Usually EPLI has its own pool of attorneys who work to defend against such claims.

- Almost every business in the United States that has employees has to handle workers' compensation issues. Most states require employers to purchase an insurance policy to handle their statutory obligations to workers who are injured or become ill due to workplace exposure. Whether your business is small or large, handling the expense and effort of meeting those statutory obligations is an ever-present challenge. When it comes to your business, you can never have too much insurance!

5. **What do you do when your business is devastated by a disaster such as a kidnapping of key personnel?**

Ask almost any executive if they would like to have personal protection, and they will tell you they neither need it nor want it. Generally, corporate America doesn't wish to be bothered by security personnel involved in their day-to-day activities. Depending on the organizations political or high-risk field, they should consider a Key Personnel Protection (KPP) plan.

Corporations have the responsibility of providing a reasonable level of safety and security for its employees. Usually, the most visible and vulnerable of those employees are its most senior executives or key positions of departments. In many instances, there is a profit motive associated with the security of key employees.

The need for a management protection plan is based on the following risk factors: Public prominence of the executive or the corporation represented; involvement in a controversial industry or business; documented threats, abusive letters, or extortion attempts directed at the executive or the enterprise; or local conditions associated with a specific geographical location or an event that creates a higher threat level.

6. **How does your company handle detecting and preventing workplace violence?**

Workplace violence is the second leading cause of occupational death in the U.S. It is the number-one killer of women in the workplace, and the number-two killer of men in the workplace. More than 1,400 work-related homicides occur each year and many acts go unreported due to fear of retaliation. Because of this, it's imperative that management understands the potential magnitude of workplace violence, how to identify potentially violent employees and non-employees (such as customers, outside contractors, and sub-contractor employees), and be able to effectively manage avoiding violent incidents before they occur.

Frequently, warning signs precede incidents of workplace violence. Training and risk prevention will assist employers in identifying the early signs of potential violence. The prevention process involves several proactive steps by the employer: Implementing effective and clear policies against violence and any threats of violence; providing education and training to all employees and managers; assessing the work environment for existing problems and modifying the work environment as necessary; and creating clear guidelines for internal investigations of employee complaints, including when to bring in an outside professional to make a psychological assessment or conduct an investigation. These guidelines allow the employer to obtain unbiased findings when an employee comes forward to management with a complaint or allegation about a co-worker.

Personnel designated to handle the security/safety policies should be prepared to: Deal with emergencies, including planning ahead and having proper communication channels set up in case of emergency; determine the best management practices and implement workplace violence prevention policy to reduce the risk of violence at work; document procedures related to potential violence; learn the warning signs and risk factors that can lead to violent behavior; manage conflict resolution techniques; and provide employees with personal safety tips and special precautions for night, weekend, and remote area employees who work outside of an office or regular place of business.

7. **Why is it important to have a protocol for proper handling of internal investigations, as well as workers' compensation and tort claims?**

Setting up a protocol for internal investigations allows your business to operate with an added layer of protection. Just as alarms and firewalls monitor external threats, having the tools and knowledge to intelligently conduct internal investigations allows you to monitor potential threats to your business that are internal. Without such preparation, your business might as well have the front door wide open to thieves and other crimes against the business.

However, some problems can exist in any workplace. For example, hostile employees and the potential for workplace violence can occur in any work environment, from a white-collar software firm to an industrial factory that manufactures electrical parts. Workplaces with diverse ethnicities have to be sensitive to possible racial tension and the potential for discrimination claims, just as businesses with a large male workforce but few females must be aware of any sexual harassment allegations and the potential for a lawsuit based on any such claims.

After identifying the areas most likely to require investigation, a person should be appointed to document all internal investigations. This includes keeping track of how an investigation begins, such as when it was first brought to the attention of management. It is very important to document key dates and times, and update management of the status of the investigation. It also includes meticulous documentation of all parties involved, including reporting parties, potential witnesses and suspects. Other important phases include determining if outside help is required, such as legal counsel, a corporate private investigation firm or law enforcement.

It is important to note that appointing an internal employee (or employees) to conduct and document investigations may require increased time. As a result, it may be more effective to hire a third-party private investigator to document and conduct the investigation. These experts deal with the crucial documentation process, know when to involve law enforcement or attorneys, and have access to many investigative resources that may not be available to a non-professional. Management should weigh the benefits of using outside resources versus the loss a key staff member's time to conduct a thorough investigation.

8. **Can inadequate records management get you sued?**

The short answer is *Yes*. When it comes to managing records, especially those that contain sensitive information, there are several key issues to keep in mind. Rapid technological advances in business have changed not only the speed in which data is exchanged, but also the amount of data that can be exchanged. This creates a greater possibility for a data breach; including the accidental loss of sensitive information and the potential for identity theft.

Business owners looking to avoid legal exposure as well as a loss of reputation should consider the following factors:

Confidentiality

Many businesses maintain sensitive information on its employees, vendors and customers. This includes names, addresses, Social Security numbers, financial transaction details and other information that could be exploited in the wrong hands. If a hacker manages to steal the names and Social Security numbers of a group of your employees, identify theft can become a liability to your company. If a competitor manages to obtain a list of your biggest clients, it can lead to all manner of allegations, including industrial espionage, anti-competitive business practices and, at worst, the loss of key clients who are embarrassed to be involved. It is of key importance to limit access to confidential information by setting up access control systems. All confidential documents should be marked as such, and employees should be aware of the company's internal policies for handling sensitive information.

Information Systems Security

Due to the continued growth of digital record retention and management, it is of key importance to have strong information systems security. This includes firewalls, individually assigned passwords and user accounts for employees with access to digital records, and often, a third-party Information Systems Security vendor, to ensure any potential soft spots and targets for data breaches are well protected. Also important: The ability of your Information Systems Security vendor to quickly alert management of any data breach, thereby identifying potential suspects and minimizing the potential damage of such an attack.

Privacy Violations

If a data breach does occur and the sensitive personal information of an employee, vendor or client is compromised, federal and state law necessitate that employers notify the affected party in a timely manner. In addition, it is often prudent to document any such notification, as this will later help protect your business from claims of negligence. It is best to consult with your internal or outside legal counsel. It would also be wise to consult the Fair Credit Reporting Act[38], the federal guidelines that govern consumer privacy rights.

---

38 http://www.ftc.gov/os/statutes/031224fcra.pdf

Public Disclosure

When obtaining, sharing or reselling sensitive information, it is legally required that businesses notify individual consumers of such actions. In addition, employers performing a background check on an applicant must disclose the scope and nature of the investigation to the consumer prior to conducting the background investigation. Employers who fail to obtain such signed authorization prior to performing a background check leave the door open to allegations of privacy violations, unfair hiring practices, etc. Public disclosure is an important consideration that should not be taken lightly.

Records Retention

The nature of certain information requires that it be confidentially stored for *no less than* or *no greater than* a certain period of time. For example, the Federal Insurance Contribution Act[39] (FICA) requires that employee records related to mandatory federal taxes be retained for at least four years. Under the Fair and Accurate Credit Transactions Act[40] (FACTA), every company that employs one or more employees is required to shred any and all documents that contain information derived from a credit report on their employees.

9. **Why is it important for your company to provide adequate training by credentialed trainers on topics such as conflict resolution, workplace violence prevention, and sexual harassment prevention?**

Employee workplace training is not only a legal obligation in most states; it also makes good business sense.

Workplace violence, sexual harassment, and communication conflicts are disruptive to the workplace and damage the work environment. The anxiety and frustration experienced by employees who work in a hostile workplace not only impacts the quality of their lives, but also the quality of their work. Ultimately, the company pays the costs associated with poor employee morale, low productivity, and sometimes even resultant litigation.

Sexual harassment abatement through workplace training is one of the best investments your company can make. The money spent on proactive employee training is substantially lower than the costs associated with defending sexual harassment claims and lawsuits.

---

39 http://www.ssa.gov/oact/progdata/taxRates.html
40 http://frwebgate.access.gpo.gov/cgi-bin/getdoc.cgi?dbname=108_cong_public_laws&docid=f:publ159.108.
    pdf

Consider this: Are your supervisors and managers quickly and effectively able to resolve issues regarding personality conflicts? Are they functioning as a team? If your business could benefit from training in these areas, you may wonder to whom you should turn; how do you select the best training provider for your firm? Where do you start? Do they have to be licensed? What are their credentials? What makes them qualified?

After you've determined your company's specific needs, find a training firm. If your business is named in a lawsuit, you and your training company will be put *under the microscope*, so be very careful and only hire a training firm capable of representing your business not only in the "classroom", but also in court if needed (the trainers could be called as a witness, so you want only those who are reputable, credible and capable of undergoing scrutiny). Be sure they meet a thorough criteria; inspection of their qualifications means asking questions. These include: How long have they been in business? Do the trainers hold degrees and credentials in the fields of expertise required? Can they provide references? Do they have valid business licenses? Do they have liability insurance? I highly recommend that prior to using a trainer, you verify their credentials and experience.

Next, schedule an appointment and speak with the trainer in advance. Be prepared with a list of questions: What exactly is covered in the training? Is the training interactive? Can the trainer provide a course outline and training materials for review? Go over their training outline in detail and make sure you are comfortable that it fits with your corporate culture. Notify your facilitator of any concerns or issues that you may be experiencing, and ask them to incorporate them into the session.

In most cases, employees will be more receptive to the information if the person communicating the information (the trainer) is an outside, third party and not a manager that the employees have reported to on a daily basis. After all, employee morale and your company's financial wellbeing are at stake, and any training can make your company a safer place to work

10. Why is it important to include pre-employment background checks, I-9 verifications, and drug testing as part of your hiring process?

Pre-employment background checks help employers to make a well-informed hiring decision and to ensure a safe workplace for all employees. The Fair Credit Reporting Act (FCRA) includes the federal guidelines that specify what background screening companies can and cannot do when performing a background report. The FCRA states the specific rights afforded to consumers (in this case, referred to as an applicant) when they are the subject of a background investigation, such as the right to dispute information, the requirement of a signed release form authorizing the investigation, and being provided with a summary of their legal rights.

Anytime an employer requests a background investigation on a prospective employee, the employer must first obtain a signed release and disclosure form from that applicant, granting authorization for the employer to perform the investigation. In addition, the employer must provide each applicant with a copy of the FCRA *Summary of Rights* and, depending on individual state law, any applicable information or disclosures required. For example, employers in California are required to provide all applicants with California's *Statement of Consumer Rights* and *Notice Regarding Background Investigations.*

Background investigations can also reveal details on an applicant's driving record, credit history, previous education, employment history, and drug use.

Another service to consider is I-9 verification. I-9 verification is the process of verifying a new employee's eligibility to legally work in the United States. The Department of Homeland Security, in conjunction with the Social Security Administration, has developed a program called E-Verify, an Internet-based system that allows an employer to use the information reported on an employee's I-9 form to determine the eligibility of that employee to work in the United States.

Current business practices encourage all employers to harbor a drug-free work place and implement a policy pertaining to drug testing. It is well known that employees that are under the influence of drugs work at a slower rate, are often late or absent from work, and are more likely to be involved in a workplace accident. Background screening companies are capable of performing 5, 9, or 10 panel tests (screening for 5, 9, or 10 different types of illicit drugs) and have streamlined the drug screening process. Most background investigations can be completed in 48 hours. Please see the *Appendix* for copies of:

- Applicant Release and Disclosure Form
- FCFA *Summary of Rights*
- California *Statement of Consumer Rights*
- Notice Regarding Background Investigation
- Pre-Adverse/Adverse Action Letter

CHAPTER S - STRATEGIC PLANNING

By Ivan M. Rosenberg and Daniel Feiman

1. **What is the difference between *strategic, tactical, operational,* and *project* planning?**

    Unfortunately there is not a general agreement on the meaning of these terms. Very often, people apply the term *strategic planning* to what is really a *tactical planning* exercise. As a result, the organization fails to benefit from the unanimity, inspiration, and creativity that are typically generated by a true strategic plan.

    Strategic planning is the longest-term planning an entity does, addressing the very reason an organization exists. It is not about what the organization or entity does (e.g., a housing authority provides shelter to those in need) but about what it wants to *produce in the world*. Two elements are required to inspire and galvanize people to creativity and grand accomplishment—a Vision in which they find significant meaning, and the perception that accomplishing that Vision is feasible. Strategic planning means developing both the inspiring Vision and how that Vision will be accomplished.

    Strategic planning generally takes into account, but is not limited by, current or near-term circumstances or predictions. Covering time periods of from one to multiple decades (how long it will take the entity to accomplish its purpose) is not uncommon.

    In contrast, *Tactical Planning* specifies how current and anticipated resources will be used to achieve near-term goals. A series of good tactical plans can be used as stepping-stones to achieving the strategic plan if they are updated and adjusted regularly.

    The availability of resources cannot be predicted far into the future, so tactical plans are typically no more, and frequently much shorter, than 3 to 5 years. However, there are pitfalls if a firm only does tactical planning:

    - Tactical planning frequently extrapolates from the past resulting in a future that is only incrementally different than the past.

179

- Tactical planning leaves everything to chance after the 3 to 5 year time period. However, the impact of both product and industry life cycles often require a longer lead-time than 3 to 5 years.

- An inspiring organizational Vision often takes a long time to accomplish. Thus, a 3 to 5 year tactical plan may cause some to lose focus, or may cause some to lose the belief that the Vision can be accomplished unless it is linked to the Strategic Plan. When today's actions are not connected to the organization's Vision through the Strategic Plan, the source of passion, the Vision loses its ability to motivate the workforce and generate its best performance.

Operational planning generally addresses goals and high-level activities for the current or next year of the Tactical Plan, including budgets and granting authorization to spend money. Operational plans are the stepping-stones to accomplishing the tactical plans, just as tactical plans are stepping-stones to achieving strategic plans.

Project planning addresses specifics of how a particular outcome of the Operational Plan (and/or Tactical Plan) is to be accomplished or the requirements of a particular capital project. It generally includes accountability, specific due dates, and the interdependence of tasks. A project plan covers a single project over weeks, months, or years.

2. **Why should you work *backwards* from a Vision statement?**

It is impossible to create a plan to accomplish something, particularly something spectacular, if you don't know what you want to accomplish in the first place. Thus you should *start* with what is desired to be accomplished (the goal, or Vision – see question 3 below), and then work backwards to ensure that the plans are connected to the present (and thus have some degree of feasibility).

When you work from the present forward, the limitations and issues of the current circumstances loom large in your thinking, thus limiting the plans you create. When working backward, there are no such limitations (anything might be possible if you gets far enough in the future). Your planning group sees possibilities and approaches that would not otherwise be seen when working from the limitations of the present forward.

When you start from the future and work backward toward today, the road to success is clearer, more attainable, and anything *seems* possible.

How about a Vision Statement?

In our experience, the need to make a difference is one of the fundamental drivers of each human being. Building on this, we assert that *the purpose of an organization is to give people an opportunity to experience making a bigger difference than they could as individuals.* If you think about it, given the overhead and complexities of an organization, it is unlikely that one would join an organization if they could make the kind of difference they want to without an organization.

An organization's Vision Statement specifies the difference that organization is committed to make, i.e., its reason for being, and its purpose. It is the source of the passion that organization members have for being in the organization. Thus, the strategic planning process should start with formulating the organization's Vision, and then work backwards to the present. The Strategic Plan provides a feasible story for how today's actions contribute to fulfilling the source of inspiration, the Vision.

3. What is the difference between vision, mission and values?

In their book *Built to Last*, Jim Collins and Jerry Porras identified two elements of highly successful companies:

> "Visionary companies are premier institutions – the crown jewels – in their industries, widely admired by their peers and having a long track record of making a significant impact on the world around them." (Pg. 1)

And

> "[A] fundamental element...of a visionary company is a core ideology – core values and sense of purpose beyond just making money – that guides and inspires people throughout the organization and remains relatively fixed for long periods of time." (Pg. 48)

We suggest that there are two elements of the "sense of purpose" referenced by the authors in the second element: Vision and Mission. Thus, three aspects of successful organizations are: Vision, Mission, and Values.

An organization's *Vision* states the difference the organization is committed to make in the world, its purpose. A Vision Statement is not about the organization itself, such as "We will be the leading supplier of widgets to the game industry." Rather, it states the *benefit* the organization is committed to provide the world, how the organization wants the world different than it is...not specifically what it will *do*. For example, a distributor of parts and devices for controlling fuels (whom we will call *ABC Supply*), such as might be found in a gas station, created a Vision Statement of "We are committed to make a safe and clean environment for all generations."

A Vision Statement is visionary, an ideal situation, something not easily accomplished but worth doing in the minds of those committed to it. Thus, it may appear impossible to others. A central belief that makes the Vision impossible we call the *Obstacle Belief*, and an example associated with the above Vision is this: "Pollution is inevitable when working with petroleum products."

To accomplish the Vision, the Obstacle Belief must be converted into something possible, we call the *Missing Possibility*. Continuing the above, an example of a Missing Possibility is: "Creating a clean and safe environment is possible with breakthrough technologies, services and knowledge."

The Missing Possibility points to the *Mission*, a high level statement of what the organization is doing to contribute to fulfillment of its Vision. An example is, "ABC Supply provides world-class energy management solutions for today and the future."

Values are guidelines on behavior. For example, a value in the U.S. military is *respect for higher authority*. There are two types of values applicable to strategic planning. *Core Values* specify behavior seen as necessary for the organization to accomplish its Mission. A person with repeated and conscious violations of Core Values, i.e., a deliberate action to sabotage the Mission, is usually asked to leave the organization. *Goal Values* specify behavior seen as highly desirable for accomplishing the Mission. Typically one is never satisfied with Goal Value performance, such as *teamwork*, seeing that one can always improve.

For example, in the case of ABC Supply, the values of Safety, Integrity, and Service are Core Values. The values of teamwork and efficiency are Goal Values.

4. **In addition to Vision, Mission, and Values, what are the other components of a Strategic Plan?**

The other components of a Strategic Plan are: Strategic Goals, Planning Horizon, Strategies and Milestones.

At some point in the future, your organization's Mission will change from *maybe impossible* to *inevitable*. *Strategic Goals* are specific measurable goals that should be used as evidence that accomplishment of your organization's Mission is inevitable...that it will happen!

The *Planning Horizon* is the date by which the organization says that all its Strategic Goals will be accomplished. Given the ambitious nature of Missions, and therefore Strategic Goals, Planning Horizons typically last multiple decades. Such a long time period, often beyond one's expected employment with a company, shifts people's perspectives from *what's in it for me* to *leaving a legacy.*

Strategies are patterns of actions over time, by which the organization intends to accomplish its Strategic Goals; for example, marketing very expensive products to a limited clientele, or marketing the lowest price product to the mass market.

In general, an organization's Vision, Mission, Values, Strategic Goals, Planning Horizon, and Strategies remain relatively stable over time.

Milestones are intermediate goals at specific time intervals that guide implementation and measure progress of each strategy. Typical near-term time intervals are 1, 3, 5 or 7, and 15 years. A Milestone is an objective, observable accomplishment. *Review proposal to Agency* would not be a milestone. *The proposal to the Agency has been reviewed and approved by senior management* is a valid milestone. Milestones must be measurable, so we can know when they are accomplished, rather than merely assuming that they are.

5. What is the *practical* application of strategic planning?

Strategic planning enables an organization to see the bigger picture. This picture includes not just *what* people are currently doing, but *why* they are doing it.

As stated earlier, the organization provides people with an opportunity to make a bigger difference than they could as individuals. The strategic plan specifies the difference that the organization wants to make in the world—their reason for existence, the inspiring Vision. If this goal harmonizes with the difference that individuals in the organization *want* to make with their lives, then the workforce will be authentically galvanized and inspired.

With a powerful common inspiring Vision, a workforce is highly motivated, more collaborative, more creative, and takes on goals that they wouldn't with a shorter timeframe, e.g., three to five year tactical goals. In some sense, the workforce becomes zealous about the organization's Vision.

Strategic planning well done helps shift people's mindsets from the urgent and near-term to the important and long-term, and from being victims of current circumstances to the authors of their own futures.

A strategic plan provides a guide for making big decisions, such as whether new products and services should be added. Circumstances change, and what was predicted when the strategic plan was written may turn out differently. Mission, Strategic Goals, and Strategies provide guidelines for the adjustment of tactics and milestones, while providing a stability and constancy over time.

A brand could be said to be the characteristics and thoughts generated in others when they hear or see your organization's name or logo. (See Chapter B – Branding for more information). A Vision and Mission help an organization get clear about what it wants to be known for, and maintains the stability of the brand over time.

Finally, the long timeframe required by starting with the Vision and working backwards, provides an insight to and permits creating a response to forces that have time frames beyond the typical three to five year tactical plans.

6. How do you get the leaders of your company interested in and committed to doing strategic planning?

The best way to get your leaders interested and committed in doing strategic planning is to make a business case for it...to show them that it is not only the right thing to do, but also the better choice. Determine the costs and benefits of strategic planning vs. not doing it. You must demonstrate that by planning strategically the firm can and will accomplish much more in the future than it has in the past.

You must quantify the benefits. Remember, what gets measured, gets done. What is not happening or is not likely to happen if things continue in the way they have? What are the threats and opportunities that require more than a three to five year response?

Unless the most senior leaders commit to take a strong stand for the planning and the implementation process, and stick with it, history tells us the initiative will fail[41]. The main reasons significant change initiatives fail include:

a) Not establishing a great enough sense of urgency
b) Not creating a powerful enough guiding coalition
c) Not having a vision rooted in shared values
d) Under-communicating the vision by a factor of 10 (or 100)
e) Not removing obstacles to the new vision
f) Not systematically planning for short-term wins
g) Declaring victory too soon
h) Not anchoring change in the organization's culture

In other words, unless you plan, implement, communicate, measure, adjust and continue your plan, it will probably fail.

---

41 Source: Kotter, John P., *Leading Change: Why Transformation Efforts Fail*, Harvard Business Review, March-April, 1995

7. What are the most common planning *pitfalls* to look out for?

The most common pitfalls to look out for in building and implementing your strategic plan include confusing *strategic* with *tactical* planning. As we previously stated, real strategic planning is very long-term, and is linked directly to the Vision of the company. A three to five year tactical plan is a tool and a good stepping-stone toward achieving the strategic plan, but it is not a substitute for it.

The next common pitfall is basing your strategic plan on current circumstances, rather than the Vision of the organization. By definition, the Vision is like the horizon; a goal to shoot for but never fully attained. Strategic planning is a creative process rather than an analytical one.

If you plan for too short a time frame, you are setting the organization up for failure. Visions take decades to accomplish, so you must plan accordingly. This is where tactics and milestones can be set, accomplished and celebrated. These periodic *victories* can help reinforce the path to the Vision succeeding.

Probably the most difficult challenge to overcome in planning is the thinking that this is a "senior management only" exercise. This is the traditional approach, which is why most organizations never achieve what they could have. We recommend that all stakeholders experience being represented at the planning process. In general, this means including the *influencers*, those who are surrounded by a group that tends to believe what they say about the organization. By influencers, we mean non-management employees who have significant influence over others by what they do and say, rather than by their title. They may be *early adopters* (first to try something new), who try something first and therefore others try it too, or *mules* (those who refuse to change) who refuse to adopt the new process so keep others from it by that decision. Often, they are the *nodes* (think of the spoke of a wheel with the *influencer's* influence radiating outward) of the organization's informal communication network. Including the influencers, if you employ a planning process with decisions made by consensus, means gaining the buy-in of the rest of the workforce is considerably easier. Including those from every level of the organization means you will receive input otherwise lost. Insights from completely different, and important, perspectives can now be included to create your unique plan, one that grows out of your organization's Vision.

Finally, senior management not only must stay involved, they must lead the initiative. Senior management must lead by example, include participants at every level, challenge the status quo, and create an atmosphere of openness, creativity and the possible.

8. **What are the *critical* components of implementation? What are the most common implementation pitfalls to look out for?**

Strategic Plans, like all plans, are vulnerable to becoming just good ideas instead of becoming a *reality*. The difference? Implementation. What is required for success is an effective Support System that will assure implementation independent of people's intentions, good or otherwise, or memory. Some of the elements of such a system are:

a. Creation and Review
    i.   Rather than only the senior executives developing the plan, the strategic planning group should represent all stakeholders.
    ii. Regular, scheduled reviews of the plan should be both quarterly and annually. Annual revisions of the plan must be calendared and completed. This is as important to your success as creating the original plan. This should not be something that is approached when there is nothing else to do. It must become as routine an expectation as reviewing operating or financial results.

b. Accountability:
    i.   For each annual goal, there should be one – and only one – person accountable for the achievement of that goal. Ideally, this person should be someone who is enthusiastic about the goal and who *wants* to make this achievement happen.
    ii. The topmost senior executive must have ultimate accountability for successful strategic plan implementation.
    iii. Ensure that senior executives are visibly "walking the talk".
    iv. Provide support for those accountable (coaching, training in leadership, team building and maintenance, etc.).
    v.   All goals must be objectively measurable against agreed upon benchmarks, whether that is internal or external.

c. Communication
    i.   Ensure that all decisions, meetings, and activities reference the strategic plan as their rationale.
    ii. Track progress on each goal and publish this internally for all to see.
    iii. Implement frequent, multi-channel, and up-to-date communication concerning progress on accomplishing the annual goals. Displays and scoreboards are particularly effective.

d. Ensure that all systems are consistent with the strategic plan
    i.   Company systems, such as job descriptions, performance reviews,

and reward and recognition systems, should be consistent with the strategic plan. For example, it is hard to implement teams if all the rewards are based on individual performance.

ii. Ensure that the organization culture is supportive of the strategies.

iii. The IT system should link operating, financial and strategic results automatically.

9. What are the differences you should expect in how your organization operates after you do strategic planning?

If you have actually taken the time to do strategic planning the right way, we say congratulations! Now what? You need to begin to implement your plan. As we mentioned in the previous answer, implementation includes reviews, accountability, communication and systems integration. Assuming you have these in place and working, this is what you *should* expect:

a) Expectation for senior leaders to "walk the talk", and visibly fess up when they don't.

b) More creativity, more reference to the Vision, Mission, and the strategic plan as a basis for decision-making and for evaluating the decisions and actions that are made.

c) Less "shooting from the hip" or decisions based on personal whimsy.

d) Less tolerance for things inconsistent or not supportive of the strategic plan.

e) Significant improvement in results: Although perhaps not spectacular results immediately, a steady improvement over time will demonstrate success.

f) Need for flexibility in tactics as moving forward, and a consistency with the Strategic Goals and strategies.

10. How can you do strategic planning *efficiently*?

Let's start off by defining what we mean here by *efficiently*. Efficiency (as explained in Chapter O – Operations) is doing things right, as opposed to effectiveness, which is doing the right thing. Or put a different way, efficiency is accomplishing the goal or task with the least amount of inputs. Wasted effort is eliminated.

Therefore, an efficient strategic planning process is one where you gain the maximum benefit from the minimum amount of time and energy expended. To do this, try these steps:

a) Clearly distinguish between strategic, tactical, operational, and project planning, and keep them consistent.

b) Document everything. Start by documenting your strategic planning process to find ways to improve upon it. (See Chapter P – Process Improvement for more information).

c) Use experienced facilitators instead of choosing the lowest cost alternative (many think they know how to lead strategic planning, even if it is not their profession).

d) Ensure all the leadership is on board both to support the planning process and to implement what results from it. Those leaders not on board need to leave the organization.

e) Ensure the workforce is authentically supportive of the strategic plan (having the influencers[42] create the plan helps considerably).

f) Create strategic goal *owners* and *champions* to focus activities toward success.

g) Give people the time needed to understand and become supportive of the strategic plan.

Organizations that have followed these guidelines have been able to not only succeed beyond what might have initially seemed possible, but have also been able to sustain this for far longer than anyone imagined.

---

42 See question 7 for a discussion concerning having influencers create the plan.

CHAPTER T - TURNAROUND

By Bette Hiramatsu

1. What is meant by *turnaround*?

Here are the most accurate definitions: *Turnaround.* (Noun): An important change in a situation that causes it to improve. Synonym: transformation.[43] *Turnaround Management.* (Term): A process dedicated to corporate renewal. It uses analysis and planning to save troubled companies and returns them to solvency...[44]

2. What are the strategic options for a troubled company?

A business in crisis has to accomplish a turnaround, or it will die. A business in crisis has three primary options:

a) Stay in business either through an out-of-court work-out or Chapter 11 Reorganization under the U.S. Bankruptcy Code.
b) Seek an outsider buyer for the entire business.
c) Liquidate the business.

There are additional alternatives within each option. Details are provided under questions 8-10 below.

Determining the best course of action depends on the root causes of the problems, the magnitude of the issues, and the extent to which changes need to be made. Other decision-making variables are: The size of the business, the number of creditors, the nature of the relationship with creditors and the complexity of the issues and lastly, access to capital.

Whether as part of the strategy to liquidate or stay in business, another option can be the sell-off of a subsidiary, division or product line as a means of raising cash. Potential reasons to spin-off assets include: the division is not a part of the core operations of the business, the division could be of more strategic value to another company, it is in a declining industry, it is underperforming or

43 MacMillan Dictionary, 2011
44 Wikipedia, 2011

unprofitable, or is in a highly competitive market. Management should preclude

cannibalizing the business by selling operations that are profitable and critical to the success of the business for the short-term benefit of raising cash. Other options, primarily for larger companies, include an equity investment in the company through an employee stock ownership plan (ESOP), debt-for-equity exchanges and the private placement of debt or stock.

3. **Should you use your existing staff, or engage outside professionals?**

When a business is facing a crisis situation, the business owners and managers are very likely outside of their range of skills. Akin to a life-threatening medical emergency where one would see an emergency room physician, a business in crisis will dramatically increase its likelihood of survival by working with a turnaround consultant who has the skill set and seasoned experience to sort through the myriad of issues, prioritize and make quick decisions under pressure with very little time to spare to resuscitate the business client before it *dies*.

Turnaround consultants are professionals who have expertise guiding businesses that are underperforming, facing financial and operational challenges or crises, and advising or leading them to the path of stability and ultimately to profitability and positive cash flow. The turnaround professional must also have the ability to effectively negotiate with the many players involved, each of which has a different agenda. These include:

a) Secured lender(s) -i.e., bank or commercial finance company;
b) Unsecured creditors -i.e., suppliers, landlord(s) and bondholders;
c) Shareholders.

To find a qualified turnaround consultant, consult the membership directories of either the Association for Insolvency and Restructuring Advisors (www.aira.org) for Certified Insolvency and Restructuring Advisors (CIRA) or the Turnaround Management Association (www.turnaround.org) for Certified Turnaround Professionals (CTP). Providing quality standards, these certifications recognize those professionals who have several thousands of hours of related experience, have demonstrated a high level of knowledge and integrity through the completion of study and exams, and have maintained the credential through continuing education.

Management should also seek the advice of a competent and seasoned bankruptcy counsel who represents *business debtors*. It is also advisable to obtain guidance from an experienced CPA who specializes in distressed situations for businesses. Tax issues may arise from the potential cancellation of debt and from the sale of assets or sale of the business. An investment banker who specializes in distressed investments should be consulted regarding a potential equity investment in the company through an employee stock ownership plan, debt-for-equity exchanges, the private placement of debt/stock and the sale of the business. For referrals to these professionals, ask your banker or commercial finance lender, attorney, or CPA.

4. **What is a turnaround plan?**

One of the first actions of a turnaround is the preparation of a turnaround plan, the road map that provides the path from crises to rehabilitation and ultimately, to re-growth. A turnaround consultant can provide a plan or offer guidance in regards to a turnaround plan (acting as the financial advisor to the president or the board of directors), or the turnaround consultant can join the company in a more full-time capacity, as the Chief Restructuring Officer for the business.

There are four distinct phases to a turnaround plan: Assessment, Implementation, Stabilization and Regrowth.

Assessment Phase

The following actions are performed during this phase: the liquidation analysis, the root cause analysis, a review of management, a SWOT (Strengths, Weaknesses, Opportunities and Threats) analysis and a review of accounting procedures. The liquidation analysis determines, on a "worst-case basis", the approximate recovery the secured creditor(s), the unsecured creditor(s), and the shareholders would receive if all assets were liquidated. The root cause analysis, after comprehensive reviews of financial and operational data and interviews with senior and mid-level managers, identifies the reasons a business is facing challenges. At the completion of this phase, a report should be prepared summarizing the findings and the recommended solutions to guide the company to become profitable and have positive cash flow.

Implementation Phase

First, you have to stop the bleeding…then you need to restructure.

The above phase generally implements the recommendations in the report prepared in the Assessment Phase. *Stopping the Bleeding,* focuses on the growth of cash by increasing efforts to collect accounts receivables, selling unnecessary assets and cutting expenses and cash outflows (see Chapter U – Underperformance

Issues for more information). *The Restructuring Phase* requires more time, because of the complexities involved with re-negotiating secured debt (or locating a substitute lender) and the restructuring of unsecured debt (trade payables and facility leases), which usually involves many players.

Stabilization Phase

After the company has survived the crisis stage, the next phase focuses on increase of profits while continuing to make incremental improvements through a more in-depth assessment. Examples include: Direct cost and product line analysis, marketing strategy, the organizational design, streamlining general and administrative functions and costs.

Regrowth Phase

This final phase concentrates on repositioning the company for the next several years or more through the orderly rebuilding of high margin sales. Regrowth could be accomplished with the development of new products, new markets, improved customer service, or more effective marketing techniques; it should result in increased market penetration with increased profitability. Financial planning is also important to ensure that the company's balance sheet grows proportionately and healthfully with the increased volume. In time, acquisitions may also become a part of the regrowth strategy so long as debt is kept in check.

5. **"Can this business be saved?" What are the key factors that make a business turnaround successful?**

According to Donald Bibeult[45], the following factors can contribute to a successful turnaround:

a) New competent management with the authority to make requisite changes
b) A viable core business with an economic purpose to exist
c) Financial resources to fund the turnaround
d) A positive attitude amongst staff motivated to implement the turnaround plan

For a turnaround to be successful, management must have a hands-on work style; they must be given the authority to make significant changes, they must increase the internal controls of the operation and they must inspire the staff to become a part of the solution.

---

45 Bibeault, Donald B., *Corporate Turnaround: How Managers Turn Losers Into Winners!*, Beard Books, 1999.

The business must have an economic reason to exist. It must be a feasible operation with a sound strategy and the ability to generate positive cash flow and profits, have large enough sales volume and it must have reasonably current equipment and a competitive location to be accessible to markets, labor pools and raw materials. Management must be also aware of past and/or future external or internal changes that could have an impact on the business.

During the initial turnaround process, there must be adequate cash, financing or access to capital to operate the business. The funds can be generated from the sale of unprofitable divisions or unnecessary assets. They could also be generated with *bridge* loans from banks or commercial finance companies, or – in the case of small or mid-sized businesses – occasionally from friends and family.

Determination and a positive, *winning* attitude by management and all employees are keys to the success of a turnaround. Attitude is the foundation of a corporate culture and if the general tone within a business is defeatist, it will be difficult to turn the company around.

6. How should you communicate the challenges of your business to your bank or commercial lender? To your trade suppliers?

With all creditors, whether the lender(s) or suppliers, it is critical to have good relationships with an open line of communication. Ignoring their queries, whether through the regular mail, voice mail or email, only creates feelings of distrust and ill will and, if not dealt with, over time may lead to lawsuits or a Ch. 7 forced liquidation. Timely, candid and effective communication is not only the right thing to do; it encourages the creditor's cooperation and buy-in with the turnaround plan and the future success of the company. Vendor support also provides the business with additional time to determine the turnaround plan, which in turn reduces the strain on cash flow.

Since at this juncture, faith in the owner/senior managers by most creditors will likely have diminished significantly, it is important to rebuild confidence in management by precluding any negative surprises with prior warning and by following through on all promises made. Communications such as this are best handled by a turnaround professional who has experience dealing with concerned lenders, unhappy unsecured creditors (vendors and landlords), etc., and can speak objectively and effectively on behalf of the business.

Before communicating with creditors, it is very important to prepare a liquidation analysis to see what each class of creditors would receive on a worst-case basis. This helps to determine the strategy for negotiations with each class of creditors.

Secured Lenders

Support from the commercial bank/commercial finance company is key to the turnaround of a business; this relationship should be viewed almost as a partnership. The secured lender is usually the largest single creditor to the business, has a lien on all assets and, if privately held, has a personal guarantee from the owner(s). If the secured lender is fully collateralized and the lender has confidence in the turnaround plan, occasionally it is possible for the bank to provide bridge financing while the plan is implemented.

Trade Suppliers

If the business fails, unsecured creditors face not only the potential write-off of debt, but also the loss of future sales. If the business succeeds, however, their debt may be repaid in part or in whole, and they have the assurance of continued business. Communication with all unsecured creditors must be handled in a reasonable way, and they should be assured that they would be treated equitably along with other creditors in their class. Unsecured creditors should also be clearly informed of what they stand to lose, should they file legal action against the company. Early in the process, vendors that are critical to the success of the business (there is no practical alternate supplier) must be identified and treated with care. An open line of communication should be developed with these critical vendors.

7. **Should you communicate the challenges of your business to your employees?**

As with lenders and creditors, an open line of communication must be maintained between management and employees. Precluding staff attrition, while keeping the employees motivated and positive, is critical to the turnaround of the business.

Should there be a bankruptcy filing, it is crucial that senior employees are made aware immediately prior to the filing. Immediately after the filing, all employees should either be met with as a group and/or they should be given a package of information. The meeting or package should provide answers to FAQs, such as how to deal with creditors and customers, as well as the impact the filing would have on compensation and benefits, etc. To preclude rumors getting out of control, management must make themselves available and visible to their employees during this critical time.

8. Should your business reorganize?[46]

As previously mentioned, the owners/managers of a troubled business have three options: stay in business and reorganize, sell the business, or liquidate. Within the first two options, there are additional alternatives. The responses to questions 8-10 in this chapter are intended to provide a general understanding of the available options. However, this information should *not* be used for making bold stroke decisions. The circumstances for each business will be different and as such, a business owner or senior manager should seek the advice of a reputable turnaround consultant, bankruptcy counsel, and/or CPA who specialize in insolvency issues before making major decisions. These insolvency professionals have a variety of mechanisms for reorganizing debt and/or liquidating company assets with varying degrees of risk to the principals. It is always best to consult one or several of these professionals before making any decisions.

Reorganization: A business can be re-organized either through an out-of-court workout or the U.S. Bankruptcy court. Both options are discussed below.

Out-of-Court Restructuring.

If it appears the business can be rehabilitated, most businesses should try to negotiate for an out-of-court restructuring of their debts with all creditors. At a ratio of 5 to 1, it is estimated that more agreements are handled out-of-court than through the bankruptcy courts[47]. In general, out-of-court workouts are less expensive, more flexible, faster and easier for the debtor as well as the creditor. It allows the debtor the privacy to work out its own financial affairs, avoids having to deal with court scrutiny or the rules of the bankruptcy code, and does not require the same level of reporting as with a bankruptcy filing. Finally, if the out-of-court restructuring is unsuccessful, the debtor still has the option of filing for relief under the U.S. Bankruptcy Code and/or liquidating the business.

The primary disadvantages of an out-of-court restructuring are:

a) Decisions are not binding on recalcitrant creditors (the *hold-outs*). Since it is usually advisable to obtain approval of the plan from substantially all of the creditors, if a few large creditors hold out – the restructuring plan is subject to re-drafting or is doomed to fail.

46 Discussions with Richard Brownstein, Esq. of Brownstein & Brownstein, Woodland Hills, CA.
47 Association of Insolvency and Restructuring Advisors, Certified Insolvency and Restructuring Advisors Study Course, Part 1.

b) Vendors may change the terms of sale to COD.

c) The company does not benefit from the automatic stay (see details on an automatic stay in the following section). However, most creditors will grant the debtor time after they see that management is pro-actively addressing its problems and that an out-of-court restructuring is in progress.

d) The debtor cannot reject executory contracts (i.e., leases).

Chapter 11 Reorganization

When the situation seems hopeless, when the business can no longer meet its debt service requirements and is unable to renegotiate its secured and unsecured debt, it may be time to file for relief under the U.S. Bankruptcy Code, Chapter 11 Reorganization. The primary advantages of Chapter 11 Reorganization include:

a) The ability to continue to operate the business

b) The automatic stay that mandates that payments cannot be demanded, collateral cannot be repossessed, most contracts cannot be cancelled, and all collection activity by creditors must cease

c) The ability to borrow funds as a debtor-in-possession

d) Executory contracts can be rejected

e) The reorganization plan can be proposed to all creditors

f) Creditors in opposition to the plan may be forced to comply with it once approved by the court

g) The unsecured pre-petition debt may be paid back with pennies on the dollar over time

The principle disadvantages of Chapter 11 Reorganization include:

a) *Time and costs*

A Chapter 11 Reorganization case usually takes much longer to close than an out-of-court restructuring. The debtor is responsible not only for the fees of its attorneys and professional advisors, but also that of the creditors committee and other committees that may be appointed. The costs can become so onerous that some Chapter 11 Reorganization cases are converted to Chapter 7 Liquidation. For that reason, most businesses with annual revenues less than $10 million should be dissuaded from filing for bankruptcy because they usually lack the economies of scale.

b) Restrictions

Many decisions must be approved beforehand by the bankruptcy court including: the use of cash collateral (proceeds and profits from the sale and income generated by secured assets), the sale of assets outside of the ordinary course of business, the salaries of officers and certain employees and hiring professionals such as attorneys, accountants and management consultants. Financial reports must be submitted regularly to the court, which places an additional burden on the already strained finance/accounting staff. Finally, representatives of the creditors committee and other committees, if any, will scrutinize the reorganization plan for the business.

c) Short time frame

Many businesses are unable to make decisions on executory contracts or to develop a credible reorganization plan within the strict deadlines of the revised bankruptcy code. In 2005, the bankruptcy code was significantly modified with the passage of the Bankruptcy Abuse Prevention and Consumer Protection Act (BAPCPA), such that a business has a maximum of 210 days from the date of filing to accept or reject executory contracts, 18 months with which to file its own plan of reorganization, and 20 months total (from the date the bankruptcy petition is filed) to obtain acceptance of the plan from creditors (under certain circumstances these time limits are even shorter).

d) Lack of financing

In the current credit environment, Debtor-In-Possession (DIP) financing for working capital during the bankruptcy period is not easily available. This is particularly true for mid-sized businesses.

e) Public admission of failure

Bankruptcies are a matter of public record, and if the company is large enough, the filing will be announced in the media. Even if it is not, business bankruptcies are frequently announced in the business section of some local newspapers.

9. When should you elect to sell your business?

Depending on the business, selling the company may create more value than by liquidating it, and bears significantly less risk than reorganizing it. The business may have more strategic value to a competitor, supplier or customer – particularly if the company has attractive attributes such as strong market share, a defensible market niche, desirable intellectual property (trademarks, copyrights or patents), or tangible assets such as real estate or proprietary equipment or processes. For small or mid-sized businesses, frequently the buyer is a competitor that is larger and stronger financially.

To determine the potential selling price of the company, a valuation of the enterprise and its component parts should be prepared by an investment banker specializing in distressed investments. The valuation may be based on several approaches, including the discounted cash flow method and multiples of cash flow and business attributes such as those listed above. To determine the value of the company on a worst-case basis, a liquidation analysis should also be prepared. Depending on existing liens and the potential for creditor lawsuits, the buyer may require that the U.S. Bankruptcy court approve the sale. This in turn mandates an auction process for the sale of the company.

10. When should you liquidate your business?[48] [49]

When the business is no longer considered a viable operation – because sales and market share have fallen precipitously, losses are worsening and there are no indications of improvement, and debts are accumulating and there is no value in intellectual property – the owners/managers may want to consider liquidating the business. There are several ways a business can shut down its operations: a self-liquidation, an Assignment for the Benefit of Creditors and relief under the U.S. Bankruptcy Code Chapter 7, and Chapter 11 Liquidation.

Self-Liquidation

A self-liquidation is the least costly way to close a business, but is advisable only when the liquidation of assets is sufficient to pay off all debts. The debtor can usually manage this process with its own staff with some guidance from insolvency counsel.

---

48 Discussions with Richard Brownstein, Esq., Brownstein & Brownstein, Woodland Hills, CA.
49 Discussions with Chuck Klaus, Business Development Manager, Credit Managers Association, Burbank, CA.

Assignment for the Benefit of Creditors (ABC)

ABCs are allowed under most state laws; court supervision will vary from state-to-state. An ABC is the voluntary transfer of all assets of a business to an assignee, an independent third party that has the fiduciary responsibility to liquidate the assets and distribute proceeds to creditors based on the priority of their claims. In an ABC, the business can continue to operate for a short period of time to complete work-in-process, and/or finish profitable jobs that will ultimately benefit the creditors. The assignee can also seek potential buyers of the business in an effort to preserve going concern value. The assignee also takes the responsibility to ensure all taxes are paid and final tax returns are filed.

Chapter 7 Bankruptcy Liquidation

The business ceases to operate on the date of filing, the U.S. Bankruptcy court appoints a trustee, the business is liquidated, and proceeds are distributed to the creditors. Due to court supervision, this process takes the longest. The principal of the company will be required to file schedules of assets and liabilities, attend hearing(s) with the bankruptcy trustee and will be responsible for filing final tax returns.

Chapter 11 Bankruptcy Liquidation

This is much like a Chapter 7, but the debtor-in-possession has the power, rather than a trustee, to liquidate its own assets. This frequently means a greater price for the assets can be obtained, which could be important for the payoff of those obligations for which the principals may ultimately be liable. Unfortunately, many of the drawbacks of the Chapter 11 reorganization still remain.

CHAPTER U - UNDERPERFORMANCE ISSUES

By Bette Hiramatsu

1. What is *underperformance?*

An underperforming company, while not in distress, lags behind its industry peers in terms of productivity, efficiency, profitability or balance sheet management. In general, it demonstrates sub-par execution with its sales and marketing strategy and production, quality or customer service management. If left unchecked, a business that continues to underperform increases its potential to fail over time. Companies that are in a near crisis or crisis situation are addressed in Chapter T - Turnaround.

2. What underperformance issues can arise as your business grows?

There are generally three stages of growth for a business[50]: Entrepreneurship, the professionally managed enterprise, and an institution.

In an entrepreneurial business (quite often a small or lower middle market business), the company's founders usually have a strong sales or technical background, are visionaries and tend to be creative in a business-sense. They usually don't understand – and may even dislike – dealing with financial issues and/or having structure, controls and systems. As the operation becomes larger and outgrows the strengths and skill set of the founder, the company faces a crisis of leadership. At this juncture, the company must either evolve into a professionally-managed enterprise by recruiting outside professionals and establishing structure and systems, or the founders must accept the fact that they will not grow or be a top-performer in the industry, which increases the risk of eventual business failure. The period before and during this transition is often very risky given the reticence a founder may have for the *new* order and to potentially have to take a backseat role to an outside professional. This period also affects the corporate culture, resulting in the loss of some employees who cannot rise to the occasion.

---

50 Bibeault, Donald B., *Corporate Turnaround: How Managers Turn Losers Into Winners!*, Beard Books, 1999.

If an entrepreneurial business makes the successful transition to becoming a professionally managed enterprise, a new set of challenges arises as the business grows and becomes more complex. The centralized organizational structure may become too cumbersome and hierarchical for lower level, long-time employees, who tend to be closer to the operation and to customers than the senior managers. This creates a crisis of autonomy, which is best solved by transitioning into a decentralized business with delegated authority (autonomy) and more formal systems for planning, control and coordination.

3. **What are the common *internal* reasons for your business to underperform?**

Imbalanced Management Team

The three primary functions of almost any business are sales/marketing, production/operations, and accounting/finance. Each of these three functions must be managed equally well and staffed appropriately; however, in many underperforming businesses the accounting and finance departments are undermanaged and staffed with employees who have insufficient skill set. The result is an imbalanced management team, which becomes one of the primary root causes of financial problems.

Inadequate Financial Planning and Cash Flow Management

Following the concept of the imbalanced management team, financial or cash flow planning is either poorly prepared, or not done at all. This frequently causes companies to become overly reliant on debt and to have no plan to address declining sales volume, slowing collections or rising inventory levels. Poor planning causes unpleasant surprises with insufficient time to develop contingency plans.

Insufficient Management Controls and Financial Analytical Tools

Again, because of the sub-par financial management team and the lack of adequate controls, changes in sales, profitability, receivables, inventory and payables can go unnoticed until management finds itself in deep trouble.

Undercapitalization

Capital or equity is the financial reserve required for a company to withstand downturns in the economy, or losses and/or hiccups in the cash flow cycle (slowing collections and/or timing differences for cash disbursements), and still remain in business. Businesses that start out undercapitalized, or become undercapitalized due to losses, are at an increased risk of collapse until profits can be earned on a sustained basis.

Too Much Debt

Excessive leverage increases the risk for failure because debt, unlike equity, must always be repaid according to a pre-determined schedule.

Operational Inefficiencies

Attributed to inertia, complacency or lack of focus, many firms become less, rather than more, efficient over time. This common situation must be addressed through a process improvement initiative or the business may be permanently harmed. (See Chapter P – Process for more on this).

Inability to Keep Up with the Changing Needs/Interests of Customers

Consumer preferences shift with the economy, demographics, new trends/fads and technology. The road to business failure is strewn with companies, such as Blockbuster Video and Borders (books), which did not foresee the impact that the Internet and technology would have on their businesses in terms of the convenience of shopping and ordering near commodity-like products online, and having product delivered either online or to one's home or workplace.

Overexpansion or Oversaturation

Expansion, if overly aggressive or if based on a passing fad, can be a risky strategy because it increases fixed cash outlays (such as rent and payroll) and can make the business more vulnerable in the event of an economic downturn. In the retail industry, care must be taken to avoid cannibalizing sales from a sister store and oversaturating the marketplace.

4. **What are the *external* reasons that can cause your businesses to underperform?**[51]

Changes in the Economy

The economy is impacted by changes in interest rates, the balance of trade, the budget deficit, the inflation rate, and by *shocks* to the system, such as the supply and price of oil and acts of terrorism. Most importantly, the economy is affected by changes in consumer spending (two-thirds of the economy) that are influenced by the unemployment rate, interest rates, the stock market, and home values.

---

51 DiNapoli, Dominic, Sigoloff, Sanford C. and Cushman, Robert F., *Workouts & Turnarounds: The Handbook of Restructuring and Investing in Distressed Companies*, Business One Irwin, 1991.

Changes in Government Legislation or Regulation

Changes in legislation and regulations have and will continue to increase the cost of doing business. Changes such as these include the handling and removal of environmental hazardous waste material, Occupational Safety and Hazard Act (OSHA) and Americans with Disabilities Act (ADA).

Changes with Competitors

Domestic competitors, who are in closer touch with the changing preferences of customers and have deeper pockets, can be quite formidable. Foreign competition, with their substantially lower cost of doing business, have in some cases caused many U.S. companies to either exit the marketplace or to move operations to foreign soil to reduce costs to be able to provide competitive pricing.

Changes in Technology

Businesses that do not plan for changes in technology with continual product improvement and new product lines become vulnerable to getting "leap-frogged" by their competitors.

Labor Issues

Collective bargaining agreements, while losing strength and power in the last few decades, can still be a force to be reckoned with. Although the employees of a business may not have union representation, vendors, customers or transportation companies may be unionized. Should there be a labor strike, there will likely be an effect on non-union businesses.

Natural Disasters

With our global economy, a natural disaster can have a significant impact on businesses locally and on the other side of the planet. As we have recently experienced with the earthquake, tsunami, and nuclear disaster in Japan in March 2011, natural (and man-made) disasters have created supply chain problems and, in some cases, temporary workplace shutdowns for U.S. factories that rely on products made in Japan.

5. **Do small to mid-sized businesses have different reasons for underperforming than large businesses do?**

In an entrepreneurial company, the entrepreneur *is* the business. Consequently, the business becomes a reflection of the entrepreneur's personality: strengths, weaknesses, expertise and passion. Accordingly, these businesses tend to have issues that are different than those of larger, professionally managed corporations. These issues are described below:

Lack of Breadth of Management Experience

Before becoming a business owner, entrepreneurs typically have had prior experience managing a sales/marketing or production/operations department, but have had little or no experience managing an entire company, including income statement and balance sheet management responsibility and being in a leadership role. As the business grows, the needs of the business can outgrow the skill set and experience of the entrepreneur. Quite often the entrepreneur is slow to recognize that it is time to bring in professional management.

Risk Takers but Not Gamblers

Entrepreneurs are generally risk takers or they would not have started up or purchased a business. Yet they are usually not gamblers, so they tend to make reasonably good choices. Over time, however, these strengths can become weaknesses if the business owner becomes unrealistically optimistic or is in denial of looming problems.

Big Spenders

Entrepreneurs can be spendthrifts, whether funds are spent on personal life style, being in love with the "latest and greatest" inventory or equipment, having *ideals of grandeur* (i.e., an aggressive but premature expansion program) or building a *Taj Mahal* (i.e., an extravagant corporate headquarters building or personal residence). Each of these actions has a negative impact on profitability and cash.

Nepotism

This is the hiring of a family member(s) or relative(s) and usually involves a double standard of performance and over-market compensation for the subordinate relative. Nepotism has a negative impact on employee morale, productivity and profitability.

Access to Capital

While outside of its control, small or mid-sized businesses can usually only access capital through banks, commercial finance companies, the U.S. Small Business Administration and friends and family. Depending on the business and industry, funding may be available through business incubators or venture capital. (See Chapter D – Debt and Chapter E – Equity for more information).

6. What are the (qualitative) early warning signs of problems?[52]

Examples of early warning signs include: frequent bank overdrafts; product or service quality is declining; the line of credit is usually maxed out; relations with banks are declining; loan covenants are close to being "busted"; the inability to make timely payments on loans, trade payables and taxes; relations with vendors are becoming strained due to slow payments and the maintenance of plant and equipment is deferred. Other examples include:

Financial Reporting Lacks Depth

Senior management is not provided with sufficient pertinent information to manage the business profitably or with positive cash flow. Remember: Management can only operate with the information they are given and cannot change what they do not know about.

Financial Reporting is not Timely

The monthly accounting should be completed by the 5th of each month and financial statements issued by the 10th, so that emerging problems can be recognized early and addressed quickly. The less current the information is, the less useful the information becomes.

Deliveries to Customers are Late

This is usually indicative of problems in production, scheduling, purchasing issues, inventory control or difficulties getting timely deliveries from suppliers due to slow payment (See Chapter O – Operations and Chapter P – Process for more information).

Customer Returns are Increasing

This is a red flag indicating potential problems in operations, quality control, or the shipping department - but also of declining employee morale.

Financing is Structured Inappropriately

Generally, the growth of current assets (accounts receivable and inventory) should be financed with current liabilities (accounts payable or a line of credit) and the purchase of long-term assets should be financed with long term financing. The mismatching of financing – for example, the purchase of high-ticket equipment financed through the line of credit – will ultimately cause a liquidity problem.

52 DiNapoli, Dominic, Sigoloff, Sanford C. and Cushman, Robert F., *Workouts & Turnarounds: The Handbook of Restructuring and Investing in Distressed Companies*, Business One Irwin, 1991.

Employee Morale is Declining/Employee Turnover Is Increasing

If employees, especially those who have historically been solid performers, begin to produce late or substandard work product, there is likely a problem with morale that, in time, causes turnover to increase. Often employees become aware of growing problems before senior management does. Absent information regarding any issues on compensation, low morale/increased turnover can indicate a loss of faith in management.

7. **What are the financial metrics (quantitative signs) that warn of looming problems?**

Sales are Declining or Flat/Market Share is Decreasing

Sales can decline due to external factors, such as a change in the economy or increased competition. Sales can also fall because of internal factors, such as: Not keeping up with changes in consumer preference or industry trends, operational problems, quality issues and customer service issues.

Profitability is Declining

Diminishing profits are usually caused by flat sales with increasing costs, costs growing faster than revenues, or declining sales with flat costs.

Gross Margins are Eroding

Gross margin is the profit, after direct expenses, measured as a percent of sales. A decreasing gross margin is an indication of a decline in the efficiencies of direct operations (i.e., productivity of laborers, overtime and the unnecessary waste of raw materials) and/or the company's failure or inability to pass on increased costs to its customers.

Operating Income Margins are Decreasing

If the gross margin is consistent, then it is likely that general administrative expenses are increasing disproportionately to changes in sales.

The Breakeven Sales Point is Increasing

The breakeven point is the sales level at which the company earns no profit and incurs no loss. The higher the breakeven point, the greater the risk to become unprofitable, should sales fall. The formula is:

Breakeven Sales Point (in $s) = (Fixed Costs + Interest Expense + Depreciation) / (1 − (Variable Costs/Sales))

Debt-to-Net-Worth Ratio is Increasing

An increasing trend in this ratio signals losses or eroding profits and/or the increased reliance on debt including trade payables.

The Turnover of Accounts Receivable is Slowing

Accounts receivable is one of the most valuable assets of any business. The slowing collections of receivables can be an indicator of lax credit and collection policies and/or the deterioration in the financial viability of some clients. The unhealthy growth of receivables ties up cash/working capital.

The Turnover of Inventory is Deteriorating

The disproportionate growth of inventory to changes in sales is unhealthy because it ties up working capital and increases holding costs. Some incorrect reasons for inventory growth are: Poor controls over inventory and purchasing, the organization of the warehouse, an inventory imbalance, eroding sales or obsolescence.

The Turnover of Accounts Payable is Slowing

If slow payments persist, suppliers could change the payment terms to COD (cash on deliver), which will only exacerbate the problems more.

The Sales per Square Foot or Sales per Employee is Declining

These ratios measure productivity. The sales per square foot statistic is typically used in the retail industry, while sales per employee is used in virtually all industries. Company results should be compared to industry norms for more meaningfulness.

Altman's Z-Score

The Z-score is a quantitative diagnostic model used to predict business failure. It was created by Professor Edward Altman of New York University and published in the *Journal of Finance* in 1968 (See Chapter Z – Z-Score for more information).

8. **What are the characteristics of ineffective management?**

There are quite a few characteristics of ineffective management, including the following:

- Management focuses more on revenues than on profitability and does not know where the business is earning a profit or losing cash flow.
- "Fires" are routinely put out rather than focusing on the root causes of problems.
- The response to incidents is passive, rather than proactive and planning for corrective action(s).
- Direct reports continually acquiesce to the CEO and do not challenge him/her.
- The CEO lacks forcefulness or, on the other hand, is too forceful.
- There are no regularly scheduled management meetings with purposeful agendas to encourage communication amongst the management team.
- Even with the existence of management meetings, the team is not cohesive, does not communicate well or does not work together to develop solutions to problems.
- Managers protect their own turf rather than sharing information and cooperating with other managers.
- Managers blame other managers, departments or past situations for current issues.
- Deadlines are constantly missed.

9. What are some proactive approaches to improving cash flow?

For all businesses, but even more so for those in an underperforming or crisis situation, these adages are highly appropriate: *Cash is king! Cash is the lifeblood to any business!* Cash buys time while a plan is developed to improve the underperforming business. To increase cash, management must first look to internal sources, making disbursements in a conservative, well thought out manner, before reaching out to external sources.

Methods to increase cash internally include: reducing assets, slowing down cash disbursements and increasing profitability. Examples of ways to reduce assets include focusing on the collection of accounts receivable, selling excess or stale inventory in bulk and selling unnecessary fixed assets.

Approaches to slow down cash expenditures include: reducing and/or cancelling purchase orders, stretching payables, requesting extended terms on a temporary basis, renegotiating payables with a payment plan, restructuring the terms of equipment loans, eliminating or reducing capital expenditures. If a capital purchase is critical to the success of the business, consider buying used or refurbished equipment from a reputable source.

Methods to increase profitability include: increasing prices, reducing direct costs and operating expenses, improving efficiencies, renegotiating labor contracts and real estate leases, closing unprofitable locations, selling divisions and subleasing unneeded space.

Ways to increase cash externally include: obtaining an accounts receivable line of credit or factoring line or – if a line of credit is already in place – requesting an increase in the line limit and/or advance rate from the lender (commercial bank or commercial finance company).

If the business is financed by a commercial bank and the bank declines the request for a larger line or increased advance rate, consider moving to a commercial finance company or factor which may provide more borrowing availability. While the interest rate will be higher compared to bank rates, sometimes it is more important to increase borrowing availability (liquidity) until the company can become stronger and more profitable. In time, the return of healthy profits should permit the company to return to a bank for financing. Lastly, an equity investment by a strategic partner should also be considered.

10. **What are some proactive approaches to maintaining the operational and financial health of your business?**

There are several ways to do this, and any of these are worth considering alone, or put together into a far-reaching strategy:

- Strengthen the financial management and staff with the appropriate level of talent.
- Beef up the depth of financial reports; insist that reports are prepared on a timely basis.
- Know the monthly and annual breakeven sales point. If the breakeven point is more than expected sales, changes must be made to preclude losses.
- Improve operational efficiencies by creating a culture of continuous process improvement primarily by eliminating waste. There are eight *deadly wastes* that can cripple many companies. These are: defects; inventory; motion; overproduction; processing; transportation; waiting time and creativity. (See Chapter P –Process Improvement for more information).
- Identify key performance indicators (KPIs) relevant to the business and for the industry. This information should be provided on a daily basis to senior and mid-level managers and should include:

sales, collections, cash balances, working capital line loan balance and backlog.

- Prepare cash flow projections using supportable and conservative assumptions, so that hiccups in the business can be anticipated before they occur and contingency plans can be developed in the event that the forecast will not be met.

- Keep in touch with the marketplace and evolving trends that affect the industry.

- Maintain open communications with the lender(s), key vendors and large customers.

- Maintain effective relations with outside counsel, CPA and consultant.

- Consider establishing a board of advisors, comprised of seasoned trusted professionals, who can provide sage advice with a different perspective.

- Realize that higher sales alone do not always create higher profits. It is better if the business has less volume and strong profits than more sales and losses.

- Update the corporate strategy each year. (See Chapter S – Strategy for more information).

- Avoid allowing any one customer to represent more than 25 percent of sales, or obtain credit insurance for receivables due from this customer(s) in the event of financial difficulties.

- Preclude having any single vendor supply more than 25 percent of inventory purchases.

- Create an atmosphere of open communications and candor amongst managers, and between managers and employees, such that employees are aware that candid dialog is more important than telling management *what they want to hear.*

- Practice MBWA daily. *Management by Walking Around,* a term coined by the legendary Bill Hewlett and David Packard of the now-famous hi-tech company they founded, means that senior management should walk around the office area or plant and chat with employees at all levels on a daily basis. The goal should be to find out what's happening, what's going wrong, and what's going right within the organization. This practice will boost morale, productivity, and the bottom line – and keep the owner(s) and senior managers *in touch* with the business.

CHAPTER V – VALUATION

By Davis Blaine

1. What is the process for valuing your business?

The following describes the essential work steps and considerations required to perform a detailed valuation of the common stock (equity) of a business.

The four essential work steps in business valuation follow this paragraph. The primary data needed for the valuation include at least the following: (1) detailed and consistent accounting records; (2) comprehensive Business Plan or detailed projections for the next three to five years; (3) objective management assessments of their company's strengths and weaknesses; industry competition; product life cycles; and external factors impacting growth and/or operating profitability.

Historical/Cost Approach - Involves summation of individual values of tangible and intangible assets, with little reliance on overall business cash flows. Useful approach only if the assets are significant to the operations, such as income producing real estate; high technology companies with significant intangible value which could be sold outright or licensed to others (often, no value is shown on historical balance sheet); and other asset holding companies.

Business Transaction - Comparison of subject firm with terms and conditions of outright sales of similar firms; adjustments required to compare for products, revenue size, customer base, market niches, capital structures, distribution sources, regulatory environment, and technology utilization.

Capital Market Approach - Contrasting subject with financial attributes of similar public companies (traded on organized capital market exchanges); from the meaningful sample of six to eight public firms, financial ratios are calculated correlated to the most meaningful ratios of the subject, next, adjustments to this price are made to reflect a control premium for a privately held subject, as well as the discounts for lack of marketability (liquidity).

Discounted Cash Flow Approach - Discounting future cash flows to the present at a rate commensurate to the risks associated with achieving these cash flows. Added to this amount is the present value of the residual value of the business.

2. **What is fair value and how might it affect your company?**

Fair Value is becoming the new standard basis for recording both asset and liability amounts on the balance sheet. The United States is now part of a worldwide effort to create an international set of standards for GAAP (Generally Accepted Accounting Procedures), such that users of company financial information can evaluate performance on a reasonably consistent set of principles.

Fair value is the price that would be received to sell an asset or paid to transfer a liability in an orderly transaction between market participants at the measurement date. The key clarification is an *exit* price, as opposed to an *entry* price (cost to acquire). Thus, the focus shifts away from buyer specific rates of return to market (outside, prudent investor) expectations of future inflows (asset) or outflows (liability).

Market Inputs

There are three levels of the fair value hierarchy of inputs, as follows:
Level 1 – observable based on quoted prices (exchanges)
Level 2 – other than level 1, but still observable via corroborating data
Level 3 – unobservable (company's data)

The fair value framework does not, however, eliminate the complexity and judgment required to estimate fair value. For example, given the proliferation of complex financial instruments that have unusual features (such as derivatives), the determination of fair value will remain judgmental and not always conclude in a consistent result.

3. **What are the key factors that create maximum business value?**

There is almost unanimous consensus that management is the most important ingredient to success and value in a business. And, it is not just at the top. There must be the requisite depth of middle management, as well as industry experience, vision, and a solid culture at all management levels. Probably the next most important factor is the firm's market share and intensity of competition. A top-three position significantly enhances value.

Following are the other features of a business that may provide quantitative evidence or qualitative assessments as part of the ultimate value:

a) Maximizing cash flow and Earnings Before Interest and Taxes (EBIT). Central to these attributes are maintaining adequate (not excessive) working capital and solid gross margins.

b) Positive and well-accepted differentiation of the products/ services. Included in this factor is the technology or IP advantages, and how long that *lead* will last. The other critical aspects are the company brand, goodwill, and time in business.

c) Another important component of value is the market niche, and *the near term growth potential.*

d) Size matters. The larger, more diversified companies attract more favorable investor interest. An economic downturn or significant industry shift, such as completely new and viable technology, is less likely to severely impact a diversified company.

e) Continually deciding to reduce customer and supply concentration is also critical to value enhancement. Except possibly in a very fragmented market segment, reliance on one or a few customers is never a recipe for long-term success.

f) As much as possible, maximize the predictability of future performance. This is only possible if management thoroughly understands the customer/revenue/profits metrics, and continually adapts improved cost efficiencies.

g) Develop and maintain both short and long term liquid capital sources.

h) The firm must implement and monitor solid to resourceful systems and procedures.

i) Insure against potential liabilities/losses, which could cast doubt on future profitability.

4. Is it possible to realistically value intellectual property (IP)?

Intellectual property (IP) is distinguished from general intangibles, such as goodwill, which have no definable useful life.

The valuation of an IP is usually the most tenuous, complex, and creative exercise of any valuation or appraisal. While some models are available for analyzing various data, there is no generic model for appraising every facet of IP.

In instances where one or two principal intangible assets comprise the essence of the company, their appraisal is almost synonymous with that of the business enterprise. The valuation of nearly any IP must isolate that portion of the overall business cash flow that is reasonably attributable to that asset.

Most often, the newer the IP, the more difficult the process. Without some historical data on use of the IP to generate income/profits or save costs, estimating IP valuation is much more subjective. The key, then, is to develop some reasonable data points about future expected cash flows. These data points become the lynch pin around which a discounted cash flow case can be constructed.

Complicating the process are the following considerations:

a) There are no rules of thumb that can provide high-level guidance or value ranges.

b) The cost to produce the technology usually bears no correlation to value, which is based on future cash flows or comparable sales.

c) The studies or market research for an industry or market niche are essential to illuminating the IP potential.

d) The extent of legal protections, such as patents, provide a basis for estimating economic useful life of the IP.

e) Certain governmental agency barriers, such as the FDA, can elongate the period until IP cash flows are realized.

f) Having the knowledge of what revenue the IP expected to generate, and whether the IP will work in the way it was intended.

5. When does your company need to value the business to satisfy Internal Revenue Code Section 409A?

Essentially, the 409A valuation is required at the time a company issues non-qualified deferred compensation (NQDC). The valuation determines if the stock grant or option is "in the money" based upon the value of a share of common stock. If it is in the money, the recipient of the NQDC is subject to income tax.

The rules cover traditional elective deferred compensation for all taxpayers - public and private companies, as well as Board members, employees and individual service providers.

Valuation Presumptions

The Regulations require *a reasonable application of a reasonable valuation method.* An approach is considered reasonable for privately held companies based upon consistent application of either of the following:

a) *Appraisal Presumption (AP)* – valuation by an *independent*, qualified appraiser, especially if performed within 12 months of an initial public offering (IPO) or the sale of the company. The Appraisal Presumption (AP) should also be obtained in the event of these circumstances:

- Board minutes suggest strategies for executing or entertaining near-term IPO or acquisition.
- Company is scheduling meetings with potential investment bankers and/or underwriters.
- Company has sought buyout or recapitalization offer.
- Company has begun a program to fulfill Sarbanes-Oxley compliance.

b) *Illiquid Stock Presumption (ISP)* - Good faith valuation known as the Illiquid Stock Presumption (ISP) may be relied upon under these conditions:

- The company is less than 10 years old.
- The stock is not subject to a put or call obligation other than right of first refusal.
- No relevant date will occur in 12 months or less.
- Valuation is written and performed by persons with significant knowledge and experience.

6. What is the purpose of a written buy-sell agreement, and how does that relate to value?

A Buy-Sell Agreement is a contract that:

- Restricts the owners from freely transferring an interest in his or her business entity, and that governs who, when, and under what terms their ownership interests may or shall be transferred.
- Defines the *triggering events*, valuation approach, price, and terms.
- Is usually between two or more existing owners of a business.

Generally, this agreement accomplishes the following:

- Establishes price and/or valuation methodology upon the occurrence of specified *triggering* events.

- Prevents unwanted individuals from becoming members of the ownership group (e.g. divorced spouses).
- Ensure a ready market for closely held ownership interests.
- Protects minority interests that lack control.
- May establish an estate tax value.

Purchase price is usually established by the following:

- *Book Value* – least accurate and not reflective of current market.
- *Fixed Price* – usually as modified by agreement of owners, least attractive method as often not changed or changed based on current owner motivation, etc.
- *Formula* – must be clearly defined, and specifics for each asset included in book value calculation, discounted future returns, or other method.
- *Appraisal* – set forth considerations, such as value criteria, how to select the appraiser, and standards for the appraiser.

7. **Under what circumstances does your company need a fairness opinion?**

A fairness opinion is a statement by a financial advisor that the consideration or financial terms in a merger, acquisition, divestiture, securities or other transaction are fair, from a financial point of view, to a company's shareholders, or a limited group of shareholders (i.e., public shareholders or non-controlling shareholders).

Fiduciaries or persons in control of a transaction must meet the test of *entire fairness*. They must address fair dealing: full disclosure, timing of deal, arm's length negotiation, and approval by an independent body or committee.

Another burden is fair price, which may include the following considerations:

- The value and form of consideration received or paid.
- The value of the subject business or securities transferred.
- Alternative form of transaction structure and consideration.
- Alternatives available that may bring more value than the proposed transaction.

- Economic and financial considerations of the proposed transaction.
- Value based upon methods that are widely accepted within the specific market segment.
- Valuation approaches: comparable public ratio and sale transactions and discounted cash flow analysis.
- Liquidation analysis may include the breakup value of the company.

Board Responsibility

The independent fairness opinion fulfills the fiduciary responsibilities of boards of directors and management. In addition, it serves as formal support for a transaction, which may later be litigated as part of a fraudulent conveyance claim. However, in anticipation of this potential liability, the fairness opinion should be supplemented with a solvency opinion.

Public company boards are held to a higher fiduciary standard. However, private companies where stock holdings are split among various entities and officers have similar issues. SEC rules require issuers and affiliates to fully inform the various holders of classes of securities.

8. **Should you value your business before you test the market to sell it?**

Believe it or not, in some cases, your own opinion of the value of your company may be low. You may not account for how a financial or strategic buyer sees the potential for growth, or can align the company with similar holdings.

However, the most important part of considering a business sale is the *considering*. You should run your business each day as if you would sell tomorrow. Most importantly, if you are committed to a sale process, you should know your primary value drivers as provided by the valuation.

Another reason to value the business is that it can inform the buyer about the value drivers. In addition, it will focus attention on other, often overlooked value considerations:

a) The value of the real estate owned by the company may be great. The proper treatment is to charge the company a fair market rental based upon a separate appraisal of the real estate, and then add the appraised value to the business value.
b) Excess assets not used in the business add to business value, such as extra cash not needed for normal working capital requirements.
c) Intellectual property owned by the firm is included in the business valuation, as are all operating assets. However, what if the inventor or the owner, outside the corporation, owns the IP? In this case, this is an

intangible value, and added to that of the tangible assets to determine the net value.

9. Is an Employee Stock Ownership Plan (ESOP) a viable exit option for a private business owner?

The leveraged ESOP is still viable. The following steps are necessary to implement an ESOP:

a) Retain qualified advisors with specific expertise
b) Conduct a feasibility study that considers each of the costs and benefits
c) Estimate the value of the company
d) Structure a transaction that considers constraints discovered in steps 1) and 2)
e) Consider the plan design and trust provisions
f) Estimate the repurchase liability
g) Obtain transaction financing
h) Implement plan administration
i) Communicate program to employees

ESOPs engender much consideration and conversation, yet usually are eliminated as a strategy. Why do most of them never get implemented? The initial costs, often in excess of $100,000, overwhelm many firms. And there are ongoing costs each year for valuation, accounting, and trust administration. Also, the value of the company and the amount to be received by the owner are too low to consummate a deal. Bank financing, the most advantageous source of capital, is very difficult to obtain. Finally, owners often decide that they do not want numerous minority shareholders, especially with direct access to sensitive financial information.

10. Why do you want to develop a Discounted Value for a Minority Interest, and why is it complicated?

Discounted value for less than control interests and illiquid investments (meaning no or limited access to free trading public markets) is how the marketplace of buyers and sellers transacts business. Reduced (discounted) prices should be established and supported by valuation experts in specific circumstances, especially when the value may be challenged by an interested party or outside regulatory body or agency.

More detailed analysis is now required. First, the requirements of the Financial Accounting Standards Board (FASB) for valuations and GAAP accounting are much more specific in terms of approaches to value. Second, the IRS has continued to contest unsupported discount analyses in Tax Court. Finally, the Court has acceded to the persuasive arguments from the IRS in challenging subjective, unsubstantiated valuations. In order to support discounts in the future, a thorough quantitative analysis must be utilized in conjunction with the empirical data. This requires a thorough understanding of modern financial models and the underlying market data.

CHAPTER W - WHAT IS NEGOTIATION VS. MEDIATION?

By Mike Young and Jeff Kichaven

1. What are negotiations?

We all negotiate every day. We negotiate things from large to small, from the important to the mundane. We negotiate with our family, our spouse, and even our dog. We negotiate just to get on the freeway during rush hour. Some of us negotiate business contracts, lawsuit settlements, even terms to bring peace between warring nations. What is this process that seems to pervade our everyday life and applies to the most mundane decisions, as well as some of the largest conflicts facing the world?

One definition, which seems to cover the bases well, sees negotiations as "an interactive communication process by which two or more parties who lack identical interests attempt to find a way to coordinate their behavior or allocate scarce resources in a way that will make them better off than they could be if they were to act alone."[53] Broken down into bite-sized pieces, the definition makes perfect sense:

An interactive communication process by two or more parties...

In other words, negotiation requires multiple parties *actively* participating in a *communication* process. The communication need not necessarily be oral or even written. *Any* type of communication will suffice, including those friendly hand gestures used by some of our commuter friends.

...who lack identical interests...

If the two parties have identical interests, there is no need to negotiate. Each party can satisfy his or her own interests without sacrificing anything. It is only when those interests diverge that a bargain must be struck.

...attempt to coordinate their behavior or allocate scarce resources in a way that will make them both better off.

Here is the essence of the negotiation process: The effort to find an outcome that leaves both parties better off. For example, assume a husband and wife want to see a movie together, but prefer different movies. By *negotiating,* the

---

53 Korobkin, *Negotiation Theory and Strategy* (Aspen 2002).

couple can search for an alternative that they would each prefer to the status quo, such as choosing a third movie they both want to see, or skipping the movie in favor of a comedy club. It is through the negotiation process that parties with disparate interests explore alternatives in the hopes of finding a solution that that leaves them both better off.

2. What is a win-win negotiation?

Those studying negotiations like to distinguish between *distributive* (or *positional*) *bargaining* and *integrative* (or *interest-based*) *bargaining*, two relatively confusing terms that nonetheless reflect two meaningfully different approaches to the negotiation process.

Distributive Bargaining

Distributive bargaining involves the process of dividing a finite resource, such as money. For instance, suppose you are interested in buying a used car that is listed for $5,000, and you offer $4,000 for it. The ensuing negotiation would decide how that $1,000 separating you and the seller would be divided or distributed. This is known as a *zero sum game*, because for every dollar one side gains in the negotiations is at the expense of the other. Both parties cannot walk away with that $1,000; they can only hope to split it in a way that is acceptable.

Integrative Bargaining

There is another way to look at the negotiation process, one that seeks not simply to divide a finite resource, but to better satisfy each party's actual needs. Consider this well-travelled but still effective example: Two kids are arguing over an orange. As the King Solomon of the family, Mom decrees that the orange shall be sliced in half, with each child getting one of the halves. Problem solved. Only now Mom has two unhappy children. Why? Because she failed to ask each child *why* he or she wanted the orange. Had Mom asked this simple question, she would have learned that one needed the entire rind to add to a cake recipe, while the other wanted the fruit for juice. By discovering each party's *underlying interests*, their true motivations, Mom would have discovered a much more elegant solution – give one the peel, the other the fruit – a result that would have left each child better off.

Where distributive bargaining focuses on positions (hence it is often called positional bargaining) – i.e., "I want the orange;" "no, *I* want the orange" – integrative (or interest-based) bargaining focuses instead on the parties' underlying interests, needs, desires, and motivations – "I want to bake a cake;" "I want to make juice." Very often, where the *positions* may conflict, these *underlying motivations* do not conflict at all.

Integrative bargaining is often called *win-win* negotiating, because by focusing on each party's underlying interests, it is possible to devise solutions that benefit everyone.

3. How should you prepare for a negotiation?

As with just about everything in life, success comes with preparation. And being prepared for a negotiation means understanding your own needs and desires, contemplating your counterpart's, and developing a negotiation strategy designed to reconcile the two.

Your Own Needs And Desires

While you may think you know what you want, a little introspection at the outset of a negotiation will pay big dividends later on. The kids in the example above each wanted the orange...at least that's what they were arguing about. But with a little self-reflection, it became clear that one really wanted to bake a cake, while the other wanted juice. The positions they were taking ("I want the orange") were masking their true underlying desires ("I want to bake a cake"; "I want to make juice"). Once the underlying desires were surfaced, a mutually satisfactory solution was easy to develop.

The same works for your business deals. Take a moment and reflect on what your true goals are for the upcoming negotiation. Dig a little deeper to discover what is it you really *need*.

Your Counterpart's Needs and Desires

After considering your own needs and desires, do the same for your counterpart. This will necessarily be more difficult, since the underlying needs and desires of your negotiating partner are probably not available with a Google search. On the other hand, in today's digital age, there is an incredible amount of information publicly available, both through official channels (such as SEC quarterly filings) and unofficial (Facebook, Internet forums, chat rooms). By making the effort to really learn about your counterpart, you just might be able to surface some of the underlying needs and desires of your negotiating partner. At a minimum, you may have enough information to make an educated guess, while identifying what additional information you would like to have to improve your analysis. Indeed, in some situations, it may even make sense to share information with your counterpart, so that you both have a better sense of the goals you are attempting to satisfy in the negotiation (easier said than done).

The Strategy

Once you have a sense for what you and your counterpart are each interested in accomplishing, develop a negotiating strategy that will help you get there. Remember, the goal is not to *beat* your counterpart in the negotiation – this is not an Olympic sport. The goal is simply to satisfy your interests, which generally requires you to satisfy your counterpart's interests as well. A successful negotiation is one in which the interests of both sides are met.

4.   How can you improve your negotiating position?

BATNA

This is perhaps the most significant negotiation tool you can develop to increase the chance you will have a successful negotiation outcome. Introduced in the book *Getting to Yes*, your BATNA[54] – Best Alternative To a Negotiated Agreement – is what you can expect to happen if the negotiation does not result in a deal.

For instance, let's assume the following: The success of your business is dependent on sourcing a certain raw material; the supplier knows of your need; and you have no option but to buy from this supplier. In the upcoming negotiation, you will have a very weak BATNA. The supplier can hold out for a very high price, because your only alternative to cutting a deal is to go out of business. Essentially, you are stuck paying whatever the supplier demands.

But with a little preparation, you can improve your negotiating position by developing a stronger BATNA. You can investigate other sources of the raw material, or develop a plan for manufacturing your product with a different material. In other words, you can create some competition for the supplier *before* your negotiations, in order to ensure that the supplier cannot hold your need against you.

While developing a strong BATNA *before* you commence may not always be possible, it is one of the few things you can do in preparing for a negotiation that will ensure your needs and interests are ultimately satisfied at the lowest possible cost.

5.   What are some common negotiation tactics?

Anchoring

Many parties prefer having their counterparts begin the negotiation by setting an initial offer or demand. However, in some circumstances, the initial offer can serve as an *anchor,* meaning it can influence how the other party views

---

54 Fisher, Roger, William L. Ury & Bruce Patton, *Getting To Yes,* 1981

the strength or his or her position, particularly when the negotiation is over something whose value cannot be measured by outside objective standards. For instance, a negotiation over a car involves an object whose value can be measured against sales of similar cars or prices determined by neutral third parties (the *Blue Book*). A negotiation over pain caused by an accident is much more subjective, and hence much more susceptible to influence by an *anchor*. The initial demand in a settlement negotiation over a personal injury, for instance, even if rejected by the potentially liable party, can nonetheless serve to influence the bargaining range, resulting in an ultimately higher settlement amount.

Persuasion

So-called *principled* negotiation seeks to find an agreement between parties based not on power or external leverage, but on generally accepted neutral standards. For instance, in a negotiation over the purchase and sale of a house, the parties look to sales of comparative houses as a guide, and then seek to persuade the other party that the house in question is either better or worse than the comparatives, based on objective factors ("this one has a built-in stove; that one has a spa," etc.). Indeed, most negotiations involve efforts to use established standards to persuade the other side to alter his or her views.

Hardball Tactics

There are nearly an unlimited number of aggressive tactics negotiators can use in an effort to drive a better bargain, including intimidation, anger, threats, physical discomfort (the bright light in the eyes, the low uncomfortable chair, the cold room), gamesmanship (good cop/bad cop), extreme emotions, and the like. What they all have in common is an effort to obtain a better deal based on issues *external* to the subject of the negotiation. Rather than convince you to pay more based on the value of the product at issue, these negotiators seek to use external forces to pressure you into making concessions.

There are numerous ways to combat these tactics. One is to simply ignore them (this often works with threats when the threats were made more out of frustration than a premeditated effort to extort concessions). Alternatively, you could address the tactic head on:

"I need a better chair, and less glare, if I'm to continue these negotiations."

"It's cold in here. If you can't turn up the heat, we'll need to take these negotiations to a different location."

"Are you two seriously playing good cop/bad cop? Why not take some time and get your negotiating strategies in synch."

You could also postpone the negotiations until the tactics cease; strengthen your BATNA; or even reciprocate with tactics of your own (which will likely prove ineffective in encouraging a productive negotiation, and will almost certainly result in a fractured relationship between the parties and a more heated process). Finally, and perhaps most effectively, you can try to counter the use of such tactics altogether by befriending your counterpart *before* the negotiations begin. It is very difficult to threaten a friend. Regardless of the response, the key is to avoid making negotiation concessions in response to external pressures (to the extent possible) and to attempt instead to refocus the negotiations on the merits of what is at issue.

But perhaps the most effective way to neutralize an opponent's use of hardball negotiating tactics is to call on the assistance of a neutral mediator. As discussed in the next question, a neutral third party can go a long way towards helping the parties engage in constructive, integrative, and ultimately successful negotiations.

6. What is mediation?

Mediation means a process in which a neutral person or persons facilitate communication between the disputants to assist them in reaching a mutually acceptable agreement.

What do you need in order to have a mediation? Well, first, you need a dispute. In the business world, people typically use mediation when litigation is pending or threatened, and lawyers are involved.

Second, you need a mediator. Mediators typically have a legal background, though some people from other backgrounds are excellent mediators as well. Mediation is a separate profession with separate skills, so professional mediators have separate, specific training and experience in mediation, not just law or their other previous field. In picking a mediator, you should ask yourself, "What are the specific challenges we – both my side and the other side – face in settling this case? Does the prospective mediator have the skills to help us meet these challenges?" While you will generally want a mediator with some familiarity with the subject matter of the dispute, you will also need a mediator with specific mediation skills to get the job done.

Finally, you need the intention to put the dispute behind you. In every dispute, you reach a point where you are ready to make it part of the *ancient history* of your life and move on. You may become willing to pay a little more or take a little less just to get it over with. If you are at or near that point, chances are that the other side is too. They have spent exactly as much time and likely as much money. That's when the mediator's skills can help you make that long-elusive deal.

7. How is mediation different from negotiation?

Mediation is a form of negotiation – a negotiation facilitated by a third person; the mediator. This makes it different than an ordinary negotiation in some beneficial ways.

Ritual

The convening of a mediation on a specific day, in a specific place, with specific people agreeing to be present, makes the mediation an event as well as a process, with almost ritual qualities. It is the day when we come together to make a deal because, after all, that is what mediation is for. This formality focuses people on the task at hand, and that focus promotes success.

Reactive Devaluation

Psychologists have identified many barriers to progress in negotiation. Perhaps the most important is *reactive devaluation* – the natural tendency to disregard the other side's ideas because they originate with the other side. "What's good for them must be bad for me," right? Well, not always. Many deals are good for everybody, and the idea has to originate somewhere. In mediation, ideas can appear to originate with the mediator, so you will be better able to evaluate the idea on its merits and make wiser choices.

Whose Turn Is It?

Psychologists have also observed that in many negotiations, nobody wants to go first and nobody wants to go last. Both sides think it to their strategic advantage to let the other side make the first, next or last move. When this happens, nobody may move, the negotiation may become paralyzed, and beneficial deals can be lost. The professional mediator has a variety of skills to create the appearance (and often the reality) of simultaneous movements, which allows the parties to make good deals they might not be able to reach on their own.

Lawyer-Client Relations

In litigation, lawyer-client relations can become strained. As the client, you may become frustrated because lawsuits take so long and cost so much. Lawyers also become frustrated when you don't understand or accept that litigation is nasty, brutish and long – even when you're in the right. When this happens, both lawyer and client suffer. A skilled mediator can help lawyers and clients get back on wavelength with each other, too, which in turn makes the negotiation between the sides that much easier.

8. Is mediation like litigation?

Yes and no. As in litigation, you have a plaintiff, a defendant and a dispute. You still have a lawyer with a fiduciary duty of undivided loyalty to protect your interests. You still want the best possible result.

In mediation, though, the parties themselves are the decision-makers, not a disinterested judge, jury or arbitrator. So the whole task is different. In litigation, your goal is to prove a point. In mediation, it is almost unheard of for the other side to concede that their point is wrong and your point is right. So the effort is futile.

Instead, the goal is to make a deal with the other side, even though your point may be valid. This requires entirely different methods of communication.

In litigation, the sides often antagonize each other. Indeed, sometimes, that is your goal. If you can anger or antagonize the other side in a deposition or trial, for example, their effectiveness in communication and persuasion will diminish and it may be easier for you to beat them. But if you antagonize the other side in mediation, will they be more likely to negotiate with you and reach a reasonable deal? Probably not.

What communication strategies are better? Here are four from *Getting to Yes* (introduced in question 4):

Separate the people from the problem.

Don't make it personal, don't call them evil, and don't make it about blame. Try to phrase the problem as a question, and start it with *what* or *how*. For example, "What is the best way for us to deal with the concerns over whether the last shipment met the specifications in the contract?"

Focus on interests, not positions.

"Splitting the difference" seems unprincipled and leaves everybody unsatisfied. Yet that is how so many negotiations end. How can you do better? Again, ask *what* or *how* questions about any proposed outcome: "What makes this result important, or beneficial, or desirable, to you?" "How will you use the proceeds of a settlement?" The answers to questions such as these may reveal interests that can be addressed in a variety of creative ways.

Invent options for mutual gain.

It won't always be as obvious or as much fun as the example of the orange but, in many cases similar options are there. In business cases, one common situation involves payment over time. A plaintiff may want a certain amount to settle a case. The defendants may say that they can't afford it. But maybe over time, they can. Maybe with proper security, the plaintiff can live with it. Voila, a deal! Litigation simply does not allow for creative negotiations of this type.

Insist on using objective criteria.

To evaluate options, ask not what you think or what the other side thinks, but rather, what is objectively reasonable. In the previous example, the question, "What is proper security for payments over time?" is often raised. Objective criteria might include, "What security would a bank require for credit along these lines?" When you make it objective, you reduce the risk of argument and increase the chances of reaching your goal, making a smart deal.

9. **Why mediate if you have a strong case?**

Everybody in litigation thinks they have a strong case. If they didn't think so, they wouldn't be wasting time and money with a lawsuit. So, why does anybody mediate?

Most importantly, litigation is not free. Winning a lawsuit has its costs, and they are not just financial, though financial costs are a big part of the overall burden. Litigation also takes time – years in some cases – and during this time, litigation can impose serious mental and emotional burdens, as well as practical business problems.

Some people just can't think about anything else when they are involved in a lawsuit! You're under attack and naturally you're going to get defensive and spend time thinking about how to defend yourself. Defendants often believe that the best defense is a good offense, and so try to put the plaintiff on trial one way or another as the litigation proceeds. So even if you are the plaintiff, you will spend a fair amount of time defending yourself as well.

Litigation necessarily focuses on past events. So, while you are spending your days and nights reviewing old files and testifying in depositions, strategizing over how to defend what you did years ago, your competitors are out there in the marketplace creating new products and services to meet your customers' needs in the present and future.

Sometimes, you can use mediation to create outcomes that litigation just can't provide, such as arranging for payment over time, renegotiating a commercial lease, or licensing intellectual property for future exploitation. Even if you can't, though, mediation lets you put conflicts over the past behind you so that you can look to the future. As legendary Hollywood lawyer Greg Bautzer was wont to say, "All's well that ends…"

10. What if you don't like the result?

In mediation, you always like the result. That's because the result is always the one you yourself choose. You either choose to settle or you choose not to settle, based on whether you think the best settlement you can negotiate is better that the alternative of not settling. You make the choice.

The key is that, in mediation, you always have the option not to settle. Sure, litigation is expensive, lengthy and disruptive, but sometimes the price of peace is just too high. The other side wants far too much or offers far too little. You couldn't live with yourself or explain it to others if you made such a bad deal. You are more at peace with the idea of going to war. If that is your informed, calm decision, that's ok.

You have a constitutional right to a jury trial, and the purpose of mediation is not to bully you out of it. After a full day of the facilitated negotiation we call mediation, though, it is amazing to see how many people settle, even though they initially thought it would be impossible.

CHAPTER X - X-RAY YOUR ORGANIZATION

By Daniel Feiman

1. What does it mean to X-Ray your organization?

When you visit the doctor for an X-ray, you are getting an internal snapshot to see if everything is working the way it should be, and that everything is in its right place. An X-ray of your company is no different; it is a look inside to see what is working, what is not and/or what is missing that should be there. Another way to put this is you look to see where you were, are and could be. Other names for this process include a *strategic assessment* or an *environmental scan.*

That said, especially in today's challenging economic times, we strongly recommend going beyond this internal-only focus and expanding your company X-ray to include an external review relative to your specific company and industry. This allows you a 360° view of the world as it impacts your company. I'll go into this in more detail later in the chapter.

2. Where do you begin an X-ray?

You should begin the X-ray process by reviewing your company's *Vision, Mission, Values* and *Goals.* (See Chapter S – Strategy for more information). Is the company living up to its Vision? Is it following its Mission to accomplish its Vision? Is everyone in the company living up to the stated corporate Values? Are the Goals SMART goals? (See question 5 for the definition of SMART).

These are tough questions when taken seriously, and the answers may or may not please you. If you, and everyone else in the company, can honestly answer "yes" to each of these, then you are right on track. Now you can move on.

However, if not, it is time to step back and reassess. Which of these is not working and why? What do you need to do to right the ship before moving forward? The vision, mission, values and goals are the foundations of any good company and need to be aligned and optimized. You know what happens to a building when the foundation isn't stable - Just look at that building in Pisa, Italy.

3. What are the best tools to use?

The classic starting point, the one that is the easiest to use, and still the most effective is the *SWOT analysis* (Strengths, Weaknesses, Opportunities and Threats). You list where your company falls under each of these.

Strengths
This is what your company is exceptionally good at, and that the market values.

Weaknesses
These are the areas that must be improved to achieve your stated goals.

Opportunities
These are the positive circumstances or elements that can be (but are currently not being) leveraged to achieve the company goals.

Threats
These are the negative circumstances or elements that must be overcome or avoided to achieve the company goals.

Below, I have expanded the traditional Opportunities and Threats sections beyond the single categories and divided them between internal and external. Experience tells us that to really understand your company, this is necessary and helpful.

SWOT Analysis	
STRENGTHS:	**WEAKNESSES:**
Operations	Operations
Marketing	Marketing
Finance	Finance
HR	HR
Customer	Customer
Other	Other
OPPORTUNITIES (Internal)	**OPPORTUNITIES (External)**
Operations	Operations
Marketing	Marketing
Finance	Finance
HR	HR
Customer	Customer
Other	Other
THREATS: (Internal)	**THREATS: (External)**
Operations	Operations
Marketing	Marketing
Finance	Finance
HR	HR
Customer	Customer
Other	Other

As a starting point for this exercise, I have listed the minimum areas you should explore for each of the six SWOT categories: Operations, Marketing, Finance, HR, Customer and Other. Use this as a guide to evaluate these specific areas and beyond. You can also add additional categories that fit your specific circumstances.

There is a caveat here: Unless everyone is completely honest in his or her contributions to these lists, you are wasting your time. The purpose of this assessment tool is to determine what has to be fixed and what you need get the company to the next level. Flatter yourself with a long list of the Strengths without completely identifying the Weaknesses, and Threats, and the company is headed for disaster.

An important tool I have had great success with over the years, one that helps companies get a clear overall picture of their marketplace as it impacts their unique situation, is the *PESTLE* analysis. PESTLE (Political, Economic, Social, Technological, Legal, and Environmental) is a true strategic scan focused primarily on the external world. It is critical, because each of these areas has an impact on your company, directly and indirectly. Many companies never think that they will be affected by these variables until something happens and they are. To do this properly, you need to seriously research each area. *What would happen to your company if there were a change to regulations or laws that affected a major supplier or customer? How have you been impacted by the current economic decline?*

For each of the six areas you should list the most important factors that have a reasonable chance of impacting your company. Then go across and make decisions on the relative *potential impact, timeframe, type, direction of the impact, and importance.* Mark the boxes accordingly and then step back and take a look at the overall matrix. *What needs to be addressed immediately and how? What might impact you that you can nothing about and how do you plan for that?*

This is also a useful tool for understanding the risks associated with every major decision you or your company makes, whether it involves market growth or decline, new products, line extensions, branding, new customers, or changes in strategic direction for a business or organization.

The model below shows a generic example of what your company might want to consider:

PESTLE Analysis on _____ (organization name) Date_____						
PESTLE Analysis factors		Implication and importance				
		Potential Impact:	Time Frame:	Type:	Impact:	Relative Importance:
		H – High			< Decreasing	! Critical
		M – Medium	S - Short-term	+ Positive	> Increasing	* Important
		L – Low	M - Medium-term	- Negative	= Unchanged	~ Un-important
		U – Undetermined	L - Long-term	? Unknown	? Unknown	? Unknown
Political						
War						
Unstable government						
Internal political issues						
Economic						
Inflation						
Currency value						
Cycles						
Social						
Ethics						
Lifestyle						
Earning capacity						
Technological						
Intellectual property issues						
Obsolecence rate						
Communication						
Legal						
Law change						
Restrictive re						
Global law conflicts						
Environmental						
Ecological						
Regulation						
Restrictions						

The next tool to consider using to understand the unique influences on your company is the *Porter's 5 Force model* (see diagram below). Developed for industry analysis and business strategy by Michael Porter of Harvard Business School in 1979, the Five Force model gives you the opportunity to review the relative *power* between your company and the other primary forces in the marketplace you currently are in or plan to be in. The greater the relative power of each of these forces (*New Entrants, Suppliers, Customers, Competitors and Substitutes)* compared to your company in a given market, the more difficult it is for you to be successful, because the combination drives down potential profitability. *Why?* Because as each, or any, of these becomes more aggressive in their actions they can, directly or indirectly, cause your company to need to lower its prices to maintain its market share, therefore, reducing its profit. Knowing your position compared to each of these other elements allows you to make more informed decisions that should lead to better results and more attainable goals.

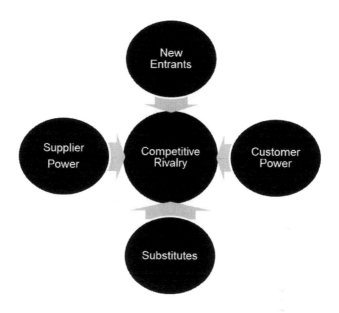

Once you have finished looking at relative power in the marketplace it is time to review *Ansoff's matrix*. Ansoff's matrix (see below) is a simple way to look at your potential growth opportunities as you see them.

They are divided between four areas: *Market penetration,* where you produce existing products or services for your existing customers; *market development,* where your existing offerings are offered to new markets; *product development,* where you look to develop offerings to your existing customers; *diversification,* where you take the bold step to enter new markets with new offerings.

Market penetration is the least risky strategy, since it will continue to use the company's existing resources and capabilities. If the market is growing, revenues will grow at relatively the same pace, if you maintain market share. If some competitors reach capacity and you don't, there may be room for further growth. Determine if your company goals match the anticipated industry growth rate.

Ansoff's Matrix

		Products/Services	
		Existing	New
Markets	Existing	Market penetration	Product Development
	New	Market Development	Diversification

Market development is riskier than market penetration since you are venturing into new markets. The key is to leverage your core competencies to optimize the results you plan to obtain. Additionally, you should adjust your expectations and the risk analysis tools you use to make decisions.

Remember, as shown in *Porter's 5 Force model*, the relative power of your customers? Well the *product development* strategy is where you are proactive, or reactive, in developing what your biggest, most important customers want/need. This choice is made when the company's strengths and relationships are related more to specific customers rather than your own products. Clearly this creates more risk than market penetration, but you gain the possibility of reaping greater rewards.

Diversification may be a reasonable choice when the higher risk of this option is offset by the probability of a relatively higher than normal return. It is considered the most risky of the four options identified in the matrix, since it requires both product and market development, and may be outside the core competencies of the company. However, when you have the skillset, the know-how and the opportunity to be a first mover into a lucrative new market opportunity, it may be too good to pass up.

4. **What company components should be included in your X-ray?**

Every business is made up of at least three components: *Operations* – what you do; *Marketing* – how you sell what you do; and *Finance* –what happens to the money. Every good review of your company needs to include a strategic review of these three critical inter-related modules of your company. (See the Chapter O – Operations for more information). These each must work well together to give you the greatest chance to achieve company goals.

Marketing needs to know the capabilities of the company (Operations). Operations needs to know what the customers want (Marketing). Marketing needs to know how much revenue they need to generate (Finance). And Finance needs to know what everything is going to cost (Operations and Marketing). Yes, this is overly simplified, but you get the point.

Take this a step further and you have one of the most widely adopted and successful tools in use today: The Balanced Scorecard (BSC). Developed by Kaplan and Norton[55], the BSC links your strategy to your goals with equal emphasis on *Finance, Customer (Marketing), Operations,* and – an additional element – *Learning and Growth (Employees).*

The basic principle is to align your business activities to your vision and strategy while monitoring company performance against strategic goals. Communications are improved since each area's results are measured against targets and published internally.

5. **Why are SMART goals important as part of an X-ray?**

Do you find that your company frequently sets goals that are not met? If you want to achieve sustainable success you must set goals with agreed-upon targets for the company to work toward. Further, these goals should be SMART goals. SMART is an acronym for:

Specific

A specific goal has a greater probability of being achieved than a general one. To set a specific goal you must answer the four *W* questions and one *H* question: *Who* is involved; *What* is to be accomplished; *Where* is the location; *Why* this is to be done, with reasons, purposes and benefits stated; and *How* will it be completed to include resources, requirements and restrictions? An example would be: "To meet 12 new prospects and close five new orders using our new demonstration model by June 30", rather than just *"sell more"*.

Measurable

SMART goals are objectively and consistently measured against agreed-upon standards, such as industry benchmarks or international best practices. Ideally, the information on the progress toward the goal should be automatically generated by your accounting system, so that the goals can be regularly compared against the targets to determine whether they were achieved or not.

---

55 Kaplan R S and Norton D P (1992) "The balanced scorecard: measures that drive performance", *Harvard Business Review* Jan – Feb pp. 71–80.

Attainable

This is the delicate balance between setting goals that are challenging enough (sometimes called *stretch goals*), yet not impossible. If they appear to be impossible, no one will actually work toward them – they give up. If they are set too low, the company will fall short of its potential. Good goals are established at that point in between these two extremes, so that they are perceived by everyone to be what is needed and yet can be accomplished.

Realistic

This concept really covers three things:

    a) You are *willing* to work toward achieving the goal
    b) You are *able* to make progress toward achieving the goal
    c) You *believe* the goal will be realized

Where these three ingredients are present together, the goal is deemed to be realistic.

Time-bound

Unless a goal has a specific timeline, it probably won't be achieved when it is needed. Therefore, every good goal has to be time-bound; some people call this a *deadline*. This has a negative connotation, so we will use the former term. Time-bound goals can include interim dates and times to measure progress against, but in the end there must be a specific date when the goal will be accomplished by, and that is not changeable. When commitment dates are regularly changed, they completely lose their meaning and the goals stop being attained.

6. **But aren't there different timelines for different kinds of goals?**

Absolutely. SMART goals need to be divided between short-term, medium-term, and long-term goals. The length between short- and long-term is for you to decide. Start by sitting down and looking at what the company has accomplished lately.

When were these goals originally set?
What is the minimum amount of time required to accomplish each of the company's most important goals?
What are they tied to?

Many companies start by looking at their operating year:
What must be completed before yearend?
Is there anything that must be completed in less time?

If yes, that may establish the short-term horizon. If not, then your operating year (12 months) may be a reasonable short-term horizon for your company.

Next, look at the longest cutoff date the company has for any goal. That may be your long-term horizon. Medium-term is what goes between the two. One company that I recently worked with set their short-term time frame at 90 days, their medium-term at 91-180 days, and their long-term at 181+ days. Another one established 18 months; 36 months; and 36+ months as their short-, medium and long-term horizons. It all depends on the industry, company and people that make up your company.

7. **As you X-ray your company, how do you decide what to do first?**

This is a question that many people ask when trying to decide how to prioritize the company's resources. I recommend a simple matrix (yes, another one). It is the *Effort vs. Impact* matrix.

The Effort vs. Impact matrix (see below) allows you to look at the relative effort required (as you see it) to perform a task or achieve a goal, and then estimate the relative impact (as you measure it) when successful.

Some of the results are obvious, such as for major, long-term projects, where the amount of effort is large and the impact to the company is significant (DE/HI). Alternatively, when little effort is needed and the result is low these become *fill in tasks* (EE/LI). Likewise, we all would love a few *quick wins* (EE/HI) that require little energy yet yield huge outcomes. And we all have a few *thankless tasks* (DE/LI) that must be done and take tremendous effort but gain us little. The *medium* items are the real grey areas for you to work in, as you see fit, between the extremes that are identified in the tool.

In a perfect world, all your efforts would be well rewarded. Until that time comes you have to look at every goal, task and project and place each of these in one of the nine squares of the matrix. By doing so, you automatically recognize the expected outcome, prioritize each and can, therefore, allocate your resources to achieve the best outcome possible.

Effort vs. Impact matrix

	Easy	Medium	Difficult
High	EE/HI	ME/HI	DE/HI
Medium	EE/MI	ME/MI	DE/MI
Low	EE/LI	ME/LI	DE/LI

Impact (rows) — Effort (columns: Easy, Medium, Difficult)

8. **Is there an X-ray that looks at how the entire company works together?**

There is an X-ray that looks at the overall company and its inter-relationships. It is the *McKinsey 7S Model.* Developed in the early 1980s by Tom Peters and Robert Waterman, two consultants working at McKinsey & Company, the basic concept of this model is that there are seven characteristics of a company that need to be aligned if it is to be successful.

The McKinsey 7S Model

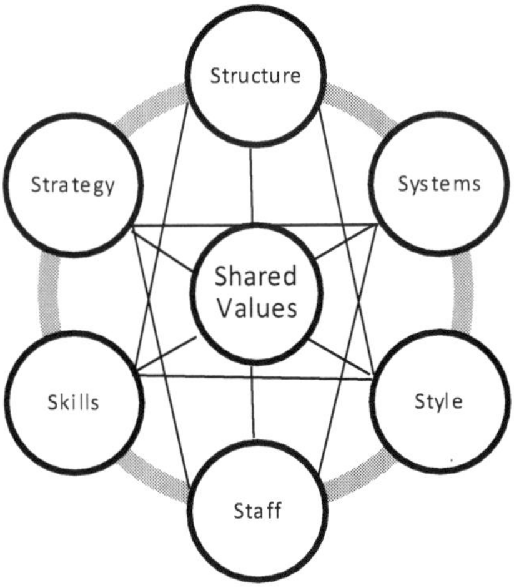

Of the seven, three are *hard* elements, because they are easier to recognize and management can directly influence them. These include: *strategy, structure, and systems.* The remaining four should be considered *soft* elements, as they can be more difficult to describe, are less tangible and more influenced by culture. They are *shared values, skills, style, and staff.* Nonetheless, these soft elements are equally as important as the hard elements if the organization is going to be successful.

9. **How do you decide when to make what you sell vs. outsourcing it?**

The classic challenge for many companies is deciding when to make what they sell and when to outsource it. If this is a problem you have faced with your company, the best practice is to combine the *subjective* approach of the *Make vs. Buy* matrix, with an *objective* formula calculation. First, look at how much the item is within your *core competency,* compared to its *strategic importance.*

The Make-or-Buy Decision

		Core Compentency		
		Low	Medium	High
Strategic Importance	High	Strategic alliance	Probably make	Make
	Low	Buy or Outsource	Neutral	Probably make

Next, ask yourself questions such as:

Is this item really within my core competency?
Could disclosing proprietary information hurt me?
What could be the impact on my quality or delivery?
What additional risks could I face?
How irreversible is the decision?

This is the *subjective* part of the decision.

The next step is to calculate a result based on four important numbers:

a) [V] – the volume needed
b) [PUTC] – the per-unit total cost from a supplier

    c)   [FC] – the fixed costs directly related to making it

    d)   [PUVC] – the per-unit variable costs of making it

Once you know these figures you can plug them into these two formulas: *CTB [Cost-To-Buy] = [V * PUTC]* and *CTM [Cost-To-Make] = [FC + (PUVC * V)]*, and calculate the *objective* part of the decision. Now you can look at the subjective and objective components together and make the best decision for the company.

10. Now how do you *read* your X-ray, and what do you do with the results?

If you have applied these tools to your company, objectively and honestly, have documented the results and communicated them to all involved, you have the basis for action plans that will take you from where you are to where the company wants/plans to be.

The action plans should be written with specifics that are measurable, what resources are needed, who is responsible to complete the item, and by what date the item will be accomplished. Try one or more of the tools provided in this chapter. See what works for your company and what you want to change.

Wasn't it Winston Churchill who said, "If you're standing still, you're falling behind?" Your customers, suppliers and competition continue to evolve; so you need to evolve also.

By Andy Pattantyus

1. What is the best way to calculate and improve financial yield?

Return on Invested Capital (ROIC) is the best way to calculate financial yield. ROIC measures the actual cash-on-cash return of an investment. Because ROIC excludes interest, depreciation, taxes and accruals, it is the truest measure of a company's financial performance. Investors want to know whether the operations of a company are creating or destroying value. To create additional value (financial yield), ROIC must be greater than the Weighted Average Cost of Capital (WACC), which includes debt and equity. The average WACC for American companies is approximately 9%[56]. If there is to be any positive financial yield at all, the ROIC must be greater than the WACC, otherwise the company is losing value and growth only serves to destroy value faster.

Investors who consider the quality of earnings will look at the financial yield from operations, which are represented on the income statement as EBITDA (Earnings Before Interest Taxes, Depreciation and Amortization). EBITDA can be increased by improving labor efficiency, and/or reducing waste, resulting in improved yields.

Inventory Turns (the number of times per year you sell your inventory and replace it) is a good indicator of operational efficiency for companies that move material. A very inefficient sales and distribution company might turn its inventory only two times per year, while the ultra-efficient fast food company might turn its inventory nearly 100 times per year. The amount of inventory on the books, relative to revenues and earnings, is also an indicator of operational efficiency. Generally, companies with huge inventories have the potential to improve financial yield by improving operations.

2. Does yield financially affect your operations?

A business is made up of a series of processes. When any of the processes are operating at less than an ideal state, it affects all subsequent processes, and

---

56 Koller, Tim, et.al., "Value: The Four Cornerstones of Corporate Finance," McKinsey and Company, John Wiley and Sons, 2011

therefore the end result. Each imperfect process step results in yield loss. The waste from a process step must be reworked or scrapped; therefore more capacity is needed. Thus, low yield in one or more key operations can have a wide range effect on operations. Consider the flowchart below, which shows a single manufacturing process step.

One Manufacturing Process Step with Support Processes

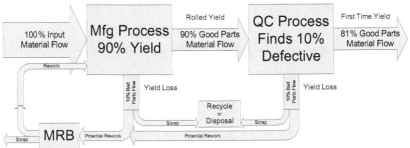

The flowchart shows how yield loss and rework introduce complexity into the material flow, which greatly increases the difficulty of capacity planning and completing to schedule.

The capacity plan must account for yield loss throughout the process, adding measures necessary to correct defective parts, which add cost without adding value. Upstream process steps of a process with low rolled yield may require 2 to 4 times as much capacity as the same process with a high rolled yield. While the yield of the beginning process step(s) may be high, extra production capacity is needed to compensate for all the yield losses in the subsequent downstream process steps. For the inefficient process, extra machines and inspection steps require extra space in the facility and people to run them. Extra capital investment in machinery and inventory reduce Return on Assets (ROA) and ROIC. The figure below, shows the accumulating effect of attrition through the process. Since latent defects can slip through any inspection, there may be additional costs to service customer repair and warranty claims. Expensive computer systems are required to manage all this inspection, rework flow and service activity. So yield has a huge impact on company operations and thus affects financial performance.

A lot of waste and yield loss is sometimes structurally embedded in a process, caused by poor product and/or process design. Thus, improving yield requires a redesign of the process and the product, requiring time and effort from the assigned human resources. However, this is an investment not an expense. Product redesigns can eliminate process steps. Changes in equipment, material and tooling can produce yield improvements at specific process steps.

In any company, the concept of yield can also be applied to almost every administrative process, such as transaction processing. Consider the process, which responds to a request for quote (RFQ) from a customer. Dozens of steps are needed to generate a quote, and many are not done right at first, wasting time and driving up the transaction cost. Transaction cost is a good measure of an administrative process in which only information is being exchanged.

3. **What is process yield, and why should you care?**

Yield is a measure of process efficiency. Percent yield is the proportion of useful output compared to a theoretical waste-free 100%. So process capability determines yield. A capable process will get it right the first time; producing a high yield. A low yield process is not as capable; therefore, it generates lots of scrap and/or rework because the process is not under control. The ideal process has no waste (See Chapter P – Process for more information). When process steps are less than ideal, they consume resources and time, and must be managed. Therefore, each necessary process step must be high yield, or produce near-perfect results on the first attempt.

As shown in the figure below, low-yield processes waste materials and time. The inspection processes used to identify defects and reverse material flows for rework add a tremendous amount of complexity to Sales and Operations Planning (S&OP) and Capacity Planning[57]. To plan capacity and labor requirements and handle raw material purchases, management systems, like Kanban cards[58], are needed. Extra manufacturing capacity is needed to handle the extra material flow, resulting in consumption of floor space, equipment, materials and labor.

The essence of high yield is low scrap and little or no rework – doing it right the first time. Raw material order quantities should be readily predicted, as well as cycle and production lead-time. Little or no rework means little or no extra capacity is needed to handle downstream defects that come back upstream. High yield is the result of capable processes. Capable processes are high quality, predictable, reliable and efficient.

First Time Yield (FTY)[58] is the best measure of real productivity at a specific process step. Rather than measure FTY, many companies measure scrap and over usage. Such measures are problematic because they become a part of the daily language, get incorporated into standard costs and disappear. Such measures fail to prompt improvement. Far better are measures that reveal the issues and cannot be jiggered. To reveal the processes that need improvement, process-by-process yield measurements and monitoring are necessary.

---

57 APICS Dictionary, 13th Edition, 2011
58 Lean Lexicon, 4th Edition, Lean Enterprise Institute, 2008

The inspection step, usually a measurement, has its own yield and process capability. Here emerges the possibility of rejecting perfectly good parts due to inadequate yield. Ideally, every measurement process has a yield of 100%; more realistically, every measurement process is less than perfect. A portion of the yield loss will be false rejections, where good parts are labeled defective by the measurement process; and false acceptances, where defective parts are labeled good. Visual inspection processes have a very low yield. Because the process is subjective and fatiguing, a bank of visual inspectors will find only 70% to 80% of the defective product, while rejecting too many good parts. Machine inspection can be fast and reliable, but only if the measurement process has been carefully designed and validated. Before trusting reported numbers, inquire about the test methods and measurements used to determine yield.

4. Why is your rolled yield so low?

Rolled Yield (RY)[59] is the proportion of units completing a process without any defects. Similarly, First Time Yield (FTY)[59] is the proportion of units successfully passing an inspection step the first time. FTY represents both the process capability of the production process and the process capability of the measurement process. See RY and FTY in the first graphic above.

Consider how rolled yield for a complete process is calculated: At each individual process step, the probability of getting a good part is less than 100%. Consider the hypothetical 4-step process in the graphic below, where each process step has a 90% probability of successful completion. We have a process with only 4 process steps, yet FTY is a shockingly low 66%.

Rolled Yield for a 4-step Manufacturing Process

Clearly, the first time yield (FTY) for the total process is dependent upon the total number of process steps, as well as the rolled yield (RY) at each process step. There are two methods for increasing FTY of the total process. The first is to improve the RY at each process step, which can be accomplished only by improving the process capability at each step. (Note: improving the process capability of an inspection process *could* decrease the FTY.) The second is to create a process with fewer steps. This can be accomplished using Design for Manufacturability and

---

59 ENG 123, "Design for Manufacturability Participant Guide," Motorola University, 1992

Assembly (DFMA), a method for reducing the number of product components and process assembly steps, or simply through *process re-engineering*. The ideal process step consumes no resources, and therefore does not exist.

Ultimately, a high FTY is a function of good design. DFMA can be applied to any product and process design, resulting in fewer moving parts and fewer process steps. Specific features are included in the design of each part to make it easier to handle, orient and inspect. For example, registration marks on a component will help the vision system perform critical inspection measurements. In administrative processes, forms and data entry screens make it easy to detect missing information and ensure completeness by filling in the blanks.

Each process step must be engineered for high process capability. This is where Six-Sigma comes in. For the purposes of this chapter, I will define a Six-Sigma process as one with process capacity greater than or equal to 2.0. This means that the Upper Specification Limit (USL) and the Lower Specification Limit (LSL) are at the +/- 6-sigma, where the process is defined by +/- 3-sigma. The more process steps, the more important process capability becomes. Imagine the FTY for a semi-conductor manufacturing process where several hundred process steps in a series are needed to make the product, and there is no opportunity for rework. To get any FTY at all, the rolled yield at each process step must be approaching 6-sigma, which permits only 3.4 defects per million parts. Many companies decide to live with low FTY, because they think they can afford to.

5. **How much yield are you giving up to lost time?**

A company implementing Lean methods to transform their factory into a Lean Visual Factory, with balanced processes and one-piece flow, can double its production within the same factory building using the same number of workers and machines. I've learned through my consulting experiences how lost time can result in a factory yield loss of 50 percent or more.

As I will discuss in the next question, *NVA to VA ratio*, time losses can be found in plain sight – the wasted moments of needless tasks, extra motions and extra mouse clicks. Since these snippets of wasted time are not clearly identifiable financial line items (like labor or materials), the waste often remains buried inside standard costs, which *accept* the waste.

Much machine time is lost to unscheduled downtime (when a machine breaks down unexpectedly) and scheduled downtime (for changeover or unstaffed shifts). Usually, this downtime is not measured; rather, it is buried in standards and normal costs. A machine capable of producing 3,000 units per shift may only be expected to produce 1,400. If 1,400 units are produced in one shift, the machine will be reported to have run at 100% efficiency.

Over the past two decades, capital-intensive companies have grown adept at measuring Overall Equipment Effectiveness (OEE)[59]. OEE reveals the root causes of wasted time, allowing the business to begin productivity improvement projects. The best way to improve a process is to stabilize it first, following up with a Lean initiative to eliminate non-value added (NVA) time, such as changeover or breakdown. The unexpected breakdown of just one piece of equipment can cause a huge yield loss, while changeover time can often take an entire shift. One shift out of five in a week is a 20 percent yield loss. Almost any machine changeover can be redesigned to require only a few minutes, using the Single Minute Exchange of Die (SMED) method[59].

A company considering investing in a bigger factory and more machinery should first consider alternative investments in reducing changeover time and improving machine reliability to reduce unplanned downtime. The return (ROIC) for spending to improve OEE will be large, compared to almost any other investment in operations.

6. What is your NVA to VA ratio?

For companies seriously considering embarking on a Lean Transformation initiative, this is the most pertinent question. The moment a customer order is accepted, the stopwatch starts running. The NVA:VA ratio is the yield on elapsed time, and reveals what proportion of the production lead time (or dock-to-dock time) is actual productive, value added time.

The ratio between Non-Value Added (NVA) and Value Added (VA) time can be greater than 100:1 for the non-Lean company. For the Lean company, NVA:VA ratio is usually less than 25:1, and can be less than 5:1. The NVA:VA ratio is a measure of yield on the elapsed chronological time from dock-to-dock. As the ratio decreases, material moves more quickly through all the process steps of the operation.

For companies that have not yet embraced a Lean Initiative, it is possible to double yield (production throughput), while keeping plant floor space and labor the same. Most companies are getting less than a 50 percent yield from their expenditures on labor equipment and facilities. After fully implementing a Lean Transformation, dock-to-dock time can be reduced to less than 25 percent of pre-Lean values, as shown in the Value Stream Map calculation results below. (A value stream map is defined as: The graphic representation of all the processes required to produce a product or service of value to either an internal or external customer. This could apply to a product group or individual products or services. It also includes the flow of materials as well as information.) The NVA:VA ratio becomes a key performance indicator (KPI) for operations management.

Key Performance Indicator - The NVA:VA Ratio

The goal of the COO of any company is to improve productivity. The performance of the COO can be measured using KPIs (Key Performance Indicators) such as the NVA:VA ratio, Inventory Turns and the rolled yield of each process. Implementing Lean practices to improve the NVA:VA ratio enables the reduction of WIP (Work-in-Process), leading to improved Inventory Turns. An honest calculation of the NVA:VA ratio requires a Value Stream Map supported by observation and measurements from the plant floor.

Typically, most discussions about yield are focused on material yield. A Lean approach will also look at yield in terms of elapsed time, which is very low. Even a fully automatic machine may stop every few minutes if the process is unreliable. Because the capacity is accepted as fait accompli, the organization sets their norms for standard costing at a very low level. In this manner, a machine running at 45 percent output is classified as a process running at 99 percent efficiency.

7. **Is your labor yielding enough?**

For a quick litmus test of productivity, divide total sales by the total number of employees. A typical manufacturing company will produce about $200,000 revenue per employee[60]. A "world class" company will produce from $225,000[60] or more revenue per employee. A few exceptional companies generate more than $1 million revenue per employee. We have seen many marginal manufacturing companies, on the verge of extinction, producing barely $100,000 of sales per employee.

---

60 Zelinski, Peter, "What is Your Shop's Sales Per Employee?" Modern Machine Shop, July 29, 2010.

Labor yield (the return on human capital) can be inefficient for two reasons. First, employees are trapped inside inefficient processes. Second, employees are inefficient due to a mix of personal accountability, lack of training, and company culture.

Redesigning the process to improve yield has been described already in this chapter, and has the potential to double the productivity. As labor productivity improves, the Direct Material portion of COGS increases[60] while Direct Labor decreases.

Adjusting the company culture for performance and accountability is more difficult. Recently, new tools and systems have become available for the measurement of people and performance, the use of which helps individuals and companies optimize human performance[61],[62],[63]. Most companies actually have about 3 times more employees than would be needed to get the job done with only 'A' players[63].

The company constantly improving labor productivity is a learning organization. At stagnating companies, the company and its employees have likely stopped learning. The learning curve[64] is a time-tested method for measuring and tracking the rate of productivity improvement of individuals, departments, locations and product lines. As a rule of thumb, productivity should improve by 10 percent to 20 percent each time cumulative production has doubled.

8. Is extra labor needed due to yield losses?

Because all yield loss reduces productivity, extra labor is needed to compensate. More workers are needed to perform rework or to produce more units at each step in which the first time yield is low. Harder to identify is the extra labor needed to: Expedite orders, operate and maintain complex MRP/ERP systems, staff material review boards (MRBs), inspect rejected parts, order extra materials and perform extra handling of materials. A large number of workers, essential to the operation, end up classified as General and Administrative (G&A), which is pure overhead. The example above shows the complexity of the processes needed to handle the yield loss.

61 Taylor, Lynn E. "The Core Values Handbook," Taylor Protocols, 1992
62 Taylor, Lynn E. "Choices: Finding Your Place of Highest and Best Contribution," Elliot Bay Publishing, 2010.
63 www.taylorprotocols.com
64 [64] Jordan, Raymond, "How to Use the Learning Curve," Materials Management Institute, 1965

9. How does material yield loss affect materials?

Material yield loss is the most visibly apparent waste on the manufacturing floor. For processes where the yield is much less than 99.73 percent, the scrap pile will be noticeable, on both the plant floor, and the income statement. Such a process has a low process capability < 1.0, and cannot stay in control. Extra materials must be ordered to compensate for the yield losses.

Material costs are highly visible on the P&L statements as Direct Materials (DM). If the company can afford the waste, as many can, the systemic waste is built into the normal cost in the standard costing system. Only unusual losses (example: a big batch is scrapped due to contamination) are captured as Direct Overhead (DOH) or Direct Variable cost.

Since direct material is highly visible on the P&L, the COO and the CFO are under constant pressure to reduce material costs. Most respond by trying to convince suppliers to lower their prices, paying little attention to internal inefficiencies. For commodity materials (example: steel sold by the pound), the market sets the cost, and there is no choice but to look to operations to improve yield.

Some types of material yield loss are unavoidable. For example, a process that stamps round beverage can lids out of aluminum strip stock will have scrap aluminum consisting of the remainder of the web, with punched holes. No matter how much the process is continuously improved, a percentage of the aluminum remains as scrap. This high-value scrap can be collected and sold to a recycler to recoup some of the loss. Handling the scrap is a reverse material flow, necessitating a reverse supply chain and management process.

10. Why don't you see yield loss in your financial statements?

A useful indicator of operational efficiency is Inventory Turns, which is easy to calculate from the company financial statements. If Inventory Turns are low, there is a good chance the material is not flowing well as a result of yield losses and poorly designed processes.

Direct Material shows up on every P&L statement, but rarely reveals information about the extra material consumed due to yield loss. The cost of excess material is usually buried into the standard cost and no further action is taken. Most accounting systems and MRP / ERP systems are not pre-configured to gather information on yield loss, but can be configured to capture and report it[65]. A good place to start is by asking whether the yield loss (scrap and/or over usage) is going to be captured and counted, and how it will be reported. Once

65 Cunningham, Jean E. and Fiume, Orest J., "Real Numbers: Management Accounting in a Lean Organization," Managing Times Press, Durham NC, 2003.

the yield report is produced, who will receive it and who will act on it? Which department budget is going to absorb the yield loss? Since information collection and reporting costs money, appropriately designed processes should support answers to such questions.

More than one author of this book has mentioned the adage, "What gets measured gets done." There's a reason for this: It's true. Proper counting of waste, and translation of counted waste into costs, are great first steps toward justifying yield improvement projects to reduce cost.

Sweeping problems under the rug is human nature. Most departments within operations are not inclined to request accounting "buckets" to track the cost of waste, because it draws attention to their own shortcomings. Moreover, the company may not properly support improvement initiatives. Ultimately, an enlightened company culture, keenly focused on waste reduction and efficiency improvement, is a prerequisite to setting up accounts to track waste. Use of Lean Manufacturing methods enables the use of Lean Accounting methods, which eliminate Standard Costing[65]. With no place to hide, Lean accounting methods reveal the waste and give the CEO, CFO and COO a critical tool to support their goal of efficiency improvement.

CHAPTER Z – Z-SCORE

By Daniel Feiman

1. What is a *Z-score?*

The Z-score is a predictive model created and first published by Dr. Edward I. Altman in 1968[66]. It is used to forecast failure in a business for up to two years in the future. This diagnostic tool is still used regularly today by financial professionals around the world, due to its high level of accuracy. The original model, designed for publicly traded manufacturing companies, combines five weighted financial ratios that evaluate management's demonstrated ability and financial strength in a straightforward linear equation. The result is a single number called the Z-score.

A Z-score less than *1.8* indicates that insolvency is likely, while scores greater than *3.0* indicate bankruptcy is unlikely to occur within the next two years. A Z-score that falls between these two parameters is in the grey area and should be carefully watched. A decreasing trend is an indication that prompt changes must be made quickly.

The estimation was originally based on data from publicly held manufacturers, but has since been re-estimated based on other sets of data for private manufacturing, non-manufacturing, emerging markets and service companies (see examples below).

2. Why is the Z-score important to your business?

It is important because it provides you with a relatively easy-to-calculate and easy-to-understand diagnostic tool to assess your own company's financial health as well as that of your suppliers and customers. You can track your company's score over time to identify deteriorating trends to enable you to take action sooner rather than later. (See Chapter T – Turnaround for more information).

If you use suppliers that are public companies or have provided financial statements, you can assess their financial health to help you to anticipate if they can continue to provide you materials or services without interruption. If a pattern

---

66 Altman, Edward I., Financial Ratios, Discriminant Analysis and the Prediction of Corporate Bankruptcy, *The Journal of Finance*, September, 1968

develops that indicates trouble is coming, you can both discuss it with them and look for alternate sources, in case you need them.

At the same time, the Z-score can be used to review your customers' financial statements (assuming they are publicly traded or have provided financial statements) to determine if trouble lies ahead. This proactive approach allows you the opportunity to help your customers realize that they may have grave challenges ahead, but most importantly, it gives you the chance to preclude or minimize potential bad debt write-offs and control your business, rather than becoming the victim of your own naiveté. You can act while there are still options, and even help your customers realize that you and they can take the appropriate action, so you are not left holding the bag.

3. **How accurate is the Z-score?**

This is a relatively accurate model. The real world application of the Z-score has successfully predicted 72% of corporate bankruptcies within *two years* of these companies becoming insolvent. Over a span of 31 years (until 1999), the model was found to be approximately 80-90% accurate in predicting bankruptcy within *one year* of the event.

4. **What are the steps you need to calculate a Z-score?**

There are basically three steps to calculating a Z-score.

Step One

Locate the eight values or variables that comprise the formula. Seven of the eight numbers are found on the company's financial statements, specifically the balance sheet and income statement. The location of each variable is listed in the far right column in the table below:

Variable	Statement	Where
a) Earnings Before Interest & Taxes: EBIT	Income statement	After operating expenses
b) Total Assets	Balance sheet	Asset section
c) Net Sales	Income statement	Top line
d) Market Value of Equity		Commons shares outstanding * market price
e) Total Liabilities	Balance sheet	Above equity
f) Current Assets	Balance sheet	Above long-term assets
g) Current Liabilities	Balance sheet	Above Long-term liabilities
h) Retained Earnings	Balance sheet	Equity section

One variable not found on the financial statements is the *Market Value of Equity*. This is calculated by taking the number of common shares outstanding (found in the Equity section of the balance sheet) and multiplying it by the current price per share in the marketplace. The current market price can be found in several resources including:

- The company's website
- Your stockbroker
- Websites, such as Google Money (www.GoogleMoney.com)
- Publications, such as the *Wall Street Journal*

The market value of equity is a market-driven number, rather than one resulting from on-going company operations, so it is constantly subject to change. Although this variable is required to calculate the Z-score, the market value of equity actually has the least impact on the overall score relative to the other four inputs based on the weighting factors.

Step Two
Calculate the following five ratios using the eight values listed above:

- *EBIT / Total Assets* – This measures operating efficiency before the impact of tax and leveraging factors. It recognizes operating earnings as being important to long-term viability.
- *Net Sales / Total Assets* – This is a standard measure of productivity or the sales generated from the investment in the company's assets. Also called sales turnover, this ratio varies greatly from industry to industry.
- *Market Value of Equity / Total Liabilities* – Large fluctuations of any variable can be a possible red flag but particularly here.
- *Working Capital / Total Assets* – Measures liquid assets in relation to the size of the company.
- *Retained Earnings / Total Assets* – Measures profitability that has been reinvested in the company since its inception and may indicate potential future earning power.

Step Three
Apply specific weights to each ratio. This is the proverbial "secret sauce". These weights were the result of Altman's detailed study of the relationship between these specific ratios and what was needed to derive at a consistent predictive result.

5. How is it calculated for public manufacturing companies?

To calculate the original Z-score multiply each of the five ratios from above by their respective weight factor as shown below:

Ratio	Weight Factor
EBIT/Total Assets	3.300
Net Sales /Total Assets	0.999
Market Value of Equity / Total Liabilities	0.600
Working Capital/Total Assets	1.200
Retained Earnings /Total Assets	1.400

The resulting number is the Z-score. So what exactly does this mean?

When the resulting Z-score is *3.0 or above*, the firm is very likely safe based on the financial data used.

When the number is between *2.7 and 3.0*, the company is probably safe from bankruptcy, but this is in the grey area so keep your eyes on this score in the future.

When the score is anywhere between *1.8 and 2.7*, the company is likely to fail within two years. This is the lower portion of the grey area, and a dramatic turnaround of the company is needed immediately to avoid any nasty surprises.

When the Z-score is below *1.8*, the company is highly likely to be insolvent soon. If a company is generating a score less than *1.8*, take immediate action to protect your company, because the company is in serious trouble and may not survive for long.

Always be careful to double-check your calculations each time you go through this process; this is only a model, not a perfect predictor of the future. Additionally, check for potential errors in your calculations. Be aware that fraud, economic downturns and many other factors could cause unexpected reversals at any time.

Here is an example of an imaginary firm's Z-score:

Figures in Millions (As of Year end)		Z Score
Working Capital	$ 12,933	
Total Assets	$ 109,022	
Total Liabilities	$ 86,386	
Retained Earnings	$ 60,900	3.93
EBIT	$ 32,008	
Market Value of Equity	$ 167,330	
Net Sales	$ 95,758	

6. Can you use the Z-score on private companies?

Yes, there is a slightly modified version of the original Z-score model that has been designed specifically for non-publicly traded companies. It also uses five ratios, and four of the five are the same as the original model. The one difference is, since the company is not publically traded, there is no way to establish a *market* price of the stock. Therefore, the fifth ratio uses the *Book Value of Equity*, found in the equity section of the balance sheet. This value will usually be significantly less than that of a public company, since it will not have the benefit of the open market trading of shares that reflect the company's financial results since inception. Further, it does not reflect the investors' anticipation of the future value (as private companies do not report their earnings publicly, and therefore have no established market price).

Additionally, the weights are slightly different:

Ratio	Weight Factor
EBIT/Total Assets	3.300
Net Sales /Total Assets	0.999
Market Value of Equity / Total Liabilities	0.600
Working Capital/Total Assets	1.200
Retained Earnings /Total Assets	1.400

Let's look at the impact of this modified model. Using the example from the company we previously looked at, if the book value of equity was $20,000 (instead of the market value of $167,330) and the appropriate weight factors are applied, the Z-score drops from the model for public companies at *3.93* to the model for private companies at *2.44*.

Without the benefit of the market value, this firm went from apparently very solid financially to reasonably all right, but not great. For this non-public manufacturing company model, a result above *2.9* is considered in the *Safe Zone*, from *1.23 to 2.9* is the *Grey Zone* or *Uncertain,* and below *1.23* is called the *Distress Zone.*

7. What about non-manufacturing and emerging markets?

For non-manufacturing and emerging markets, there is yet a third model. This model relies on four variables and four weights:

Figures in Millions (As of Year end)		Z Score
Working Capital	$ 12,933	
Total Assets	$ 109,022	
Total Liabilities	$ 86,386	
Retained Earnings	$ 60,900	**2.44**
EBIT	$ 32,008	
Book Value of Equity	$ 20,000	
Net Sales	$ 95,758	

Obviously the one element that is missing here is the *Sales to Assets* ratio. Our imaginary company with this model reflects:

Ratio	Weight
Working capital / Total Assets	6.56
Retained Earnings / Total Assets	3.26
Earnings Before Interest and Taxes / Total Assets	6.72
Book Value of Equity / Total Liabilities	1.05

With this model, scores greater than *2.6* are considered in the *Safe Zone*, while scores between *1.1 and 2.6* are considered in the *Grey Zone* and with less than *1.1* in the *Distress Zone*.

Figures in Millions (As of Year end)		Z Score
Working Capital	$ 12,933	
Total Assets	$ 109,022	
Total Liabilities	$ 86,386	**4.82**
Retained Earnings	$ 60,900	
EBIT	$ 32,008	
Book Value of Equity	$ 20,000	

8. **So is this the same thing as the *Beneish M-score*?**

While the Altman Z-score attempts to predict the probability of a company going bankrupt within the next two years, the M-score attempts to identify whether a company has manipulated its earnings. It was created by Professor Messod Beneish[67] and is a mathematical model that uses eight financial ratios in the standard model and five in the modified version.

The variables are constructed from the company's financial statements, and create a score to describe the degree to which the earnings have been manipulated.

---

67 The Detection of Earnings Manipulation; Messod D. Beneish; June 1999

Students from Cornell University using the M-score correctly identified Enron as an earnings manipulator long before experienced financial analysts did.

9. **What goes into determining an M-score?**

The M-score is based on a combination of the following ratios:

DSRI – Days' Sales in Receivables Index

This measures the ratio of days' sales in receivables versus the prior year as an indicator of potential revenue inflation. The DSRI is calculated by dividing accounts receivable to sales in the current period by accounts receivable to sales from the previous period. A DSRI equal to or above 1.465 is a red flag for inflating the value of receivables.

(Accounts Receivable$_t$ / Sales$_t$) / (Accounts Receivable$_{t-1}$ / Sales$_{t-1}$); ≥1.465 = Asset overstatement, or inflating the value of receivables

GMI – Gross Margin Index

The GMI compares profit from the previous period with the current period. A firm with a declining gross margin is more likely to manipulate earnings. With a GMI equal to or above 1.193, there is an increased risk that fraud will occur in the future.

(Sales$_{t-1}$)- (Cost of Sales$_{t-1}$) / (Sales$_{t-1}$) / (Sales$_t$)-(Cost of Sales$_t$) / (Sales$_t$)

≥1.193 = Economic difficulty

AQI –Asset Quality Index

Asset quality is measured as the ratio of non-current assets other than plant, property and equipment to total assets. An AQI equal to or above 1.254 is a red flag for improper capitalization of expenses.

[1-((Current Assets$_t$) + (Net Fixed Assets$_t$)]/(Total Assets$_t$))] / [1-((Current Assets$_{t-1}$)+(Net Fixed Assets$_{t-1}$)]/(Total Assets$_{t-1}$))]; ≥1.254 = Improper capitalization of expenses.

SGI – Sales Growth Index

This measures the ratio of sales this year compared to the prior year. While sales growth is not itself a measure of manipulation growth, companies are likely be under pressure to manipulate to keep up appearances. The SGI is determined by comparing current period sales with the previous period. A SGI equal to or above 1.607 is a red flag for fictitious revenues.

$(Sales_t \, / \, Sales_{t-1})$; ≥ 1.607 = Revenue recognition: fictitious revenue

DEPI – Depreciation Index

This is measured as the ratio of the rate of depreciation versus the prior year. A slower rate of depreciation (DEPI greater than 1) may mean that the firm is revising useful asset life assumptions upwards, or changing their depreciation method to one that is income friendly. Therefore, a DEPI equal to or above 1.077 is a red flag for both inflating the useful life of assets and increasing income.

$[(Depreciation_{t-1}) \, / \, (Depreciation_{t-1} + Net \; PPE_{t-1})] \, /$ $[(Depreciation_t) \, / \, (Depreciation_t + Net \; PPE_t)]$; ≥ 1.077 = Earnings manipulation: inflating the useful life of assets and increasing income.

SGAI = Sales, General and Administrative Expenses Index

This is based on the assumption that analysts would interpret a disproportionate increase in sales as a negative signal about firm's future prospects. The SGAI compares the relationship between SGA expense and sales in the current period with the previous period. A SGAI equal to or below 1.041 is a red flag for a disproportionate increase in sales.

$(SGA \; Expense_t \, / \, Sales_t) \, / \, (SGA \; Expense_{t-1} \, / \, Sales_{t-1})$; ≤ 1.041 = Earnings manipulation

LVGI – Leverage Index

This is intended to capture debt covenants incentives for earnings manipulation. The LVGI compares the relationship between total debt and total assets in the current period with the previous period. A LVGI equal to or above 1.111 is a red flag for earnings manipulation, due to incentives from an increase in leverage.

$[((Long \; Term \; Debt_t) + (Current \; Liabilities_t)) \, / \, (Total \; Assets_t)] \, /$ $[((Long \; Term \; Debt_{t-1}) + (Current \; Liabilities_{t-1})) \, / \, (Total \; Assets_{t-1})]$; ≥ 1.111 = Earnings manipulation

TATA – Total Accruals to Total Assets

This assesses the extent to which managers make discretionary accounting choices to alter earnings. The TATA is calculated by the sum of the change in working capital, less the change in cash, less the change in current taxes payable, less depreciation and amortization; divided by total assets. A TATA equal to or above 0.031 is a red flag for revenue recognition fraud.

$(\Delta Working\ Capital)-(\Delta Cash)-(\Delta Current\ Taxes\ Payable) =$
$(\underline{Depreciation\ and\ Amortization})$
$(Total\ Assets)$; ≥ 0.031 = Revenue recognition

10. Does the Beneish M-score work?

Beneish used all the companies in the Compustat database between 1982-1992 to develop his model. He was able to correctly identify those who manipulated 76% of the time while only incorrectly identifying 17.5% of non-manipulators.

The basic Beneish M-score formula includes eight variables that are weighted together according to the following: -4.84 (the *plug number*) + 0.92*DSRI + 0.528*GMI + 0.404*AQI + 0.892*SGI + 0.115*DEPI - 0.172*SGAI + 4.679*TATA - 0.327*LVGI.

There is also a five variable version that excludes SGAI, DEPI and LEVI, which were not considered significant in the original Beneish model. The values include a plug number of -6.065 + 0.823*DSRI + 0.906*GMI + 0.593*AQI + 0.717*SGI + 0.107*DEPI. With both versions a score greater than -2.22 indicates a strong likelihood of a firm being a manipulator.

Please see an example of an imaginary company on the following page:

INPUT VARIABLES	2010	2009
Net Sales	$93,281	$93,669
CGS	$51,355	$48,703
Net Receivables	$1,124	$970
Current Assets (CA)	$72,726	$67,539
PPE (Net)	$1,734	$1,970
Depreciation	$1,597	$1,322
Total Assets	$85,585	$84,001
SGA Expense	$32,416	$32,990
Net Income (before Xitems)	$5,658	$9,038
CFO (Cash flow from operations)	$7,975	$2,836
Current Liabilities	$26,158	$26,176
Long-term Debt	$485	$596
DERIVED VARIABLES		
Other L/T Assets [TA-(CA+PPE)]	$11,125	$14,492

		Variables	
		5	8
DSRI	1.164	0.823	0.920
GMI	1.068	0.906	0.528
AQI	0.753	0.593	0.404
SGI	0.996	0.717	0.892
DEPI	0.838	0.107	0.115
SGAI	0.987		-0.172
Total Accruals/TA	-0.027		4.679
LVGI	0.977		0.327
Plug		-6.065	-4.840

M = -6.065 + .823 DSRI + .906 GMI + .593 AQI + .717 SGI + .107 DEPI

M-score (5-variable model)　**-2.89**

M = -4.84 + .920 DSRI + .528 GMI + .404 AQI + .892 SGI + .115 DEPI
-.172 SGAI + 4.679 Accrual to TA - .327 Leverage

M-score (8-variable model)　**-2.53**

INPUT VARIABLES	2010	2009		
Net Sales	$93,281	$93,669		
CGS	$51,355	$48,703		
Net Receivables	$1,124	$970		
Current Assets (CA)	$72,726	$67,539		
PPE (Net)	$1,734	$1,970		
Depreciation	$1,597	$1,322		
Total Assets	$85,585	$84,001		
SGA Expense	$32,416	$32,990		
Net Income (before Xitems) CFO	$5,658	$9,038		
(Cash flow from operations)	$7,975	$2,836		
Current Liabilities	$26,158	$26,176		
Long-term Debt	$485	$596		
DERIVED VARIABLES				
Other L/T Assets [TA-(CA+PPE)]	$11,125	$14,492		
			Variables	
		5	8	
DSRI	1.164	0.823	0.920	
GMI	1.068	0.906	0.528	
AQI	0.753	0.593	0.404	
SGI	0.996	0.717	0.892	
DEPI	0.838	0.107	0.115	
SGAI	0.987		-0.172	
Total Accruals/TA	-0.027		4.679	
LVGI	0.977		0.327	
Plug		-6.065	-4.840	

M = -6.065+ .823 DSRI + .906 GMI + .593 AQI + .717 SGI + .107 DEPI

		=-6.065+(0.823*B23)+(0.906*B24)+(0.5
M-score (5-variable model)	-2.89	93*B25)+(0.717*B26)+(0.107*B27)

M = -4.84 + .920 DSRI + .528 GMI + .404 AQI + .892 SGI + .115 DEPI

  -.172 SGAI + 4.679 Accrual to TA - .327 Leverage

		=-4.84+(0.92*B23)+(0.528*B24)+(0.
		404*B25)+(0.892*B26)+(0.115*B27)-
M-score (8-variable model)	-2.53	(0.172*B28)+(4.679*B29)-(0.327*B30)

Conclusion:

The best ways to use these two models to manage your business is to apply them regularly to your own business as well as your clients/customers. Since the Z-score forecasts insolvency within the next two years, you are forewarned of potential financial problems. If the result is a score of three or higher, you have reason to feel good about your business or the account.

On the other hand, by calculating the M-score, you can determine whether or not your client appears to be manipulating their earnings. While not a direct sign of bankruptcy, it is very troubling if there are indications they are doing so. Again if you can calculate that they are not, you can have renewed confidence in the relationship.

Used together, you have a much better understanding of your customer than perhaps they do themselves, and you can proceed with the relationship confidently.

ACKNOWLEDGMENTS

It is said that anything worth doing is worth doing well. And in order to do something well it takes perseverance, patience, and planning. It also takes a dedicated team.

All of the co-authors of this book put in quite a bit of effort to adhere to my vision of what this book should be and how it should address the twenty-six topics. It was not always easy – nor did we always agree – yet somehow, it came together as you see it here. And I am pleased. I thank them all.

I must pay particular thank you(s) to Bette Hiramatsu, Rick Norris, Ivan Rosenberg and Lee Schwartz for their help in several areas, including reaching out to secure endorsements for the book, as well as their marketing efforts. I also need to thank Lee for agreeing to put our next book on hold to complete this one. There are only so many creative impulses one can respond to at any one time.

I want to thank Julien Sharp for her editorial eye, suggestions, and challenges. She and her team made this book better. I also would like to thank Dan Yeager of Nu-Image Design for his cover design and manuscript layout. The *Build It Backwards* brand lives on through our cover art.

In addition to the above, I am particularly grateful to my wife, Robin, for her constant support, objective critiques and honest assessment of this project at every step of this process. In addition to everything else, she was our videographer on the YouTube video series (which you can find on *THE Book on…BUSINESS from A to Z*). This book would not have been possible without her.

GLOSSARY

Amortization – The periodic expensing of an intangible asset over time, which records the decline of the asset's value over some expected period of time

Asset Based Lender (ABL) – Lenders that calculate loan availability based a predetermined percentage (advance rate) of eligible assets

Buy Cycle - The process buyers go through to select and purchase a product or service

The phases involved include awareness, information, assurance and loyalty. The buy cycle is now the focus of marketers (instead of the sales cycle), because the Internet has put buyers, not sellers, in control.

Call Option – A financial contract between two parties

The buyer of the call has the right, not the obligation, to buy an agreed quantity of a financial instrument at a set price and time. The seller is obligated to sell if the buyer so decides.

Cash Cow – A product in a declining market; the last stage of the product lifecycle

The owner of the product should not spend much money marketing the product, but "milk it" for all it's worth as demand for the product slows down

Core Deposits – Non-interest bearing demand deposits and bank money market deposits

Covenant (Affirmative or Positive vs. Negative) – An Affirmative or Positive Covenant is one the Borrower agrees to do something such as provide financial information, maintain minimum financial ratios, etc. A Negative Covenant is something the Borrower agrees not to do such as incur other loans, engage in other nonrelated business, enter into conflicting agreements, etc.

Disruptive Innovation – An unexpected innovation that changes forever the way people do things or think about things

The Internet changed the way people shop and buy products and services; as a result marketers must provide content about their products online, where buyers research and many purchase.

Effective Debt – Total liabilities less debt subordinated to the lender

Effective Tangible Net Worth – Net Worth less Intangible Assets plus debt subordinated to the lender

ESOP (Employee Stock Ownership Plan) – A qualified employee benefit that provides for investing in the employer stock; often used to finance a purchase from the principal owner(s) and align interests of company's employees and shareholders

Factor – Lender who purchases specific account receivables for a discount

FDIC – Federal Deposit Insurance Corporation

Funded Debt – Debt from lenders (as opposed to trade creditors or accrued liabilities)

Flanker Brand – A new brand introduced by a company that already has an existing brand in the category, allowing the company to capture a larger share of the total market by offering different brands

The term usually refers to a lower-priced offering that enables the company to capture the lower-end of the market, but can also refer to higher priced offerings, or refer to flavors, product size or product type. Example: Old Navy is a low-priced flanker to The Gap brand for Gap Inc., while Banana Republic is a high-priced flanker.

Fraudulent Conveyance – The transfer of property to another party to defraud a creditor; the offended party no longer has access to the property as collateral for the debt

Hard Money Lenders – Sources of loans to unproven borrowers or companies with high leverage or poor performing; these loans are generally expensive and collateral dependent.

Inside Sales – Inside sales people work from a desk and communicated with prospects using the phone and other technology such as email and online meetings to sell products and services. Hiring of inside sales people is increasing and technology replaces the need for sales people to travel to prospects.

In the Money – Reference to options to purchase stock

Put Options (most common) are worth exercising when the exercise price is above the market price, meaning the option has value.

Kanban – A method of Just-in-Time production that uses standard containers or lot sizes with a single card attached to each

It is a pull system in which work centers signal with a card that they wish to withdraw parts from feeding operations or suppliers. The Japanese word *kanban*, loosely translated, means card, billboard, or sign but other signaling devises such as colored golf balls have also been used. The term is often used synonymously for the specific scheduling system developed by the Toyota Corp. in Japan.

Lead Nurturing – Lead nurturing is the art of providing the right information and content online for prospective buyers in various stages of the buy cycle: awareness, information, assurance and loyalty

Leverage – Can be referred to as balance sheet leverage normally defined total liabilities divided by net worth (or Effective Debt divided by Effective Tangible Net Worth) or cash flow leverage normally defined as EBITDA (Earnings Before Interest, Taxes, Depreciation and Amortization) divided by total funded debt (funded debt is the total of monies borrowed from lenders)

LIBOR (London Interbank Offering Rate) – An internationally utilized rate index utilized in commercial loan transactions

Marketing – The process of identifying and defining customer needs and wants, the target audiences a company can serve, products and services that fit the target audiences' needs, and communicating information about the products and services to support the buying cycle

Marketing Persona – Tells a story about each customer segment a company serves

Marketing personas are often given real names and are written in a very realistic manner to bring the persona of a customer segment to life.

Marketing ROI (Return On Investment) – Calculated by dividing the sales revenue generated by marketing by the cost of the marketing activity

It makes sense to calculate ROI for each different marketing activity for comparison purposes as well as for your marketing department as a whole.

Mezzanine Debt – Financing with attributes of both equity and debt

It is often subordinate to bank debt in terms of rights to assets, as well as the receipt of interest and principal.

Mindshare – The share of a prospect's mind that is taken up thinking about your brand, product or services

Staying in front of prospects and customers with value-add communications and marketing increases your mindshare.

Niche Marketing – A business identifies a part of an industry or specific buyers that have special qualities, and markets only to that audience

Niche marketing is a good strategy for any company; changing to a niche strategy in a mature market is a way for a business to better compete when a market reaches maturity.

Porter's 5 Forces – A model used to assess potential profitability, opportunity and risk based on five key factors within an industry

The five factors include how powerful your customers are (can they negotiate lower prices – think Walmart), how powerful suppliers are (can they raise prices), how much competitors are a threat, whether or not there are significant substitutes that may lessen demand for your product, and how much competitive rivalry exists in a marketplace.

Preferred Stock – Stock that ranks above common stock in a liquidation scenario and has a preference on dividends

Price Elasticity – The change in demand for your product will decrease more (more elastic) when there is a price increase if customers believe that there is lots of competition out there, if they are apt to change suppliers easily, or if it appears that your product does not have a competitive advantage

Price Sensitivity – Customers are more sensitive to price increases if they know there are substitutes readily available or if there are competitors in the industry

Prime – A publicly available and commonly utilized rate index for commercial and consumer loans

Product Lifecycle – Products have a lifecycle, including an introductory phase, a growth phase, a mature phase and a declining phase. The lifecycle timeline looks like a Bell Curve, meaning that the introduction and growth phase show a rapid increase in sales; the mature stage shows flattening of sales growth and decline is where the sales decrease. Different marketing strategies and tactics apply depending upon where a product is in its lifecycle.

Put Option – A contract between two parties to exchange an asset at a specified cash amount or strike price, by a predetermined future date; owner of the put has the right, but not the obligation, to sell the asset by the future date

Repurchase Liability – The emerging, future liability (company's legal obligation) to repurchase stock distributed by ESOP to employees

Reseller – The marketing channel for some companies, in which a related company bundles and resells a product or service in with its offerings to make a more robust solution

Retail – A marketing channel commonly used for consumer products; is either a brick and mortar store or an ecommerce site on the Internet

Reviewed Financial Statement – The level of scrutiny provided by the CPA when preparing a financial statement

In a "Reviewed" statement the CPA performs a higher level over scrutiny and testing than a "Compiled" statement, but less than when preparing an "Audited" statement.

Revolving Line of Credit – A loan that is interest-only until maturity (normally one to two years)

It allows the borrower to borrow and repay as needed (or up to its borrowing base if formally monitored) until maturity assuming the borrower remains within the contractual loan terms.

Sales Agent – Typically an individual or company with connections in an industry that allow them to represent a product or service to businesses in the industry; sales agents typically make a commission when they make a sale

Sales Cycle – The sales cycle *used* to be the focus of marketing

How can marketing and sales control the cycle and accelerate the sale? Today, because control is in the buyer's hands due to increased availability of information online, the focus is on the buying cycle and leading buyers through various phases of buying.

SEC (Securities and Exchange Commission) – the government agency that regulates all issues regarding publicly listed securities

Senior Debt Holders – Lenders with a priority position in the borrower's assets, often evidenced by a UCC 1 filing

Social Media – Websites that allow individuals and companies to create profiles and share information and content about their company, products and services, and industry

Solvency Opinion – Involves valuation and cash flow tests, considering a proposed transaction, to determine if:

- The sum of the company's assets at a fair valuation exceeds its liabilities
- The present fair salable value of the company's assets exceeds the amount that will be required to pay its probable liability on its existing debts as they become absolute and matured
- The company has sufficient capital with which to conduct its business
- The company has not incurred debts beyond its ability to pay such debts as they mature

Supply Chain – Shows the entire chain of businesses that are involved in producing a final product or service

For example, a laptop supply chain would include: The vendors for all of the components the providers of any external processing, the manufacturer with its assembly and packaging operations – to the point of consumption.

SWOT Analysis – An analysis of a company's strengths, weaknesses, opportunities and threats

A SWOT analysis involves looking at internal factors (for example strength of distribution channel, weakness of lack of brand awareness) and external factors (opportunity first company to market, threat low barrier to entry into the market), and then identifying an action plan to leverage strengths and opportunities and minimize weaknesses and threats.

Tight Loan Structure – Refers in general to the loan terms

A "tight structure" is one where the lender is more closely controlling and or monitoring loan disbursements, collateral amounts and the borrower's financial condition.

Turnaround – A big improvement; a dramatic improvement to a bad or unsatisfactory situation

Synonym: reversal

Turnaround Management – A process dedicated to corporate renewal

It uses analysis and planning to save troubled companies and returns them to solvency.

UCC Liens – Liens filed under the Uniform Commercial Code

US Treasury Yield Curve – Curve made by plotting time out to 30 years on the horizontal access and the US Treasury Note rates on the vertical axis

Value-Based Pricing – Based more on the perceived value by the customer of the product, as opposed to being based on the costs that go into a product

If the customer does not perceive value (sometimes customers don't know what they don't know), a business must calculate the value of the solution and demonstrate that to the customer.

Voice of Customer – A practice in which, through rigorous investigation and research, a business uncovers their customers' wants and needs and presents them in priority order

Wallet Share – The process of communicating with customers to sell additional products and services

It is 5 to 10 times more expensive to sell to a new versus an existing customer, so recently much attention has been on "increasing wallet share" with existing customers.

Wholesaler – Buys products in large volume and sells at a discount to parts of the supply chain in an industry, but not the end user

Traditionally, wholesalers leveraged relationships within industries that the seller of a product did not have access to. With the Internet, some leverage their geographic location nearer manufacturing bases.

APPENDIX

DISCLOSURE AND AUTHORIZATION
IMPORTANT -- PLEASE READ CAREFULLY BEFORE SIGNING AUTHORIZATION
<u>DISCLOSURE REGARDING BACKGROUND INVESTIGATION</u>

[   ] ("The Company") may obtain information about you from a consumer reporting agency (CRA) for employment purposes. Thus, you may be the subject of a "consumer report" and/or an "investigative consumer report" which may include information about your character, general reputation, personal characteristics, and/or mode of living, and which can involve personal interviews with sources such as your neighbors, friends, or associates. These reports may contain information regarding your credit history, criminal history, social security verification, motor vehicle records ("driving records"), verification of your education or employment history, or other background checks. You have the right, upon written request made within a reasonable time after receipt of this notice, to request disclosure of the nature and scope of any investigative consumer report. Please be advised that the nature and scope of the most common form of investigative consumer report obtained with regard to applicants for employment is an investigation into your education and/or employment history conducted by Employers Choice Online, 8138 2nd Street, Downey, CA 90241 (800) 424-7011, or another outside organization. The scope of this notice and authorization is all-encompassing, however, allowing   to obtain from any outside organization all manner of consumer reports and investigative consumer reports now and throughout the course of your employment to the extent permitted by law. As a result, you should carefully consider whether to exercise your right to request disclosure of the nature and scope of any investigative consumer report.

<u>New York applicants or employees only:</u> You have the right to inspect and receive a copy of any investigative consumer report requested by [   ] by contacting the consumer reporting agency identified above directly.

ACKNOWLEDGMENT AND AUTHORIZATION

I acknowledge receipt of the DISCLOSURE REGARDING BACKGROUND INVESTIGATION and A SUMMARY OF YOUR RIGHTS UNDER THE FAIR CREDIT REPORTING ACT and certify that I have read and understand both of those documents. I hereby authorize the obtaining of "consumer reports" and/or "investigative consumer reports" by the Company at any time after receipt of this authorization and throughout my employment, if applicable. To this end, I hereby authorize, without reservation, any law enforcement agency, administrator, state or federal agency, institution, school or university (public or private), information service bureau, employer, or insurance company to furnish any and all background information requested by **Employers Choice Online, 8138 2nd Street, Downey, CA 90241 (800) 424-7011**, another outside organization acting on behalf of [   ], and/or [   ] itself. I agree that a facsimile ("fax"), electronic or photographic copy of this Authorization shall be as valid as the original.

<u>California applicants or employees only:</u> By signing below, you also acknowledge receipt of the NOTICE REGARDING BACKGROUND INVESTIGATION PURSUANT TO CALIFORNIA LAW. Please check this box if you would like to receive a copy of an investigative consumer report or consumer credit report at no charge if one is obtained by the Company whenever you have a right to receive such a copy under California law. ☐
<u>Minnesota and Oklahoma applicants or employees only:</u> Please check this box if you would like to receive a copy of a consumer report if one is obtained by the Company. ☐

Last Name:	First:	Middle Name:
Alias Names:		
* Social Security #: — —	* Date of Birth: — — 19	*(YEAR OF BIRTH IS VOLUNTARY)*
Drivers' License #:	State of Drivers License	
Current Address:	Home Phone #:	Cellular Phone #:
City / State / Zip code:		
Signature:	Date:	

*PROVIDING YEAR OF BIRTH IS STRICTLY VOLUNTARY. THIS INFORMATION WILL ALLOW ECO TO PROPERLY IDENTIFY YOU IN THE EVENT WE FIND ADVERSE INFORMATION DURING THE COURSE OF A BACKGROUND INVESTIGATION. YOUR INFORMATION WILL NOT BE USED AS HIRING CRITERIA.

NOTICE REGARDING BACKGROUND INVESTIGATION
PURSUANT TO CALIFORNIA LAW

[   ] (the "Company") intends to obtain information about you from an investigative consumer reporting agency and/or a consumer credit reporting agency for employment purposes. Thus, you can expect to be the subject of "investigative consumer reports" and "consumer credit reports" obtained for employment purposes. Such reports may include information about your character, general reputation, personal characteristics and mode of living. With respect to any investigative consumer report from an Investigative Consumer Reporting Agency ("ICRA"), the Company may investigate the information contained in your employment application and other background information about you, including but not limited to obtaining a criminal record report, verifying references, work history, your social security number, your educational achievements, licensure, and certifications, your driving record, and other information about you, and interviewing people who are knowledgeable about you. The results of this report may be used as a factor in making employment decisions. The source of any investigative consumer report (as that term is defined under California law) will be Employers Choice Online, 8138 2nd Street, Downey, CA 90241 (800) 424-7011. The source of any credit report will be Employers Choice Online, 8138 2nd Street, Downey, CA 90241 (800) 424-7011.

The Company agrees to provide you with a copy of an investigative consumer report when required to do so under California law.

Under California Civil Code section 1786.22, you are entitled to find out from an ICRA what is in the ICRA's file on you with proper identification, as follows:

- In person, by visual inspection of your file during normal business hours and on reasonable notice. You also may request a copy of the information in person. The ICRA may not charge you more than the actual copying costs for providing you with a copy of your file.

- A summary of all information contained in the ICRA's file on you that is required to be provided by the California Civil Code will be provided to you via telephone, if you have made a written request, with proper identification, for telephone disclosure, and the toll charge, if any, for the telephone call is prepaid by or charged directly to you.

- By requesting a copy be sent to a specified addressee by certified mail. ICRAs complying with requests for certified mailings shall not be liable for disclosures to third parties caused by mishandling of mail after such mailings leave the ICRAs.

"Proper Identification" includes documents such as a valid driver's license, social security account number, military identification card, and credit cards. Only if you cannot identify yourself with such information may the ICRA require additional information concerning your employment and personal or family history in order to verify your identity. The ICRA will provide trained personnel to explain any information furnished to you and will provide a written explanation of any coded information contained in files maintained on you. This written explanation will be provided whenever a file is provided to you for visual inspection.

You may be accompanied by one other person of your choosing, who must furnish reasonable identification. An ICRA may require you to furnish a written statement granting permission to the ICRA to discuss your file in such person's presence.

APPENDIX

California Statement of Consumer Rights

You have rights when an investigative consumer report is obtained on you. You can find the complete text of the law governing Investigative Consumer Reporting Agencies at California Civil Code §§1786 – 1786.60 (the "Investigative Consumer Reporting Agencies Act" or "ICRA"). The ICRA is designed to promote accuracy, fairness, and privacy of information in the files of every "consumer reporting agency" (CRA).

The following is a summary of the provisions of Section 1786.22, which you are required to receive when an Investigative Consumer Report ("ICR") will be obtained about you:

- You have the right to contact the agency that made the ICR and get information from that agency. You can do this in one of the following ways:

  1. You can go to the agency in person during the normal business hours. You can bring someone with you. That person may be required to present identification. You may be required to sign a paper allowing the agency to discuss your file with or to show your file to this person.

  2. You may receive a copy of your file by certified mail, if you have given written notice to the agency that you want information mailed to you or to another person you want to receive the file. You will be required to provide identification when you write for your file.

  3. You may be able to discuss your file over the telephone if you have give written instructions to the agency and have provided identification.

- You have the right to receive a copy of your file or your ICR from the agency. You may be charged the cost of duplication.

- You have the right to have trained personnel at the agency explain any information contained in the ICR or your file.

- You have the right to a written explanation of any codes or abbreviations used in your ICR, so you can understand the report.

You also have rights under federal law in regard to your Report. A copy of those rights is given to you with this California statement of consumer rights. Many of these rights are also included within California law. Under federal law, your report is a consumer report, not an investigative consumer report, unless the report contains information obtained from a personal interview, in which case it is an investigative consumer report under federal law.

279

Para information en español, visite www.ftc.gov/credit o escribe a la FTC Consumer Response Center, Room 130-A 600 Pennsylvania Ave. N. W., Washington, D. C. 20580.

A Summary of Your Rights Under the Fair Credit Reporting Act

The federal Fair Credit Reporting Act (FCRA) promotes the accuracy, fairness, and privacy of information in the files of consumer reporting agencies. There are many types of consumer reporting agencies, including credit bureaus and specialty agencies (such as agencies that sell information about check writing histories, medical records, and rental history records). Here is a summary of your major rights under the FCRA. **For more information, including information about additional rights, go to www.ftc.gov/credit or write to: Consumer Response Center, Room 130-A, Federal Trade Commission, 600 Pennsylvania Ave. N.W., Washington, D.C. 20580.**

- **You must be told if information in your file has been used against you.** Anyone who uses a credit report or another type of consumer report to deny your application for credit, insurance, or employment - or to take another adverse action against you - must tell you, and must give you the name, address, and phone number of the agency that provided the information.

- **You have the right to know what is in your file.** You may request and obtain all the information about you in the files of a consumer reporting agency (your "file disclosure"). You will be required to provide proper identification, which may include your Social Security number. In many cases, the disclosure will be free. You are entitled to a free file disclosure if:

    - a person has taken adverse action against you because of information in your credit report;
    - you are the victim of identify theft and place a fraud alert in your file;
    - your file contains inaccurate information as a result of fraud;
    - you are on public assistance;
    - you are unemployed but expect to apply for employment within 60 days.

    In addition, by September 2005 all consumers will be entitled to one free disclosure every 12 months upon request from each nationwide credit bureau and from nationwide specialty consumer reporting agencies. See www.ftc.gov/credit for additional information.

- **You have the right to ask for a credit score.** Credit scores are numerical summaries of your credit-worthiness based on information from credit bureaus. You may request a credit score from consumer reporting agencies that create scores or distribute scores used in residential real property loans, but you will have to pay for it. In some mortgage transactions, you will receive credit score information for free from the mortgage lender.

- **You have the right to dispute incomplete or inaccurate information.** If you identify information in your file that is incomplete or inaccurate, and report it to the consumer reporting agency, the agency must investigate unless your dispute is frivolous. See www.ftc.gov/credit for an explanation of dispute procedures.

- **Consumer reporting agencies must correct or delete inaccurate, incomplete, or unverifiable information.** Inaccurate, incomplete or unverifiable information must be removed or corrected, usually within 30 days. However, a consumer reporting agency may continue to report information it has verified as accurate.

APPENDIX

SAMPLE ADVERSE ACTION LETTER

Date

Ms. Jane Doe
Human Resources Manger
XYZ Corporation
123 Any Street
City Name, State 00000

Re: Adverse Action Letter

Dear _____:

We regret to inform you that **XYZ Corporation** is unable to offer you employment), or (**XYZ Corporation** will terminate your employment effective _____), or (XYZ Corporation has decided not to offer you a promotion)].* This decision was based in whole or in part on information contained in a report from Employers Choice Online, 8138 2nd Street, Downey, CA 90241 (800) 424-7011, a copy of which was previously given to you. The agency did not make this employment decision and is unable to supply you with specific reasons why the decision was made. Under Section 612 of the Fair Credit Reporting Act, you have the right to obtain a free copy of the report if you submit a written request to the agency identified above no later than 60 days after you receive this notice. Under Section 611 of that Act, and state law you also have the right to dispute with the consumer reporting agency the accuracy or completeness of any information in the report.

Sincerely,

Ms. Jane Doe
Human Resources Manger
XYZ Corporation

Identify any adverse action taken on the basis of the consumer report.

California applicants or employees only **(this section applies only if the report referenced above is a credit report):** You have the right to obtain a free copy of your credit report within 60 days from the consumer credit reporting agency which has been identified on this notice and from any other consumer credit reporting agency which compiles and maintains files on consumers on a nationwide basis. Under California law, you also have the right to dispute with the consumer reporting agency the accuracy or completeness of any information in the report.

SAMPLE "BEFORE" ADVERSE ACTION LETTER

Date

Ms. Jane Doe
Human Resources Manger
XYZ Corporation
123 Any Street
City Name, State 00000

Re: Pre Adverse Action Letter

Dear _____:

On *Date goes here*, you authorized XYZ Corporation to obtain consumer reports and/or investigative consumer reports about you from a consumer reporting agency. Enclosed please find (1) a copy of the report we obtained from Employers Choice Online, 8138 2nd Street, Downey, CA 90241 (800) 424-7011 , (2) a summary of your rights under the Fair Credit Reporting Act and (3) California Statement of Consumer Rights.

You may identify any errors, inaccuracies and/or otherwise respond to the information contained in the report within ten calendar days from the date of this letter. 1 If you choose to do so, you must contact the Company at [Insert appropriate contact information]. If you wish to dispute the accuracy of the information in the report directly with the consumer reporting agency (*i.e.*, the source of the information contained in the report), you should contact the agency identified above directly.

Sincerely,

Ms. Jane Doe
Human Resources Manger
XYZ Corporation

NOTE: 1 EMPLOYER WILL AFFORD NEW YORK APPLICANTS AND EMPLOYEES UP TO 5 BUSINESS DAYS AFTER RECEIPT OF THIS LETTER OR UP TO 10 CALENDAR DAYS AFTER THE DATE OF THIS LETTER, WHICHEVER PERIOD IS LONGER.

CONTRIBUTING AUTHOR, EDITOR AND PUBLISHER

 **Daniel Feiman**, MBA, CMC˚ and Visiting Professor, is the Founder and Managing Director of **Build It Backwards,** a consulting and training firm based in Redondo Beach, CA. He teaches "ordinary companies how to create extraordinary results" by leveraging his expertise in *Strategy, Finance* and *Process.* Mr. Feiman has provided expertise as a management consultant for more than 16 years, after a long and very successful career in commercial banking. He works internationally with cutting edge start-up companies, as well as industry-leading multi-national firms; where he facilitates strategy, finance and process improvement projects, improving business effectiveness in a wide range of industries.

Daniel is an internationally recognized seminar leader who has worked with firms such as Apple, Credit Suisse, Hilton Hotels, Institute for Supply Management (ISM), Mattel, PEMEX (México), Promigas (Colombia), Reliance (India), the Small Business Development Center (SBDC), TRW and the University of Manchester (UK), among many others.

Daniel is the Publisher of the *Build It Backwards* series, and author of numerous published articles, white papers (available at www.BuildItBackwards.com) and business books. Daniel is also a reviewer for the New York Journal of Books.

He is adjunct faculty at the University of California, Los Angeles (UCLA) Extension Department (since 1990) and the Visiting Professor in the University of Huddersfield's (UK) Business School. He has also been interviewed on various television and radio shows. dsfeiman@BuildItBackwards.com

* CMC© (Certified Management Consultant) is the certification mark awarded by the Institute of Management Consultants USA and represents meeting the highest global standards and ethical canons of the profession. Less than 1% of all consultants have achieved this level of excellence.

CO-AUTHORS' BIOS

Here are the co-authors of this fine book:

Jennifer Beever is the *CMO for Hire,* who drives B2B marketing results through research, analysis, marketing planning, implementation, and marketing department development to grow revenue for her clients. Jennifer founded New Incite, a marketing consulting firm located in Woodland Hills, California, in 1997. She is an Inbound Marketing Certified Professional, and a Certified Management Consultant (CMC) with the Institute of Management Consultants USA (IMC USA). She also serves on the national board of the Association for Strategic Planning (ASP) and is a past-president of ASP's Los Angeles and IMC USA's SoCal chapters. Jennifer received her MBA from Pepperdine University's Graziadio School of Business, and her BA from Colby College in Waterville, Maine. jenb@newincite.com

Davis Blaine is Chairman of The Mentor Group, Inc. and Mentor Securities, LLC (FINRA registered). He is an expert in the accounting, tax, and financial aspects of acquisitions, recapitalizations, valuations and appraisal. Davis has frequently lectured and written on technical valuation issues, and has counseled many clients on buying, selling, or raising capital. In addition, he has prepared companies for public and private investment, strategic partnership, and joint ventures. dblaine@TheMentorGrp.com

David Cohn is a Managing Director of Diamond Capital Partners. After 40 years as a business owner and an investment banker, David brings a concentration of many completed deals in manufacturing, distribution, aerospace, and engineered plastics. David has co-founded two previous Investment Banking Firms, along with operating an investment banking division for City National Bank, based in Beverly Hills. Cohn has served on major boards, including the Association for Corporate Growth (ACG), and currently serves on the board of the Association of Merger and Acquisition Advisors (AMAA). He currently serves on the CM&AA faculty, which delivers M&A certification classes at DePaul University and Pepperdine University, and is on the speaking roster for the California CPA Education Foundation. He is certified by FINRA as General Securities Principal and Representative. Davis is a graduate of Washington University School of Business. DCohn@DiamondCapitalPartners.com

Kim D. Defenderfer has 25 years of commercial banking experience. He began his banking career with First Interstate Bank in 1987, and joined Mellon 1st Business Bank in 1996, where he held various positions, including Executive Vice President and Chief Administrative Officer. Kim joined California United Bank in 2009 to manage the Bank's South Bay Regional Office. He has always directly handled a portfolio of clients in addition to his other responsibilities. Kim is a Board Member of Upward Bound House, a nonprofit located in Santa Monica providing transitional housing services for families with minor children, and an Advisory Board member for California State University Dominguez Hills College of Business and Public Policy. Prior to beginning his banking career, Kim owned a solar water heating sales and installation company, lived in France and England for 18 months, and was a logger in Oregon. He obtained his undergraduate degree from the University of Oregon and his MBA from the Anderson Graduate School of Management at UCLA. kdefenderfer@gmail.com

Bruce Dizenfeld has been a business lawyer and strategist for over 30 years, with emphasis in structuring collaborative and strategic ventures. He has represented clients in all phases of transactions across diverse industries, with significant experience in the technology and health care fields. Bruce has written numerous articles on various aspects of business organizations, including licensing, risk management, intellectual property and finance. He was also Editor-in-Chief of the California Health Law Digest and a Co-Editor of Financing Techniques for Small and Emerging Businesses. Bruce has been named a Southern California Super Lawyer for 2006-2011, as published in Southern California Super Lawyer Magazine and Los Angeles Magazine. Bruce received his BA from the University of Southern California and his JD from the University of California, Los Angeles. bdizenfeld@tocounsel.com

Paula Frazier is an internationally recognized referral-marketing expert with over a decade of experience in helping people build powerful personal networks that produce high quality referrals. Paula is honored to be one of six elite Master Trainers for the Referral Institute®, an international referral training and consulting company. She is also a long time Executive Director for BNI®, the world's leading business networking organization. Paula's networking articles are regularly featured online. She has also contributed to books such as Building The Ultimate Network and Brainsbook on Networking and is also acknowledged in the New York Times bestseller, Truth or Delusion—Busting Networking's Biggest Myths. paula@bniswva.com

Christie Harper is president and founder of Brand Endeavor, a brand-consulting firm that brings world-class brand solutions to small and mid-size organizations, including non-profits, higher education and companies in the healthy living, financial services, and technology industries. She has more than 15 years of experience in branding and marketing, both inside companies and with agencies, including work with global brands such as Lexus, Microsoft, Chevron, Technicolor, Amgen, the City of Beverly Hills and UCLA. Christie earned a B.A. in Communications from UCLA, and an M.A. in Communication Management from The Annenberg School at USC. christie@brandendeavor.com

Joe Herold is Principal of the Herold Consulting Group, a human resources, organization and leadership consulting firm. Joe has over 25 years of coaching experience in human resources leadership and organizational and leadership effectiveness, as well as senior leadership in high-tech design environments, sales and service centers, manufacturing operations and corporate offices. Joe has experience is multiple industries, including High-Tech, Consumables Distribution, Energy, Health Care, Entertainment, R&D/Engineering and Aerospace. He uses his proprietary "Hierarchy of HR Value" model to help clients evaluate and focus their HR and leadership capabilities. Joe is a recent member of the Human Resources Roundtable at the Anderson School of Business at UCLA, and is on the advisory board to the Master's Program in Human Behavior at the University of Southern California. jherold@heroldconsulting.com

Bette Hiramatsu is a seasoned turnaround and restructuring consultant who has focused primarily on mid-sized businesses that are underperforming or facing financial and/or operational challenges. Since 1991, Bette has guided the owners and senior managers of mid-sized manufacturers, wholesalers, retail chains and service companies on finding the path to profitability and positive cash flow through creative problem solving, strategic planning, financial forecasting, current asset management, process improvement, cost cutting and strengthened balance sheet management. Additional areas of expertise include the restructuring of unsecured debt and the re-negotiation of leases. Prior to becoming a management consultant, Bette was a commercial lender and Vice President for ten years with Union Bank and Chemical Bank. Bette earned a B.S. in Business Administration from the University of Southern California and a MBA from the UCLA Anderson School of Management. She is also a Certified Insolvency and Restructuring Advisor (CIRA). bette@bhiramatsu.com

Jeff Kichaven is an independent mediator with a nationwide practice based in Los Angeles. He currently serves as a Director of the Los Angeles County Bar Association's Center for Civic Mediation. In the American Bar Association, Jeff has chaired the ADR Committees in the Section of Business Law, the Section of Intellectual Property Law, and the Tort, Trial and Insurance Practice Section (TIPS). He has served as President of the Southern California Mediation Association and as a Trustee of the Los Angeles County Bar Association. Jeff recently completed a term as Chair of the Entertainment Law and Intellectual Property Section of the Los Angeles County Bar Association, and currently serves as Chair of the Insurance Law Section of the Orange County Bar Association. He has been named California Lawyer Attorney Lawyer of the Year in ADR, has taught the Master Class for Mediators for his Alma Mater,

Harvard Law School, and has received a Special Award for Excellence in Mediation from the Asian Pacific American Dispute Resolution Center. Jeff frequently writes and speaks on ADR topics. Many of his articles can be found at his website, www. jeffkichaven.com. jk@JeffKichaven.com

Patricia A. Kotze-Ramos is a successful entrepreneur with a passion for business. She is founder and President of Diversified Risk Management, Inc. (DRM), a full service private investigation agency with a large range of correlated services specifically for employers, headquartered in Southern, California. Patricia is an expert on workplace investigations, litigation strategy, and investigative procedures. She has conducted corporate investigations, managed security services and provided human resources consulting for over 27 years. Her leadership and years of expertise have contributed to DRM successfully handled thousands of employment, civil and criminal matters related to clients' personnel issues. Together with DRM's staff of professionals, Patricia has grown DRM into an international company conducting business in 43 U.S. States, Canada, Mexico and other countries. pkotze@drminc.us

Called the "father of modern networking" by CNN, Dr. Ivan Misner is a New York Times bestselling author. He is the Founder and Chairman of BNI, the world's largest business networking organization. His newest book, Networking Like a Pro, can be viewed at www.IvanMisner.com. Dr. Misner is also the Sr. Partner for the Referral Institute, an international referral training company. misner@bni.com

Rick E. Norris, JD, CPA. He founded his CPA practice, now known as Rick E. Norris, Accountancy Corporation, in 1992. His firm consults to a variety of small and medium-sized businesses on a variety of strategic planning and business topics. Rick sits on the California CPA Society Entertainment Industry Conference Planning Committee, which is held annually in Los Angeles, CA. He is also is President of the Los Angeles chapter of the Association for Strategic Planning. He is co-founder and CFO of the Foundation of Local Arts, which sponsors art and music events with the goal of raising money for K-12 school art programs. Rick has published articles in the California CPA Society magazine, among other periodicals, and writes weekly for his company blog. In addition to his publications, Rick speaks frequently at various events in the area of personal and business financial matters. Rick earned a BS from UCLA. After receiving his Certified Public Accountant certificate, he earned his JD from Southwestern University School of Law. RNorris@ricknorriscpa.com

Andy Pattantyus, founder and President of Strategic Modularity, Inc. (SMI), is passionate about helping clients set goals, prepare plans and eliminate waste, thus allowing companies reach their greatest potential. Andy and his associates solve business problems by combining technical innovation with strategy, system design, facility design, human resource management, project management and accounting. An efficient business perspective combined with a mix of strong technical skills enables Andy and his team to improve a company's health. Andy holds 6 patents, a BS and an MS in Mechanical Engineering from Virginia Tech, and an MBA from Case Western Reserve University. andyp@strategicmodularity.com

Barry Pogorel is a pioneer of breakthrough performance. He founded Crossroads Transformational Consulting Inc. to develop and coach leaders to produce unprecedented results. He and his colleagues introduced this approach into the business dialogue 30+ years ago. Barry has led breakthrough initiatives for some of the world's leading companies in Asia, Australia, Europe, the Middle East, and America. His work transcends both culture and industry, since it deals with the physics of human beings working together to produce unprecedented outcomes. For many years, Barry has been a sponsor of organizations dedicated to ending hunger, empowering "youth at risk" (gang members), and bringing about international cooperation. He is also an accomplished artist, and has exhibited paintings and sculptures in various museums and galleries, including The Whitney Museum of American Art in New York. He has two masters degrees from the University of California and a post-graduate degree from Darden School of Business, University of Virginia. The theme that runs through his life is empowering greatness in leadership. barry@crossrsoadstc.com

Dr. Ivan M. Rosenberg, the President and CEO of Frontier Associates, Inc., supports leaders in achieving breakthrough results in organizational performance. His engagements have included facilitating creation of strategic plans that inspire and coalesce disparate stakeholders, creating teams and partnerships of conflicting parties, coaching C-level executives, and transforming organizational cultures to support change initiatives and mergers. Although he has served many middle-market aerospace firms, Ivan's clients range from start-ups to Fortune 500 companies in a wide variety of industries, including city and federal agencies. He founded a national software company, led an international franchisor to profitability, and was a university professor, in addition to serving on many non-profit, for-profit, and government boards. He has graduate degrees in Electrical Engineering, Computer Science, and Management. irosenberg@ frontier-assoc.com

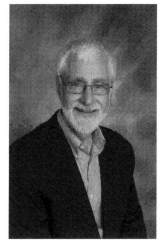

Jerald Savin is the Founder and Chief Executive Officer of the Cambridge Technology Consulting Group, Inc., and a seasoned management consultant with over 30 years of business technology consulting experience. He combines the professional disciplines of management consulting, business information technology and public accounting, a unique combination among information systems specialists. In addition to his information technology consulting practice, Jerald teaches at various universities and professional organizations, including UCLA and the California Society of Certified Public Accountants.

He is a Certified Management Consultant®, a Certified Public Accountant and a Fellow of the Institute of Management Consultants. In addition, he is the former Chairman of the Institute of Management Consultants (IMC), former Lead Trustee to the International Council of Management Consulting Institutes (ICMCI), former Chairman of IMC's Governance and Audit Committee and member of the Information Systems Audit and Control Association (ISACA). jsavin@ctcg.com

Lee Schwartz, Principal of the Schwartz Profitability Group, uncorks the operational bottlenecks of manufacturing and distribution companies, boosting bottom line results. Lee's efforts have led to corralling runaway costs, fixing broken processes, streamlining work flows and employment of best practices for smaller family run companies to Fortune 500 firms covering a multitude of industries. Prior to launching his successful consulting practice in 2001, Lee spent over 20 years with distribution and manufacturing companies, primarily in senior management positions of CEO, President and COO. Lee also advises Boards of Directors in strategic planning and operational best practices. He has served on a Board for the Council of Supply Chain Management Professionals and currently is an active member of APICS. Lee graduated from UCLA with a degree in Economics. lee@schwartzpro.com

Gene Siciliano CMC CPA is an author, speaker, consultant and management coach. He is the founder and president of Western Management Associates, a 25-year old financial management advisory firm based in Los Angeles. Known internationally as Your CFO For Rent®, Gene and his firm help CEOs and owners of privately owned companies build financial strength and shareholder value through applied knowledge and process improvement. Gene also helps non-financial CEOs and senior executives understand and successfully apply financial concepts to their companies and their careers. His books on business and personal finance are available in bookstores and online. gene@CFOforRent.com.

Ted Whetstone is a big believer in looking at life and business, differently. "Some of the greatest breakthroughs in history were the result of thinking from a highly unique perspective," Ted says. "Once you shift perspective, you change everything." Based in Santa Monica, California, Ted is passionate about inspiring and channeling the creative mind. As a business innovator, he helps companies create breakthrough products, ideas, and thinking to maximize their strategic advantage and financial gain. From start-up entrepreneurs to worldwide leading companies, he uses unconventional models and methods to help his clients harness their own power to innovate. Ted asserts that the difference between survival and greatness lies within us, and is currently writing a bold new book about expanding the operating system of the human mind. A graduate of Cornell University, Ted holds a bachelor's in materials science and engineering. ted@tedwhetstone.com

Michael D. Young is a full time mediator with Judicate West in California, and served as an adjunct professor in Negotiations and Mediation at the University of Southern California Law School for nearly a decade. He was a member of the California State Bar's Standing Committee on ADR, and is a Distinguished Fellow and executive officer with the renowned International Academy of Mediators. A former intellectual property and employment litigator and mediator with the national law firm Alston + Bird, Michael remains very active in the dispute resolution community, speaking publicly, serving on State and Bar ADR Committees, and publishing on the use of ADR in the resolution of complex disputes. Some of his articles can be found at www.MikeYoungMediation.com. mike@mikeyoungmediation.com

WANT MORE? LOOK FOR THESE OTHER TITLES IN OUR BUILD IT BACKWARDS SERIES:

HOW TO REALLY OBTAIN FINANCING FOR YOUR BUSINESS

THE Book on…Improving Productivity by Fair Means or Foul

THE Book on…Business From A to Z

THE Book on…Continuous Process Improvement

THE Book on…Business From A to Z II

THE Book on…Leadership

THE Book on…Strategy: From Planning through Implementation

THE Book on…Where to Go When the Bank Says No

THE Book on…Financial Modeling

THE Book on…Budgeting and Forecasting

THE Book on…Accounting: Making Sense of the Numbers

Made in the USA
Charleston, SC
04 October 2013